CASTLE
OF THE
EAGLES
ESCAPE FROM
MUSSOLINI'S COLDITZ

MARK FELTON

ICON

First published in the UK in 2017
by Icon Books Ltd, Omnibus Business Centre,
39–41 North Road, London N7 9DP
email: info@iconbooks.com
www.iconbooks.com

This edition published in the UK in 2017 by Icon Books Ltd

Sold in the UK, Europe and Asia
by Faber & Faber Ltd, Bloomsbury House,
74–77 Great Russell Street,
London WC1B 3DA or their agents

Distributed in the UK, Europe and Asia
by Grantham Book Services,
Trent Road, Grantham NG31 7XQ

Distributed in Australia and New Zealand
by Allen & Unwin Pty Ltd,
PO Box 8500, 83 Alexander Street,
Crows Nest, NSW 2065

Distributed in South Africa
by Jonathan Ball, Office B4, The District,
41 Sir Lowry Road, Woodstock 7925

Distributed in India by Penguin Books India,
7th Floor, Infinity Tower – C, DLF Cyber City,
Gurgaon 122002, Haryana

ISBN: 978-178578-282-4

Typeset in Janson Text by Marie Doherty

Printed and bound in the UK
by Clays Ltd, St Ives plc

CASTLE
OF THE
EAGLES

To Fang Fang
with love

ABOUT THE AUTHOR

Mark Felton has written eighteen books on World War Two including *Zero Night* ('the story of the greatest escape of World War II has been told for the first time' – *Daily Mail*) and *The Sea Devils* ('A thrilling page-turner ... it will leave your fingernails significantly shorter' – *History of War*). His *Japan's Gestapo* was named 'Best Book of 2009' by *The Japan Times*. He also writes regularly for publications including *Military History Monthly* and *World War II*. After a decade spent working in Shanghai, he now lives in Norwich.

Visit www.markfelton.co.uk

Contents

A NOTE ON THE TEXT

Most of the dialogue sequences in this book come from the veterans themselves, from written sources, diaries or spoken interviews. I have at times changed the tense to make it more immediate. Occasionally, where only basic descriptions of what happened exist, I have recreated small sections of dialogue, attempting to remain true to the characters and their manners of speech.

Prologue

The short, wiry man with the grey military moustache, known to everyone simply as 'Dick', sat slightly uncomfortably between two companions on a stone bench that had been warmed by the bright Tuscan sun. He wore a plain grey civilian suit and on his back was a bulky homemade rucksack that looked fit to burst. Stuck in the waistband of his trousers was a peculiar wedge-shaped block of wood with a metal hook protruding from its narrowest side. The terrace where the three men sat was pleasant, stretching along the western side of the castle's central keep, and actually consisted of a lower and upper terrace enclosed by an eight-foot-high, thick stone perimeter wall, the top of which was crenellated with medieval battlements. The prisoners used the lower terrace for exercise while the guards watched them easily from the upper terrace, any danger of fraternising neatly eliminated.[1]

The castle, built of grey stone, sat imperiously atop a high rocky hill near the village of Fiesole, five miles from the Renaissance splendours of Florence. It was a gloomy Neo-Gothic reconstructed medieval fortress, the slopes of its lofty perch planted with cypress, pines and shrubs.

Beyond the huge wall was a sheer drop of some 30 feet to the solid bedrock below, upon which the great castle had been constructed many centuries before. Two tall battlemented towers rose up at the castle's northern end, overlooking the main gate and road down to the nearby village, a smattering of tiled roofs and little fields huddled at the foot of the hill. The views from the Castle's terrace were stunning – rolling green hills that stretched away to Florence. On a good day one could see the golden dome of the Basilica di Santa Maria del Fiore shimmering in the sun like a precious jewel.

Dick's heart was racing. He was waiting for a window of opportunity that would be measured in just a handful of seconds. That was all the time he had to make his daring bid for freedom. It was risky to attempt such a thing in broad daylight, but he had no choice. At night Dick and his fellow prisoners were confined to their rooms in another part of the castle and denied access to the terrace.

Tuscany was hot and sultry in late July 1942, and Dick sweated inside his suit as he waited for the signal to go. His keen blue eyes carefully watched as his comrades moved into their positions to assist his escape.

Suddenly the signal was given. Dick didn't hesitate. He stood up on the bench, facing the wall, raised his arms above his head and stiffened his legs. His comrades on either side took hold of his legs and, as they had practised so many times before, launched Dick skywards. Dick stretched his arms up until his fingertips found the bottom of the guards' walkway and then he pulled with all his might, his comrades pushing on the soles of his feet until he was out of reach. With a supreme effort Dick fought to gain the platform, his short legs pedalling in the air as his arms took the strain. With panic rising like a wave inside of him, 53-year-old Lieutenant-General Sir Richard O'Connor, the hero who had defeated the Italians in Africa and taken 130,000 prisoners into the bargain, gritted his teeth and pulled for all he was worth. One of the unlikeliest escapers of the Second World War was about to try one of the most daring escapes in the history of war.

CHAPTER 1

The Prize Prisoner

'After nine months as a member of his staff, when we left England I admired and respected Air Marshal Boyd. After two and a half years of prison life with him, living in the same house, often in the same room, I admired and respected him a hundred times more. I knew him then to be a great and simple man.'

Flight Lieutenant John Leeming

John Leeming cursed loudly as his shoulder connected painfully with one of the Wellington bomber's internal struts, his stomach lurching as the stricken plane pitched and rolled alarmingly through the air as it headed for the earth. The wind screamed like a typhoon through a large and jagged hole in the Wellington's floor, one of several caused by cannon shells from the swarm of Italian fighters that had suddenly pounced on them without warning.[1] Leeming kicked at a heavy grey steel strongbox with one of his long legs, edging it towards the lip of the hole until, with a final push of his boot, the box flew out of the aircraft, plummeting towards the Mediterranean far below. One more box remained, and Leeming, dressed in his blue RAF officer's uniform with pilot's wings above the left breast pocket, his legs aching from his awkward position on the plane's floor, began to kick at it wildly until it followed the other boxes out through the hole. Then Leeming lay on the floor for a few seconds, listening to the roar of the dying engines as the wind blew everything that wasn't secured around the Wellington's interior like a mini tornado. *I've just thrown away £250,000*, thought Leeming, shaking his head in silent

1

disbelief. 'A quarter of a million of pounds sent to the bottom of the sea!' he muttered aloud. In Leeming's opinion, the war had suddenly taken a dramatically strange turn for the worse.

'Brace for impact!' came Squadron Leader Norman Samuels' frantic yell from the cockpit. 'She's going in hard!' Leeming was instantly jerked out of his private reverie, rolling on to his stomach and grabbing hold of anything solid-looking that would support him. He glanced behind him and saw his boss, Air Marshal Owen Tudor Boyd, 'a short, broad-chested, and powerfully built'[2] man with short greying hair and a neat moustache, doing likewise, his normally genial face set with a determined grimace. Boyd caught his eye and mouthed something, but Leeming couldn't hear what it was above the racket of the whining, guttering engines and the ceaseless wind. Leeming glanced back at the hole through which he had just deposited the cash boxes. The azure of the sea had been replaced by green rolling hills and fields. 'Sicily,' muttered Leeming to himself. The Wellington was now very low. Leeming closed his eyes and awaited the end.

*

A strange quietness followed the terrific violence of the crash landing. Leeming lay on his side in the broken fuselage, his hands still grimly gripping a spar. The air was dusty and there was a ticking noise coming from one of the engines as it cooled. Then Air Marshal Boyd, Leeming and the four crewmen began to stir, groaning and occasionally crying out in pain from their injuries. Leeming dragged himself out of the fuselage with the others. His arm hurt like hell.

Once outside, Leeming surveyed the Wellington. The plane was a complete wreck: one of its huge wings had broken off, its nose was smashed in, and the big propeller blades had been bent back on themselves by the force of the impact. For several hundred feet behind the Wellington the Sicilian landscape had been gouged and churned up by the crash landing. Leeming narrowed his eyes against the glare of the sun, which was warm on his smoke-blackened face. Boyd slowly stood and walked, slightly unsteadily, around to the cockpit where he began fumbling in his pockets, pulling out some papers and his cigarette lighter. Leeming soon realised that the Air Marshal was trying to set fire to the plane. It was a vital task, considering what Boyd had been carrying aboard among his personal kit. His private papers would comprise an intelligence treasure trove if they were to fall into the hands of the enemy. They, along with the plane, had to be thoroughly destroyed before the Italians arrived to investigate and take the Britons prisoner.

Leeming reflected on the journey that had landed him unexpectedly in the hands of the enemy. They had taken off from RAF Stradishall near Haverhill in Suffolk on 19 November 1940 bound for Cairo via the airfield at Luqa in Malta. Once in Egypt, the 51-year-old Boyd was to assume deputy command of Allied air forces under Air Chief Marshal Longmore.[3] The appointment of the energetic Boyd to the Middle East came at a time when Britain was struggling to maintain its position in Egypt against a huge Italian assault.

Benito Mussolini had entered Italy into the war on Germany's side in late June 1940, after witnessing Hitler's triumphs in Poland and against the Western Allies in France and the Low Countries. *Il Duce* undoubtedly thought that Italy might be able to snatch a few of the victory laurels for herself on the back of Germany's defeat of France and the ejection of the British from the Continent. But the Italian entry into the war was particularly worrisome for Britain in the Mediterranean, a traditional bastion of British power. The large and powerful Italian fleet and the massive Italian army in Libya posed serious threats to the British Empire's lifeline, the Suez Canal, as well as to British bases at Malta and Gibraltar. Already seriously run-down as the best equipment was siphoned off for the defence of Britain against a possible German invasion, the small British garrison in Egypt was vulnerable and difficult to supply. Mussolini had ordered the invasion of Egypt in early August 1940, and by 16 September the Italian 10th Army had occupied and dug in around the Egyptian town of Sidi Barrani. Outnumbered ten to one, the small British force under General Sir Claude Auchinleck had begun planning for Operation Compass, a series of large-scale raids against the Italian fortresses that would be led by a plucky and aggressive general named Richard O'Connor. Owen Boyd was being sent to Egypt to attempt to revitalise and reorganise the RAF's response to the Italian threat. Boyd seemed the ideal choice – a pugnacious First World War decorated flyer whose last post had been leading RAF Balloon Command, providing vital barrage balloon cover for Britain's cities.

But now, eleven hours after leaving England, Air Marshal Boyd's plane was a battered wreck lying in a Sicilian field. After they had dodged German flak near Paris, Wellington T-2873 from 214 Middle East Flight had headed out over a wet and stormy Mediterranean towards Egypt, with a scheduled refuelling stop at Malta.[4] But an apparent navigational error and consequent fuel shortage had brought the Wellington too close to the island of Sicily where it was immediately pounced upon by alert Italian fighters and forced down.[5] Questions would be asked as to why Boyd's plane had been sent unescorted to the Middle East by such an obviously dangerous route, especially as he was one of the few senior officers that were privy to the secrets of Bletchley Park and the 'Ultra' intelligence emanating from cracking the German Enigma code.[6] It was for this reason that Boyd, still shaken up from the crash landing, struggled to burn the aircraft and his private papers that had been carried aboard.

The boxes full of banknotes that Leeming had kicked overboard into the sea had been loaded under guard in England. They had been destined for the British headquarters in Cairo as well, vital operating funds for various hush-hush sections that conducted 'butcher and bolt' operations behind enemy lines. Once the Wellington had been hit, Boyd had pointed at the small pile of grey boxes and yelled at Leeming: 'Get rid of it, John! We're going down in enemy territory!'[7] Shortly afterwards Leeming, his heart heavy at the sacrifice, had kicked out the quarter of a million pounds, ironically enough

4

money in 1940 to buy a replacement Wellington three-and-a-half times over.[8]

It had only been because of the direct intervention of Prime Minister Winston Churchill that Boyd had been on the plane. Air Chief Marshal Longmore had requested a different officer be appointed his deputy, Air Vice-Marshal Arthur Tedder, but the Prime Minister had rejected Tedder and approved Boyd's promotion instead.[9] With Boyd having been taken prisoner, Tedder would now assume Boyd's post anyway.

*

Boyd looked up from his frantic job of setting fire to the front of the plane and spotted movement. A motley collection of Sicilian peasants, dressed in their traditionally colourful open-necked shirts, broad waist sashes and trousers worn with puttees up to their knees, were gingerly approaching the crash scene, armed with wood axes. They had been cutting down trees near the village of Comiso. 'Stop them, John,' shouted Boyd at Leeming. Leeming turned and stared at the peasants. With their axes slung over their shoulders, moustachioed faces and old-fashioned clothes, they looked like the kinds of rogues who had been at Blackbeard's side. Leeming swallowed hard and stood rooted to the spot. Boyd's booming and irritated voice repeated his order. *Is this how it ends for me*, thought Leeming gloomily, *I survive a plane crash only to be murdered by Sicilian cut-throats?*

Focusing his mind, Leeming followed his friend's order and began walking towards the Sicilian peasants. He touched the .38 calibre Webley revolver that he wore in a holster around his waist, but then thought better of it. He didn't relish waving a gun in the face of these well-armed locals, particularly a gun that only held six shots when there were fifteen armed Sicilians. Instead, he reached into his shirt pocket and pulled out a battered packet of Woodbines and a stub of pencil and started to draw a Union Jack.[10] Holding up his artwork before the Sicilians, he noticed how the sun glinted off the sharp axe blades that were slung over their shoulders. The peasants soon gathered around him in an excited, chattering mass as they debated loudly what to do.[11] Suddenly, over Leeming's shoulder the cockpit of the shattered Wellington burst into flames with a loud 'whoomph', startling the Sicilians who began running around, yelling and shrieking excitedly. They were clearly worried about explosions, probably thinking that the Wellington was equipped with a full bomb load. Leeming took the opportunity to retreat to where Boyd, Squadron Leader Samuels, Flight Lieutenant Payn, Pilot Officer Watson and Sergeant Wynn had gathered near the aircraft's tail.[12] Thick black smoke poured from the front of the plane, blotting out the harsh sun, as the flames devoured the Wellington's interior. Boyd smiled at his handiwork.

Leeming, determined to salvage his personal kit before the rest of the plane was engulfed, climbed back inside the fuselage. Grabbing the kit, he was suddenly lifted out of the aircraft as if thrown by a huge hand, landing in a winded pile on the grass. Squadron Leader Samuels had managed to arm a special explosive device designed to destroy the plane's sensitive equipment shortly before they had crashed, and this had detonated just as Leeming grabbed his kit. Leeming had had enough. He lay on his back on the grass attempting to recover his composure, the pain in his arm bothering him, listening to Boyd attempting to coax the Sicilians back over in a loud, impatient voice, telling them in English that there were no bombs on board. His efforts were suddenly undermined when the flames reached the oxygen cylinders carried aboard the Wellington, which promptly exploded, spraying shrapnel through the air. Leeming, Boyd and the others jumped to their feet and ran after the Sicilians, anxious to put as much distance as possible between themselves and the rapidly disintegrating plane.[13]

*

It had already been a long road for Leeming, at 45 years old one of the oldest Flight Lieutenants in the RAF. Born in Chorlton,

Lancashire in 1895, Leeming had demonstrated an early talent for writing, publishing his first article at the age of thirteen. He was later to write many bestselling books, some indulging his fascination with aviation. While at school he witnessed some of the early efforts at powered flight and quickly became hooked. In 1910, aged fifteen, Leeming had built his first glider, and he continued to build and fly gliders throughout the 1920s. Moving on to powered aircraft, Leeming had achieved lasting fame in 1928 when he and Avro's chief test pilot Bert Hinkler became the first people to land an aircraft on a mountain in Britain. They selected 3,117-foot-high Helvellyn in the Lake District for their stunt, managing to set down and take off again in an Avro 585 biplane. Leeming had founded Northern Air Lines in 1928, and he was instrumental in finding a new airport site for Manchester at Ringway.

In the early 1930s Leeming had branched out into horticulture, building a stunning garden at Bowden, writing bestselling gardening books and creating the character 'Claudius the Bee' for the *Manchester Evening News*. Walt Disney bought the film rights. With the onset of war in 1939 Leeming had been commissioned into the RAF and appointed as aide-de-camp to Air Marshal Boyd. Though separated by a considerable difference in rank, Leeming at 45 and Boyd at 51 were close in age and united by their fascination with flying, going back to childhood for both men. They were to become close friends and comrades during the coming years of adversity.

*

'You know,' declared Air Marshal Boyd to Leeming, Samuels and the other RAF crewmen who were sitting inside a tiny house before a large audience of excited villagers, 'all this is highly irregular.'[14] Boyd, who was seated on the only chair inside the hovel, was referring to the fact that the Sicilian peasants had yet to disarm them. The Air Marshal was a stickler for the rules and regulations, and dealing with civilians, particularly *foreign* civilians, was wearing what remained of his patience thinner. Each Briton still wore his service revolver on a webbing gun belt around his waist. Boyd, noted Leeming, sat in the centre of the room 'like some medieval monarch holding Court, we grouped like courtiers around him, the crowd of chattering villagers facing us.'[15] Boyd, stern-faced and clearly not impressed by the situation, decided upon a 'proper' gesture. It was inconceivable that no one had yet demanded that they surrender. 'We'd better hand over our revolvers,' he stated, resolutely making up his mind.

Boyd slowly rose from his chair and reached into his holster, pulling out his pistol, Leeming and the Wellington's crew following suit. But if Boyd had expected a formal surrender ceremony he was soon disabused of the notion as a peasant instantly snatched the proffered sidearm from Boyd's outstretched hand, while other Sicilians crowded forward in a noisy tumult. The British revolver was worth a considerable sum of money to the impoverished locals, who soon descended into a pushing and shoving mob who competed loudly and increasingly violently for ownership.

Boyd, not content to see his surrender gesture reduced to a farce, acted swiftly to restore order. He suddenly launched himself into the crowd, his squat, broad-shouldered frame bulling through the riotous locals and roaring at the peasant who had taken his pistol: 'Give it to me!' Though the Air Marshal was rather diminutive, the peasants reacted to Boyd's force of personality, drawing back from the red-faced and shouting foreigner in fear. It was a magnificent display of sheer bravado on Boyd's part, but entirely in keeping with his strong character. 'Give me that!' shouted Boyd, snatching the pistol from the peasant who'd originally pinched it. He broke it open and emptied the shells into his other hand before snapping the pistol shut and handing it back. 'Now you'll be safe,' Boyd explained to the confused peasant, enunciating each word in the loud manner many English use when addressing foreigners. 'Silly devils! You might have shot yourselves!'[16]

Shortly afterwards a unit from the Royal Italian Navy arrived from a nearby base and formally took Boyd and his companions prisoner. This time the 'surrender ceremony' was a good deal more dignified, and Boyd was satisfied. The Britons were conveyed by car to the Italians' base where they were given an enormous meal before being taken on to the town of Catania, on Sicily's east coast.[17] Their journey into an uncertain captivity had commenced.

*

Darkness had fallen by the time the car carrying Boyd and Leeming arrived at Catania. Their fellow captives were being separately conveyed to another camp.

'Dear me,' muttered Boyd under his breath as he looked out the car window. 'The place is lit up like a bally Christmas tree.' Both RAF officers were struck by the ineffective local blackout, with shops still brightly lit and even streetlamps on in places. Boyd did a fair amount of tut-tutting under his breath as they drove by, making comparisons with the British blackout. Eyebrows were raised further when Boyd and Leeming were summoned to see 49-year-old Major-General Ettore Lodi, the handsome and rather serious officer commanding the 3rd Air Division 'Centauro' and the senior Italian on Sicily.[18] Lodi was deeply proud of his 'blackout', and took pains to point out to Air Marshal Boyd that many of the city's street lamps were extinguished. Turning to Boyd, through an interpreter he asked for his professional opinion of his efforts. The Air Marshal, 'one of those honest people who say what they really think',[19] told him.

A red-faced General Lodi and his ADC personally showed the exhausted RAF officers to their quarters. Each man was given a bedroom, sharing a spartan bathroom. After being left alone for a while, the Britons heard someone moving around outside the door to Boyd's room. Intrigued, Boyd and Leeming cracked the door slightly and peeked out. Standing in the corridor was a bored-looking Italian soldier armed with a rifle and fixed bayonet. Using sign language, Boyd managed to ascertain that the sentry was to remain on duty outside the door all night. This news seemed to strike Boyd as an affront.

'The poor chap won't be relieved all night, John,' said Boyd, his brow deeply furrowed by this further evidence of Italian military inadequacy. 'It's just not on, John, not on at all.'

During his previous commands, Boyd had built up a sterling reputation as an officer that genuinely cared for the welfare of those serving under him. Typically of the man, Boyd now extended this solicitude to his enemy.

'The poor devil can't stand there all night,'[20] he said, still baffled by the incompetence of it all. Suddenly he made up his mind and strode across his room, snatching up one of the warped wooden chairs that they had been issued with and handed it to the sentry, indicating that he should sit. The astonished sentry, his eyes round with amazement, took the chair from Boyd.

'*Grazie, grazie,*' said the sentry over and over, making little bowing movements before finally sitting down.

'Not at all, my dear chap,' said Boyd, grinning, as he closed the door.

'That Lodi devil ought to be relieved of his command, John,' said Boyd once the door was shut. 'Can you imagine a *British* officer treating his chaps in such a fashion?' Leeming admitted that he couldn't and sat on his bed while the Air Marshal pottered about the room muttering about 'incompetence' and 'slovenliness' until he finished hanging up his uniform and retired to bed.

After a little while they heard a key being gently turned in the door and for the first time their situation sank in – they were prisoners of war. 'There seemed something grim and final about the turning of the key,'[21] wrote Leeming. For a long time he stared into the darkness, unable to sleep and more than a little apprehensive about what the morrow would bring.

*

'My God! I'm slipping, John!' the voice from outside the window said in a fierce whisper. It was the dead of night and Air Marshal

Boyd was clinging for dear life to a rickety drainpipe that ran outside his bedroom window down to a drain at the foot of the building. Leeming leaned out of the open window and grasped his boss by both arms. 'I'll pull you in, sir,' he gasped, attempting to take the strain. But it was easier said than done. For a few seconds it was touch and go, as Leeming thought that he would have to make a decision between dropping Boyd the twenty feet to the stone courtyard below or risking being dragged out of the window by the weight of the Air Marshal's dangling frame. But, after much struggling and cursing, Leeming managed to pull Boyd up to the ledge, where the exhausted Air Marshal clambered back inside, the beam of a sentry's torch settling momentarily upon Boyd's struggling legs and posterior as they disappeared over the window ledge. Seconds later the bedroom door burst open and several Italian soldiers rushed over to subdue the two struggling RAF officers. This first attempted escape from the Italian HQ at Catania, where Boyd and Leeming were imprisoned for several weeks, had been precipitated by Leeming's pre-war reading of thrillers featuring dashing cat burglars who shinned like cats up drainpipes to crack safes and steal jewels. 'What we failed to realise was that at our age climbing down a drainpipe was a precarious and difficult feat,'[22] wrote Leeming later with commendable understatement. Only after this false start did Boyd realise that they had gone about the thing the wrong way. 'Further experience would have suggested the use of sheets,'[23] he would comment, without a trace of irony.

Leeming was constantly amazed by his boss's ability to soldier on. Boyd's career had effectively come to an end when his plane had been forced down in Sicily. If he had reached Egypt he could have expected eventually to have taken full command of the RAF in the Middle East, to have been promoted to Air Chief Marshal and in all likelihood to have received a knighthood. As it was, those honours and more besides were to go to the man that Churchill had originally blocked from the post, Arthur Tedder. While Boyd would languish in captivity, Tedder would rise to fame, eventually becoming Deputy Supreme Allied Commander under General Dwight D. Eisenhower.[24]

The fortunes of war were further compounded for Boyd when he received a letter from London while a prisoner at Catania, informing him that as he had only held the rank of Air Marshal for seventeen days before capture, and as 21 days were required *before* confirmation of promotion, he was hereby demoted to Air Vice-Marshal and his pay was concomitantly reduced. But Leeming never heard Boyd utter a single word of complaint. Instead, the tough old dog started plotting his next escape. Considering what he had lost, it is small wonder that Boyd was so determined to get back home and back into some position of influence over the course of the war.

The drainpipe episode earned Leeming and Boyd a transfer to Rome, with the crew of their shot-down Wellington joining them. The headquarters at Catania was never designed to hold prisoners of war, and Boyd had by now learned that the Italian press had dubbed him 'Italy's Prize Prisoner'.[25] Clearly, Mussolini intended that his prize should be secured somewhere more appropriate – a location where shinning down drainpipes in the dead of night might be less of an option.

Boyd and Leeming finally left Catania in a battered military bus provided by General Lodi, who was thrilled to see the back of them, bound for the port of Messina, their suitcases crammed full of enough Italian toilet paper to last them for at least a year: almost as soon as Boyd had arrived at the Catania HQ, he had started stealing the toilet paper. Leeming was initially nonplussed by his boss's new pastime.

'Damned primitive,' said Boyd, pointing at their joint bathroom. 'And this is an HQ, John. Imagine what a prison camp is going to be like. No, we need to prepare for every eventuality and err on the side of caution.' So caution dictated that the two of them pinch every roll of lavatory paper that the Italians provided. Leeming later wrote that the Italians must have been considerably baffled by this strange behaviour. Each morning when they inspected the prisoners' toilet they discovered an empty lavatory roll hanging on its spool, and duly replaced the paper. Each morning, an entire fresh roll was gone. British intestinal habits must have quietly amazed and fascinated their captors, Leeming would surmise.

Whether Boyd and Leeming would need all that pilfered toilet paper now that they had departed from Lodi's HQ, only time would tell. For now, their ultimate destination remained top secret.

CHAPTER 2

A Gift of Goggles

*'The Italians were hatefully full of themselves, for they had
had a bumper week with a galaxy of generals in the bag...'*

Major-General Adrian Carton de Wiart

On the evening of 6 April 1941 two cars sped across the Western Desert, headed for Tmimi, Libya. The first, a Lincoln Zephyr, carried the past and present commanders of the Western Desert Force, Lieutenant-Generals Sir Richard O'Connor and Sir Philip Neame, along with another seasoned desert campaigner, Brigadier John Combe, and a driver. Behind them, a Ford Mercury held Neame and O'Connor's batmen, Neame's aide-de-camp Lieutenant the Earl of Ranfurly, and a driver.[1]

The desert campaign that had been going so well for the Allies at the beginning of the year had suffered an alarming reversal of fortunes since the Italian forces had been joined by Germany's *Afrika Korps*. Now, with their headquarters at Marawa in danger of being overrun by the rapidly advancing Germans, Neame, O'Connor, Combe and their aides had taken the decision to evacuate and withdraw to Tmimi.

Dick O'Connor had arrived in Libya just days before, Sir Archibald Wavell, British commander-in-chief in the Middle East, having decided that he needed to call upon the talents of his finest desert general once again. It was not that Wavell lacked confidence in the present commander of the Western Desert Force, the indomitable and brilliant Neame, it was just that Neame lacked desert experience while O'Connor had virtually written the book on North African campaigning.

O'Connor had first joined the army in 1909, and had returned from the First World War with a Military Cross and the Distinguished Service Order and Bar, indicating the second award of a decoration that ranked only one place below that of the Victoria Cross. He had gone on to command a brigade along the fiercely dangerous Northwest Frontier of India in 1936 and faced down the Arab Revolt in Jerusalem in 1940. But it was his performance in Africa that had established his reputation. With his short grey hair and neatly trimmed white moustache, 'General Dick', as his contemporaries fondly knew him, had taken command of the Western Desert Force with the ominous task of trying to stop the massive Italian invasion of Egypt. With a force much smaller than his opponent, O'Connor had done just that, launching Operation Compass on 9 December 1940. In two days the British had smashed the Italians at Sidi Barrani. O'Connor had then pushed the Italians back into Libya.

In January 1941, he had reorganised Western Desert Force then struck the Italian fortress of Bardia. It fell after two days of fighting. On 21 January O'Connor's forces had captured the strategically vital port of Tobruk. In February Beda Fomm had fallen, O'Connor capturing 20,000 Italians for the loss of just nine British and Australians killed and fifteen wounded. In a stunning run of victories over ten weeks, O'Connor's force had captured 130,000 Italian and Libyan troops and almost 400 tanks.[2] But it was O'Connor's very successes that had changed the course of the war in North Africa in the Axis' favour. Hitler had been so alarmed by British successes in the desert that he had decided that he must support Benito Mussolini before Italy was completely knocked out of the war. In February 1941, while the British Army shuffled its pack, making O'Connor General Officer Commanding British Troops in Egypt and appointing Neame to Western Desert Force, advance elements of Major-General Erwin Rommel's *Afrika Korps* had begun to disembark at Tripoli.

On 31 March 1941 Rommel had struck, launching a surprise counteroffensive that threw the Western Desert Force on to the defensive and saved the Italian Army. Matters had been compounded for the British by Winston Churchill's insistence on sending men and materiel to Greece to aid the futile struggle there – Wavell simply didn't have the units with which to stop the combined German–Italian offensive and was soon forced to give ground.

With O'Connor no longer in command of Western Desert Force, the new man had struggled to manage what was soon shaping up to be a losing battle. Fifty-three-year-old Lieutenant-General Sir Philip Neame was a sapper, commissioned into the Royal Engineers in 1908. Serious, of average height, precise and quietly humorous, Neame hailed from the Shepherd Neame brewing dynasty in Kent. A man of immense personal courage, during the Battle of Neuve Chapelle in France on 19 December 1914 he had single-handedly held up the German advance for 45 minutes by lobbing grenade after grenade at large numbers of enemy troops while a battalion of the West Yorkshires evacuated their wounded. For this extraordinary feat of arms Neame had been awarded the Victoria Cross. Even more incredibly, he had followed this up a decade later by winning a Gold Medal for shooting at the 1924 Paris Olympics, the only VC to ever have become an Olympic champion.

During leaves from the army Neame had pursued his other twin passions – exploring and big game hunting. He'd explored 'all sorts of strange places where the natives were anything but friendly ... climbed mountains in the wildest parts of the world, [and] shot all the most especially difficult kinds of big game.'[3] In India, Neame had been clawed and almost killed by a Bengal tiger, and still proudly carried the scars.

Nicknamed 'Green Ink' by some of his contemporaries for his rather affectatious use of a green pen on all his correspondence, Neame had commanded a brigade in India between the wars before being appointed Commandant of the Royal Military Academy

Woolwich in 1938, charged with turning out new officers for the army.

When Wavell, in desperation, had offered the newly knighted O'Connor command of Western Desert Force on 3 April 1941 he had refused, explaining that 'changing horses in midstream would not really help matters.' At Wavell's request, though, O'Connor had agreed to 'advise' Neame, bringing with him the 46-year-old Brigadier Combe, lately commanding officer of the 11th Hussars, a regiment that had first won widespread public fame during the Charge of the Light Brigade in 1854. In true cavalry style, Combe had commanded a flying column consisting of out-of-date Rolls-Royce and Morris armoured cars that had cut off the Italian retreat at Mersa el Brega in early 1941.[4] A good-looking man of medium height with brown hair and the ubiquitous military moustache, Combe had, like his boss, been awarded the DSO and Bar for his desert exploits and was tipped for higher command.

Following the decision to withdraw to Tmimi, the bulk of XIII Corps headquarters staff had left Marawa by 8.30pm. Only then had O'Connor, Neame and their closest aides left.

Their little convoy had originally consisted of three cars. Bringing up the rear of the convoy had been a Chevrolet Utility containing General O'Connor's aide-de-camp, Captain John Dent, a driver and most of the senior officers' baggage and bedding. Dent, though, had lost the other two cars an hour after starting out as they threaded their way through slow-moving columns of retreating British trucks.[5]

Now, Neame ordered his driver to turn off the main road to Derna and take a shortcut that he knew to Martuba. The driver was exhausted, and Neame took the wheel himself. The two big American cars thundered on through the dark desert night along the dusty road. After ten miles Brigadier Combe spotted a signboard that had been stuck to an old jerrycan beside the road and suggested that they stop and examine it. Neame refused, claiming that he knew the road and not to worry.

After driving for a further two or three miles General O'Connor was becoming uneasy, noticing that the position of the Moon indicated that they were heading north rather than east. He voiced his concerns to Neame several times, until Neame finally stopped and allowed his driver to take the wheel again. They resumed the journey, the officers nodding off in their cars until the drivers alerted them to another slow-moving convoy ahead.

In the second car Lord Ranfurly spoke to his driver about the convoy of trucks that was difficult to make out in the dim light as the cars were fitted with blackout-shielded headlights. A dashing Scottish aristocrat, the athletic 27-year-old Earl of Ranfurly, known as Dan to his friends and serving in the Nottinghamshire Yeomanry, was the sixth holder of the earldom.[6] He was possessed of a very formidable and determined wife. Refusing to be left behind in England when Dan went off to war, Hermione, Countess of Ranfurly, broke every army rule and protocol and managed to get herself to Cairo where she was able to see her husband when he went on leave.

Up ahead, Neame's car came to a halt. Ranfurly stuck his head out of the passenger window in the car behind and listened. Mingled with the sounds of the trucks' engines was distant shouting – foreign voices. But it was too indistinct to attribute nationality.

'Must be Cypriots,' said Ranfurly uncertainly to his driver. The British had conscripted many Cypriots to drive supply trucks in the Middle East. 'Just hang on here a minute,' he continued, opening the door and walking over to Neame's car. About to confer with Brigadier Combe, who had climbed out of the front passenger seat of Neame's car, suddenly Ranfurly was aware of movement. A figure came out of the gloom and thrust an MP-40 machine pistol at his middle.[7] Combe's face dropped in astonishment.

'*Hände hoch, Tommi*,' growled the German. Ranfurly slowly raised both arms above his head. The German soldier, uniform coated in desert dust and wearing a tan-coloured forage cap, shouted for help.

Combe quickly turned to the car window and roused the dozing

Neame and O'Connor. Combe reached into the glovebox and pulled out a hand grenade, stuffing it into his clothing.

'Get down on the floor and remove your badges of rank,' hissed Combe urgently at the generals.[8]

General O'Connor, looking around wildly as more Germans came running up to the cars, hastily unclipped his service revolver from its lanyard before shoving it inside his shirt, and then pulled off his rank slides.[9] Seconds later, the car doors were wrenched open by German soldiers. '*Raus, raus,*' yelled a German sergeant, pointing a Luger pistol at the officers.

The Britons were herded at gunpoint into a nearby hollow, where they would remain under guard for three nights. On the third day Neame and O'Connor revealed their identities to the commanding officer of the 8th Machine Gun Battalion, *Oberstleutnant* Gustav Ponath.[10] He hardly dared to believe his luck. Within minutes Ponath was on the radio to Rommel with very good news indeed.

Ponath packed the senior prisoners off, with their ADCs and batmen, in a truck to Derna where they were handed over to the Italians, who had command authority over the North African theatre.[11]

In one fell swoop a massive blow had been dealt to the Allied cause. The Western Desert Force was suddenly deprived of its commander and the desert genius assisting him just at the most critical moment of Rommel's offensive. The shock almost paralysed the British chain of command, deeply depressing General Wavell when he heard the terrible news.

*

Mechili, Libya wasn't much of a place – just a name on a map of the barren Western Desert. Brigadier Edward Todhunter would describe it as 'a horrible little place in the desert'.[12] But it was where Michael Gambier-Parry's war was to take a very bad turn for the worse.

On 25 March 1941, forward patrol units of Major-General Gambier-Parry's 2nd Armoured Division had been attacked and

El Agheila taken. Things had then gone quiet for a week before Rommel struck again on 1 April. The 2nd Division had been forced to withdraw, moving east towards Egypt in stages, fighting continuous sharp engagements with *Afrika Korps* panzer regiments. Rommel launched a pincer attack on the British division, using the Italian 10th *Bersaglieri* Regiment and elements of the German 5th Light Division and the 15th Panzer Division. The British and Indian troops, the latter the 3rd Indian Motor Brigade under the command of Brigadier Edward Vaughan, were exhausted by the pace of the operations and increasingly demoralised. On 4 April, Gambier-Parry, or 'G-P' as he was known to his friends, was given orders to block the Western Desert Force's open left flank, but it was realised that though brave, the 2nd Armoured Division was inexperienced, short of personnel, ammunition and signal equipment; furthermore, G-P's command of the division had left a lot to be desired. Among higher command there had been mutterings concerning a 'lack of urgency and grip of the situation'.[13]

By the time G-P and his divisional HQ arrived at Mechili, 60 miles south of Derna, on the evening of 7 April, they were at the limits of their endurance.[14] The 2nd Armoured Division, in the words of one senior commander, 'more or less fell to pieces.'[15]

Forty-one-year-old Brigadier Todhunter was with G-P as the 2nd Armoured Division's 'Commander Royal Artillery'. His command group received sporadic shelling from German artillery on the morning of 8 April, as well as plenty of long-range machine gunning. This lasted all day until the evening, when the intensity of German shelling suddenly increased in ferocity and infantry began probing the perimeter. The British troops beat the Germans off this time, but casualties were mounting and the strategic situation was deteriorating all along the divisional front line as Rommel brought his armour to bear.

Todhunter had only been made a brigadier the month before, while he had been on leave in Cairo. Born into a landed family from

South Essex, Todhunter had joined the Royal Horse Artillery in 1922 after leaving Rugby. He had thick, dark, oiled-back hair and wore black-framed spectacles that made him look more like a university professor than a tough and experienced soldier. Sent back to the front line in Libya, he had joined Gambier-Parry's staff with the rank of Temporary Brigadier.

The British began to move again at first light on 9 April, always east towards Egypt and safety. Todhunter was tasked with organising some defence for divisional headquarters, Gambier-Parry and his staff having moved up to the front 'unprotected and without any knowledge of how close the enemy were'.[16] But Rommel was upon them instantly. 'As soon as it was light enough to see we ran into really heavy shellfire,' wrote Todhunter a few days afterwards. 'Lots of it and fairly big stuff and a little further on we ran into a lot of machine guns and anti-tank guns.'[17] Moving in their large Dorchester command vehicles, the division's senior officers decided to turn the column south in the hope of outwitting the Germans, before resuming their withdrawal to the east. With G-P and Todhunter were Brigadier Vaughan (known to all as 'Rudolph') and his Indian soldiers and Colonel George Younghusband, a senior cavalryman and kinsman of the famous Edwardian explorer Sir Francis Younghusband, the conqueror of Tibet. Younghusband was GSO1 (General Staff Officer Grade 1), responsible for directing the battle and signing off Gambier-Parry's orders. Younghusband had already impressed higher command, which noted that he 'gave confidence'.[18]

'Things looked pretty gloomy,' wrote Todhunter at the time with commendable understatement. The withdrawal manoeuvre was doomed to failure as the British ran straight into large numbers of German tanks shortly after setting off.

Todhunter's Dorchester had just crested a slight rise in the ground when six German tanks confronted him and his men. Infantry were firing machine guns, and anti-tank guns had opened up on the British column as well, brewing up several British tanks and armoured cars in a confused engagement. Within seconds German bullets peppered Todhunter's vehicle, some armour-piercing rounds passing between his legs. One punched a hole right through his attaché case. Suddenly there was a terrific crack and the Dorchester rocked on its springs, smoke and dust filling the cabin. An anti-tank round had struck home, passing clean through the vehicle like a hot knife through butter.[19] Todhunter and his staff hastily baled out, taking cover as the German panzers closed in. Within a few minutes it was clear that the headquarters of the 2nd Armoured Division, and those units helping to defend it, were not going anywhere. They were surrounded. Men began to raise their hands.[20]

Dust and smoke billowed across the hot battlefield as about 2,000 British and Indian troops laid down their arms over a large area and columns of German troops moved up to take their surrender. Todhunter's staff captain turned to him.

'Sir, there's a good chance we can get away now, in all this confusion,' he said, slightly wild-eyed.

'I agree,' replied Todhunter, looking about in all directions. 'Look, you wander off and leave me. I'll follow in a couple of minutes. At the moment I'm a bit too conspicuous in this bloody red hat.'[21] He touched his field cap, its middle band the bright red reserved for colonels and higher. His shirt collar was also adorned with red tabs.

'But sir,' protested the captain.

'Go on … get going!' exclaimed Todhunter, clapping him on the shoulder. 'I'll be there presently.'

The captain reluctantly walked off, away from the approaching Germans, gathering men as he went. He managed to slip through the German encirclement and would make it to the British base at Mersa Matruh a few days later with 51 comrades, having also collected eight abandoned vehicles along the way to speed his escape.[22]

For Todhunter, his war appeared to be over. Another officer who escaped the encirclement reported a few days later that Todhunter 'was last seen in the filthiest temper and using appalling language.'[23]

His foul mood was more than shared by all the other officers and men who were now 'in the bag'.

*

An hour later, Michael Gambier-Parry stood and watched as a battered Horch staff jeep bounced its way across the rocky desert floor towards him. G-P hooked his thumbs into his gun belt, the holster now empty of its heavy service revolver, and waited. Standing beside him were three other British officers, the red tabs on the collars of their grimy shirts and red hatbands indicating their elevated ranks. Dozens of other British officers and men stood close by three large Dorchester command vehicles, giant armoured boxes on wheels the dimensions of those normally found beneath transport planes. Several British armoured cars and trucks lay scattered across the desert, badly shot up or still emitting plumes of black smoke into the clear blue sky, evidence of the ferocious battle that had ended not long before. German soldiers stood around cradling rifles and machine pistols in their arms, while medics from both sides tended to casualties wrapped in blankets on the dusty ground or propped up in the shade of trucks.

'What do we have here, chaps?' muttered Todhunter at Gambier-Parry's elbow, his eyes fixed on the large staff jeep that had drawn to a creaking halt close by. Todhunter adjusted his spectacles, removing his cap to run the back of one hand across his sweaty forehead.

The others remained silent, George Younghusband reaching into his hip pocket to retrieve a silver cigarette case. He offered it around, but only Todhunter helped himself to a smoke, the stiff desert wind whipping the smoke away as he lit up behind cupped hands.

A German soldier, one of several dressed in the sand-coloured uniform of the *Afrika Korps*, dashed forward to the staff vehicle and quickly yanked open the passenger side door. A medium-sized, middle-aged German officer hauled himself out of his seat, one hand steadying a pair of large binoculars that hung around his neck, the other adjusting a button on his knee-length black leather great-coat that was grimy with desert dust. Several other field cars and half-tracks ground to a halt close by and staff officers, many festooned with map cases and signal pads, joined the senior German, who strode towards Gambier-Parry with an air of determination.

'Well, I never …' exclaimed Younghusband as he recognised the German general.

'Gentlemen,' said a young *Afrika Korps* captain formally, in good English, 'allow me to present *Generalleutnant* Rommel.'

The Desert Fox, his keen dark blue eyes twinkling with good humour beneath the peak of his field grey service cap, stopped before Gambier-Parry, a friendly grin creasing his weather-beaten, tanned face.

'General,' said Rommel, touching the peak of his cap with one gloved hand.

'Sir,' replied Gambier-Parry, returning Rommel's salute. G-P's companions followed suit. So this was the great Rommel, thought G-P, looking the German over with renewed interest. The Britons watched as Rommel adjusted a patterned civilian scarf that was tucked around the collar of his coat, noticing the Knight's Cross and the First World War Blue Max that he wore beneath. Rommel spoke to a young captain who was standing beside him.

'My general presents his compliments,' said Rommel's interpreter, *Hauptmann* Hoffmann, 'and asks for your names please.'

'Gambier-Parry, Major-General, commanding 2nd Armoured Division.' Rommel nodded, tugged off his right glove and proffered his hand. Slightly taken aback, G-P shook it. The German's grip was firm and as dry as the surrounding desert.

'Brigadier Todhunter,' said G-P, pointing to the officer beside him, 'Brigadier Vaughan, and Colonel Younghusband.' Hoffmann made quick notes on a signal pad as Rommel's eyes scanned each man's grimy face. Then he said something in German to his interpreter.

'My general enquires whether there is anything that you need?'[24]

For the next few minutes Rommel and the senior officers chatted amiably enough through Hoffmann. It was clear to G-P and his officers that Rommel was a decent sort, and certainly no strutting Nazi. His concern for their welfare and comfort would make a lasting impression on the British officers.

'My general requests that you, General Gambier-Parry, join him for a meal, if you are in agreement?' asked Hoffmann. G-P was somewhat surprised but accepted nonetheless. It was a surreal end to an extraordinary day that had seen the British suffer a crushing defeat. The past couple of days had delivered to the enemy a host of demoralised British senior officers, all victims of the Desert Fox's tactical genius and aggressive handling of his small panzer force.

*

When Major-General Gambier-Parry arrived for dinner, he discovered that the Germans had erected a tent for the occasion. G-P seated himself opposite the Desert Fox, and over the next hour the two men, through the interpreter Hoffmann, swapped stories about the First World War, the desert, enjoyed good wine and at the end settled back to smoke 'excellent cigars'.[25] G-P was no stranger to the desert. An uncle of his, Major Ernest Gambier-Parry had been part of Kitchener's expedition to Egypt to avenge the death of General Gordon at Khartoum, and he had published a book on the campaign in 1895, six years before G-P was born. G-P's first personal experience of the desert had come in the First World War, when after winning a Military Cross in France and serving at the bloodbath of Gallipoli, he had fought the Turks in Mesopotamia. In 1924 G-P had transferred to the Royal Tank Corps, been a staff officer in London before becoming a brigade commander in Malaya. In 1940 the government had dispatched G-P to Athens as Head of the British Military Mission to Greece before promoting him to Major-General and assigning him command of the 2nd Armoured Division in North Africa.

As G-P rose to take his leave he noticed that his general's cap, which he had left on a map table outside the tent's entrance, was missing. He told Rommel, whose face took on a hard expression. Following Rommel outside, he watched as the Desert Fox made heated enquiries with junior officers until a few minutes later a young soldier was sheepishly brought before him holding G-P's cap. Rommel was furious, giving the soldier a loud tongue-lashing concerning appropriate souvenirs and military conduct, before returning the cap to G-P with an apology.

G-P felt that he should in some way thank the Desert Fox for dinner and the fuss that had been made over his errant cap. Thinking quickly, he reached into his hip pocket and retrieved a pair of plastic anti-gas goggles and presented them to Rommel. The Desert Fox was clearly touched by the gesture, and immediately placed them around his own service cap.[26] There they were to remain for the rest of his life, completing the image of the desert warrior that was to appear in so many photographs and newsreels before Rommel's untimely death in October 1944.[27]

Rommel permitted G-P, Todhunter and Vaughan to keep their Dorchester armoured offices and later on 9 April the prisoners, aboard whatever of their vehicles were still in running condition, were escorted by German half-tracks and motorcycle combinations to the airfield at Derna, where they bedded down for the night. The next day the Germans took the 2,000 prisoners to old barracks in Derna. On arrival they were surprised, and not a little relieved, to discover that they were to be handed over to the Italian Army.[28]

*

'It's quite simple,' said General Neame in a low voice. 'We take over the aircraft and fly it to our own lines.'[29] General O'Connor nodded vigorously, his whole demeanour since capture one of dogged determination to escape. General Gambier-Parry and Brigadiers Combe, Todhunter and Vaughan listened carefully to the plan during the short exercise time that the Germans permitted their prisoners each day at Derna. The group of senior British officers strolled around a dusty parade square in the dirty old barracks complex, puffing on pipes and cigarettes as they went over Neame's plan.

'Phil's right. It's obvious that the Jerries are going to shift us to Germany, and soon,' said O'Connor to the brigadiers. 'We've worked out a plan to hijack the plane that takes us to Berlin.' The fear was that the generals, because of their high ranks and command responsibilities privy to a vast amount of top-secret information, might be handed over to the Gestapo once pressure had been put on the Italian authorities under whose nominal authority they remained for the time being. At the very least, they could expect detailed and long interrogations by German military intelligence. The intelligence windfall for the Germans could potentially change the course of the war for Hitler.

The plan was outlined. It did seem remarkably straightforward, if somewhat reckless. The generals believed that they would be sent north to Germany in stages, accompanied by their ADCs and batmen. O'Connor had managed to fool the Germans into assigning a captive RAF pilot as his aide-de-camp since the disappearance of his actual ADC Captain Dent in the desert. O'Connor still had a fully loaded service revolver hidden on his person, and Brigadier Combe a primed hand grenade. The Germans, perhaps intimidated by the exalted ranks of their new prisoners, and concerned that every military courtesy be extended to them, had been loath to search Neame's party too thoroughly. The Germans also underestimated the resolve of the British generals to attempt to escape – such behaviour was considered virtually unthinkable by both the Germans and the Italians. Neame had, in the meantime, managed to find and hide a small hammer. The rest of the senior officers and their batmen would have their fists.

Neame's plan was brutally simple. Once airborne, and at a given signal, the POWs would spring into action and overpower the German guards inside the aircraft's cabin, and then O'Connor's

RAF ADC would replace the German pilot in the cockpit. The aircraft would then be flown to Allied lines in Egypt.[30] Everyone was keyed up for the operation, Lord Ranfurly writing that it was 'exciting waiting'.[31]

*

The Italians' bag of prisoners was not yet quite full. To it would be added one of the most extraordinary and larger-than-life characters in the history of warfare. And, like Air Vice-Marshal Boyd and Flight Lieutenant Leeming, this particular prisoner was to arrive quite unexpectedly from the sky, at the same time as General Neame and his friends were plotting to escape North Africa by air.

'We're going to have to ditch, sir, prepare for a landing on water!' was the last thing that Major-General Adrian Carton de Wiart heard from the cockpit of the Wellington bomber that was supposed to be taking him to Yugoslavia. De Wiart had been furiously attempting to struggle into a parachute harness, a stream of expletives flowing from beneath his salt-and-pepper moustache, when the call came through his headphones. He was relieved, as he didn't think that he could have squeezed his very tall frame through the small escape hatch set into the bomber's belly to parachute clear. De Wiart used his only hand to grip his seat tightly.

The 62-year-old warhorse had just been personally appointed by Churchill to head the British Military Mission in Yugoslavia. His journey there was by air via Malta. De Wiart's plane had been headed for Egypt, thereafter to turn north for Yugoslavia, when the emergency had struck. Both engines had inexplicably died, and De Wiart would later suspect sabotage as the cause. Running through his mind as his plane started to go down were the words of Air Marshal Sir Jack Baldwin when they had met on an airfield at Newmarket, Suffolk, two days before: 'Don't worry, old chap. I've sent 94 Wellingtons to the Middle East and only one failed to arrive.'[32]

De Wiart had thought that his war was over long before he

stepped aboard the Wellington in Suffolk, and the Yugoslavia mission had appeared to be his final service for King and Country before he was pensioned off. As the Wellington began its death dive towards the ocean below, De Wiart found that he was not scared. But this was probably because the word 'scared' was not in his vocabulary. He had already faced death over a dozen times in a military career that stretched back to the Boer War, and the general consensus of opinion was that the only thing that could kill Carton de Wiart was Carton de Wiart.

Tall, lean, balding and covered in scar tissue, De Wiart was half British, half Belgian, hailing from an aristocratic Brussels legal family. Rumoured to have been the illegitimate son of King Leopold II, De Wiart's brushes with death had begun in 1899 when he had disappeared from his studies at Oxford to enlist as a trooper in the British Army. He took a bullet in the stomach in South Africa, and after sufficient convalescence in England and the mollification of his Belgian lawyer father, who was angry with him for having abandoned his studies, De Wiart gained a commission in the cavalry. By 1901 he was back fighting the Boers. In 1907 he became a British citizen, and spent his leaves at shooting parties in various aristocratic castles around Europe, marrying an Austro-Hungarian noble, Countess Friederike von Babenhausen, daughter of Prince Karl Ludwig of Babenhausen, in 1908.

When the First World War broke out De Wiart showed his mettle at the Battle of Shimber Berris while commanding a unit of the famed Somaliland Camel Corps. De Wiart was shot twice in the face, losing his left eye and part of an ear, and in the process winning a DSO. Sent to London for recuperation, De Wiart checked himself into a nursing home on Park Lane. He would return to the same home after each fresh injury, 'becoming such a frequent occurrence that they kept his own pyjamas ready for his next visit'.[33] Henceforth sporting a black eye patch (a glass eye provided to him by doctors was thrown out of a taxi window when it proved uncomfortable),

De Wiart was sent to France where he was a battalion and then a brigade commander.

During the course of his service on the Western Front, De Wiart was wounded an astonishing *seven* further times. The list of his wounds is staggering: shot through the skull and ankle on the Somme, through the hip at Passchendaele, the leg at Cambrai, and the ear at Arras. He lost his left hand to shellfire in 1915. In fact, his hand was so mangled that De Wiart actually bit off some of his pulped fingers after a surgeon failed to help him. The entire hand was later amputated above the wrist. It is perhaps unsurprising that this bullet magnet eventually won a Victoria Cross in 1916 at the age of 36. During an attack, three of the brigade's battalion commanders were killed, so De Wiart, as the last lieutenant-colonel still on his feet, took command and constantly exposed himself to German fire as he organised, cajoled and encouraged the brigade forward, armed only with a walking stick. The brigade won the day, capturing the ground assigned to it.

At the conclusion of the First World War, De Wiart, missing an eye, parts of both ears, a lung and his left hand summed up his experiences succinctly: 'Frankly, I had enjoyed the war …'[34] But now, trapped in a diving Wellington bomber in April 1941, Carton de Wiart had not yet made up his mind whether he was going to enjoy his second world war.

De Wiart had only a hazy recollection of the Wellington hitting the water. When he regained consciousness he was being pushed through a hatch into the freezing cold sea, which instantly revived him. De Wiart and the RAF crew took refuge on the plane's wings, nursing their injuries. It was dark and the aircraft's rubber dinghy was punctured and useless. They were about a mile and a half off the North African coast. One crewman had a broken arm, the pilot a busted leg. But there was a cold northerly wind blowing rapidly inshore, and they soon found themselves about half a mile from the coast. Then, with a groan and several sharp cracks, the Wellington's fuselage suddenly broke in two and started to sink. De Wiart helped the injured pilot to swim towards the shore. The little group made it but landed straight into the hands of Italian native police.

'Lower that rifle immediately!' boomed De Wiart in Arabic, picked up as a child in Cairo where his father had practised law for a while. The native policeman obliged, a little startled by the forbidding presence of the tall British officer, hatless, shoeless and brandishing his only remaining possession, a bamboo cane inside which De Wiart had had the forethought to secrete a roll of banknotes. De Wiart, looking like a shipwrecked pirate with his eye patch and empty sleeve, questioned his captor.

'Where are the British forces?' he demanded, continuing in forceful Arabic.

'They go,' replied the policeman, 'they left here yesterday.'

De Wiart confounded their bad luck. If the Wellington had managed to stay airborne for a few more minutes De Wiart and the crew could well have come ashore in friendly territory.

Soon after, a local Italian priest arrived and led the British party to a small café, where he provided them with food and drink before arranging to take them to hospital. During their ride on a truck to the hospital, De Wiart tried to persuade his captors to take them to the British lines, but they were unmoved. They knew that the Italians would shortly arrive to reoccupy the town and they were determined to ingratiate themselves by handing over their impressively high-ranking prisoner.

As a doctor patched them up they heard the unmistakable sound of an aircraft out to sea. Looking outside, De Wiart and his party could see a British aircraft circling in the early morning light, evidently searching for them.

'Sabotage, sir. I have no doubts,' said the young pilot, his broken leg now set in plaster, to De Wiart as they watched the newly arrived British plane making its pointless sweeps over the sea. 'It's very unlikely that a Wellington would fail on one engine, let alone two, such a short way out from Malta.' De Wiart agreed. After a while the British search plane disappeared from view. 'We cursed that punctured rubber dinghy,' De Wiart wrote; 'our hearts sank low as the drone of the plane faded into the distance.'[35]

De Wiart resolved to escape, and quietly spoke to the RAF crewmen. They'd wait till darkness and then, once the native police had relaxed, slip off and try to make their own way down the coast to safety. But it was not to be. Two hours after arriving at the hospital the calm was interrupted by the sound of a field car pulling up outside the entrance. In strode two Italian staff officers, their polished jackboots ringing on the hospital's tiled floor. After questioning De Wiart, they announced that he was to accompany them to Bardia. Handed a pair of sand shoes, De Wiart bid farewell to his RAF crew, who, the Italians assured him, would be treated as prisoners of war and sent to a camp. He was later to discover that the pilot was shot, though for what reason remains a mystery.

The Italians officers drove De Wiart to Bardia where the mayor provided him and his escort with an excellent lunch. The party then drove on to the city of Benghazi, where De Wiart was ushered into a small hotel room and left under guard for the night.[36]

The night in that small, stuffy hotel room was one of the longest of De Wiart's life. 'Often in my life I had thought that I might be killed,' he wrote, 'and though death has no attraction for me, I regard it more or less phlegmatically. People who enjoy life seldom have much fear of death, and having taken the precaution to squeeze the lemon do not grudge throwing the rind away. But never, even in the innermost recesses of my mind, had I contemplated being taken a prisoner. I regarded it as the calamity that befell other people but never myself.'[37] It was a situation that Generals O'Connor, Neame and Gambier-Parry also had to come to terms with, along with the brigadiers and colonels who were captured with them. Each reacted in different ways.

'Though I never think of the Italians as great warriors,' wrote De Wiart of that time, 'they did seem to be having all the luck.'[38]

*

Neame's very daring plan was spoiled two days later when a *Luftwaffe* staff officer arrived to inform him and O'Connor that they were indeed flying to Berlin, but that they were not to be accompanied by any of their other staff or military servants. Still armed with the revolver and the hammer, O'Connor and Neame settled themselves on to a wooden bench seat that ran the length of the Junkers Ju 52's cabin, but any notions of attempting a hijacking were quickly dispelled. German soldiers armed with MP40 machine pistols took post at either end of the plane and watched the generals like hawks during the flight across the Mediterranean, which was made at a wave-skimming height of just 50 feet to avoid British fighters.

Just before Neame had boarded the Ju 52 at Derna airfield, he had spoken to an Italian officer and asked him to lodge a protest with his own headquarters. The British officers had been captured in an Italian theatre, and should by rights be handed over permanently to the Italian Army and kept in Italy, not taken to Germany.

When the plane landed at Messina in Sicily to refuel, Neame's protest seemed to have worked, for a heated argument developed between the *Luftwaffe* officer who was escorting them and some senior Italian officers, until Neame and his cohorts were bundled off the plane and handed over to the Italians.[39] It was a quiet victory for Neame, who had saved the senior officers from lengthy Gestapo interrogations once inside the Reich, and Italian military pride had been restored as Mussolini now possessed a host of British generals with which to underline before his people the prowess of Italian arms in the desert.

CHAPTER 3

Mazawattee's Mad House

'You know, these people don't know why they are at war with us.'

Air Vice-Marshal Owen Tudor Boyd
Sulmona, 1941

Flight Lieutenant John Leeming lay flat on the roof of the large house. He was dressed in his RAF uniform, its dark blue colour perfect night-time camouflage. His face had been blackened with soot from his room wood burner. He had been watching the garden for a couple of hours and cramp was starting to set in to his arms and legs. It was very quiet, just the occasional puff of wind stirring the trees and shrubs down below. Every so often one of the Italian guards would light a cigarette, the glow of a lighter or match providing a pinprick of bright light for a few seconds. The surrounding mountains and hills were difficult to make out, just tall gloomy backdrops to the little drama being played out at the villa.

Leeming strained his eyes to check various parts of the garden, looking for patches of shadow that could be used to conceal a body. Snatches of conversations between the guards drifted up to Leeming's hiding place. There were a lot of guards, their steel helmets reflecting the weak moonlight as they stood or paced around the perimeter of the house. Too many guards, thought Leeming.

His nocturnal observations at an end, Leeming carefully slid away from the edge of the roof back towards a trapdoor that led into the loft. Suddenly, his shoe caught on a loosened tile. It lifted and, before Leeming could catch it, banged back down with a loud crack.

Leeming's heart rate increased and he pressed himself into the roof, closing his eyes. He lay absolutely still, barely daring to breathe, trying to make himself as small as possible. Down below a guard snapped on a handheld torch, running its bright beam along the edge of the roof. Leeming squeezed his eyes even tighter shut and gripped the tiles around him. Any second now there would be a shout and then the sound of a rifle being cocked. Time seemed to slow down. But then the light suddenly shut off. There was no shout, no metallic click. Leeming listened as the sentry resumed his methodical patrol, his boots crunching loudly on a gravel path. Leeming waited for three minutes until his heart rate slowed before resuming his crawl back to the trapdoor and safety.

*

A few weeks earlier Leeming and Air Vice-Marshal Owen Boyd had sat inside a freezing cold railway carriage as it was slowly hauled higher into the mountainous Abruzzi region towards its destination: the small town of Sulmona, about 100 miles east of Rome. It was snowing outside the windows, thick drifts lining the railway tracks and causing several delays to their journey.

After disembarking from the train at Sulmona station, the two Britons had been hustled into a waiting car and driven two miles to their new home, the Villa Orsini. Along the way they passed walls adorned with a recurrent Fascist exhortation to the population: '*Credere! Abbidire! Combattere!*' ('Believe! Obey! Fight!'). As the car passed through the three-storey villa's large gates, Boyd and Leeming saw Italian soldiers with rifles slung over their shoulders, bundled up in steel helmets, greatcoats and mittens stamping their feet and blowing on their hands. The place looked well guarded.

The house itself was impressive. Before the grand entrance was a large marble fish pond surrounded by ornamental railings, its surface icy and frozen. The villa was a square building of buff-coloured stucco, its hillside garden scattered with classical statues[1] that were now half buried in snow. Stepping inside the house through a pair of elaborately carved wooden doors, Boyd and Leeming took in their new surroundings. The entrance hall floor was marble and before them stood a grand staircase. On first impressions, it appeared as though the prisoners had fallen on their feet, but closer inspection soon revealed that the Villa Orsini was badly designed and rather dilapidated.[2]

No one seemed to have had the forethought to actually inform the commandant that Boyd and Leeming were coming, so the villa was in a considerable state of disarray, with harassed Italian soldiers darting about, supplies piled in various rooms, and the commandant, a squat, rotund and permanently perspiring colonel, shouting orders in an excited voice above the din. Fortunately, out of this chaos emerged one man who seemed to know what he was doing, and who, ironically, was to become a friend to all of the British prisoners that were held in the villa over the next few months. Lieutenant Baron Agosto Ricciardi was a tall and elegant dark-haired man in his mid-twenties, from Naples.[3] He spoke excellent English, having had a British governess as a child, and he immediately put Boyd and Leeming at their ease. The contrast between the calm and collected Ricciardi and the excitable and loud commandant was stark. Ricciardi made sure that the two prisoners were served a hot meal after their long journey from Rome. They would soon take to calling this affable young Italian officer 'Gussie'.[4]

Two bearded young soldiers dressed in Italian uniforms stripped of insignia waited in silence on the prisoners as they sat at the polished mahogany dining table. Boyd was immediately suspicious, worrying that his captors might be able to speak English and listen in on his conversations with Leeming, perhaps hoping to glean some intelligence useful to the Italian war effort. Leeming took the initiative and decided to conduct a test, asking one of the mess waiters for something in English. He was stunned when the man replied without a hint of an Italian accent – rather it was a soft Scots burr that greeted his question.

'So you *do* speak English,' said Boyd, startled.

'I ought to, sir. My name's McWhinney. Sergeant, RAF.'[5]

McWhinney quickly introduced his serving partner, Sergeant Ronald Bain. The tough-looking Bain grinned, explaining that he was an observer and had been shot down over Libya. There was a third RAF sergeant, Baxter, also at the villa, cooking for the prisoners. An air gunner, Baxter had ended up in the sea when his Sunderland flying boat had been shot down. McWhinney had been a member of Baxter's crew. The three men had been plucked from *Campo 78*, a large prison camp at Sulmona that housed 3,000 British and Commonwealth officers and men captured in North Africa. McWhinney and his comrades had been taken up to the villa to act as domestic help for the new senior officer prisoners.[6] It was soon apparent that the three RAF sergeants were keen to assist with any escape attempts, and possessed some useful skills that Boyd and Leeming were to utilise in the near future.

*

Though ornately decorated, the Villa Orsini had stood empty for years before it was commandeered as a POW camp by the Italian government, so Boyd and Leeming spent the first few weeks of their imprisonment rehanging doors, unblocking taps and generally trying to make the place habitable. 'The Italian Government owes us a large bill for repairs,'[7] commented a grinning Boyd to Leeming when the work was finally complete. But at least the views were splendid, with a backdrop of tall mountains to the east and very high hills in all the other directions.[8] A high wall bounded the garden, with a pleasant terrace in front that looked out over the valley below, and the high mountains in the distance.[9]

The situation of their confinement was a little strange. Two British officers and three NCOs were held inside the large villa, guarded by two dozen Italian soldiers under the command of a man whose surname was so unpronounceable to the Brits that Boyd and

Leeming took to calling him Colonel 'Mazawattee'. The word, which they felt was a close approximation phonetically, was borrowed from the brand name of a colonial tea, and was derived from a conjunction of the Hindi word *mazaa* ('pleasure' or 'fun') and the Sinhalese *vatta* ('garden'). The commandant's single goal in life was peace and quiet, and not the hefty responsibility of guarding senior officer prisoners for *Il Duce*. Rome kept a weather eye on both the commandant and his charges, and the commandant felt the pressure keenly. But it appeared that Rome had appointed the worst possible officer for the task, as Boyd and Leeming soon discovered that Mazawattee was both idle and muddle-headed.[10] Were it not for the calm organisation and tactful diplomacy of Lieutenant Ricciardi, there would have been no surprise if tensions had escalated between the more Fascist elements of the Italian guard and their British captives.

Leeming took charge of the house, organised the orderlies and made sure that Boyd was properly looked after.[11] His natural flair for organisation, coupled with his good working relationship with Lieutenant Ricciardi, meant that things ran relatively smoothly.

Boyd was distinctly unimpressed by Colonel Mazawattee, and he began to demand all sorts of changes to the villa and to the prisoners' standard of living, demands that simply piled more stress on to the fat little man's already sagging shoulders. Mazawattee was slovenly in appearance. The Britons observed that he was often exhausted by having to waddle up the hill to the villa from his quarters nearby and would arrive at the sentry post by the gate mopping sweat from his brow and his meaty jowls with a soiled handkerchief. He could barely summon the strength to return the sentry's salute, until there came a time when the sentries simply stopped saluting him altogether. Ironically, the guards were punctilious about saluting Boyd and Leeming, much to their secret delight.[12]

The relationship between Mazawattee and Boyd was not helped by Boyd's disconcerting habit of speaking his mind. Mazawattee oper- ated on a system of agreeing with everything Boyd said or suggested, usually with a huge and unconvincing grin plastered across his sweaty face, without actually following up with any firm action. When Mazawattee failed to deliver, Boyd would write him a sharp note, to which Mazawattee would reply, claiming that he had been called away on important business or was on leave in Rome. Relations became so difficult that Mazawattee, when he was compelled to visit the villa for some reason, would tiptoe beneath Boyd's bedroom window in the hope that the Air Vice-Marshal wouldn't see him and confront him with yet more complaints or demands. Such comic-opera behaviour did little to improve Boyd's opinion of either Mazawattee or the Italian Army in general.

But the flip side to Mazawattee's strange behaviour were his excruciating attempts to curry favour with Boyd.

'Perhaps you would like some pet to occupy your time, no, *Generale*?' he asked Boyd one day, completely out of the blue.

'Perhaps a little bird in a cage, no?' he continued obsequiously, mopping his face with his soiled handkerchief. Boyd declined gently, both he and Leeming thinking that a caged bird was about the least appropriate gift to give to a prisoner of war.[13]

Eventually, a form of tranquillity descended upon the villa when Mazawattee realised that it was best to leave the day-to-day needs and complaints of the prisoners to Baron Ricciardi. Boyd and Leeming had both grown to appreciate 'Gussie's' attentiveness, and they had both taken to the Baron's stunning white puppy, Mickey. A cross between a St Bernard and a white sheepdog, Mickey accompanied them on the daily constitutional walks that Ricciardi arranged for the prisoners in the local vicinity, and as he grew into a huge dog he was a friend to both the Britons and the Italians in equal measure.

*

The unreality of life at the Villa Orsini was summed up by the 'incident of the machine gun'. Some official in Rome decided that the villa's guards needed heavy firepower to back up their rifles and pistols in the unlikely event of Boyd and Leeming attempting to escape, as they had at Catania, and so they sent Mazawattee a crated Fiat-Revelli 35 tripod-mounted machine gun. The guards were thrilled to be sent such a powerful weapon, and chattered away like excitable schoolboys around the opened packing case containing the oiled and wrapped gun parts. But there was one big problem: none of the officers or men guarding the prisoners had the slightest idea of how to assemble their new toy. The next day Boyd and Leeming were summoned to see Mazawattee in his office.

'I have a rather difficult problem, *Generale*. Perhaps you can help me,' said the commandant rather sorrowfully to Boyd. He asked Boyd, with a hangdog expression on his face, if the prisoners could help the guards to assemble the machine gun. Boyd, straining to keep a straight face, assured the commandant that of course he would help and that he was sure one of the British sergeants had the necessary skills. Mazawattee's face lit up and he clapped his hands together with relief, loudly proclaiming his thanks in Italian while Boyd turned to Leeming and raised his eyebrows, Leeming struggling to maintain his composure.

Sergeant Baxter, a trained armourer, was detailed by Boyd to remove the machine gun parts from their packing case, clean them of grease and assemble the weapon. Several Italian guards stood around watching Baxter work, fascinated and excited as the gun took shape on blankets spread out on the ground. When Baxter was finished the mean-looking black metal machine gun sat on its tripod with a box of ammunition belts ready beside it. The guards clapped Baxter on the back or shook his hand, loudly proclaiming his genius. Baxter strolled over to Boyd, who was leaning against a wall watching proceedings. The guards took no notice; attention was focused entirely on their new gun. Baxter took a grease-stained hand out of his pocket and opened his fist as he passed by Boyd, revealing two small springs in his palm.

'Good man,' muttered Boyd under his breath, 'lose them.'

'Sir,' replied Baxter, a conspiratorial grin creasing his face. If the Italians ever tried to fire their new machine gun, they were in for a surprise.

*

Boyd and Leeming soon discovered that there were two types of Italian that guarded them: sneering Fascists and men who were either neutral or sympathetic to the British. Fortunately, the soldiers who were simply doing their war service and had no personal or polit-ical animus towards the British heavily outnumbered the hardened acolytes of Mussolini. The Britons learned that the way to get rid of the Fascists was through their mail. The authorities in Rome were always concerned about fraternisation between the guards and the prisoners and monitored the prisoners' mail carefully, so the Britons would write in glowing terms about a particular Fascist guard in their letters home, praising his decency and generosity. It usually only took two or three notes written in this vein by the five British prisoners before the authorities in Rome quietly posted the offending soldier somewhere else, quite often to the front line in Libya.

Two English-speaking Italian NCOs, Warrant Officer Maresciallo and Sergeant Conti assisted Baron Ricciardi with keeping an eye on the prisoners. The 60-year-old Maresciallo soon impressed Boyd and the other prisoners as essentially harmless: 'a really lovable old rogue' was how Leeming described him.[14] Maresciallo had spent his working life in a travel company. Leeming suspected it was his long years of dealing with agitated and tired travellers that gave him his reassuring manner. A great raconteur, Maresciallo enjoyed telling risqué stories.

Sergeant Conti was only 21, and had been raised under the Fascist regime. He could quote Mussolini verbatim, and talked a lot of rub-bish about an Italian master race, but neither Boyd nor Leeming thought him much more than a brainwashed and essentially harmless youth. The highlight of his week was Wednesday morning, when his Fascist military magazine arrived. He would sit reading the stories,

his lips silently moving, before getting worked up at the manufactured heroics and accosting one of the prisoners with lurid tales of
battlefield heroism.[15] No one took Conti seriously. Leeming thought
that he was 'a decent, kindly boy, willing to help anyone. All the
Fascist education had done was to confuse and muddle his mind,
leaving his fundamental nature as it was.'[16]

*

The routines of imprisonment at the Villa Orsini provided the prisoners with the first notion of escaping. Their guards had settled into
predictable activities. Lieutenant Ricciardi, though watchful, was not
hostile to them, and Boyd and Leeming in particular were afforded
some freedoms within the grounds of the villa that could be exploited
for their own purposes. It was also apparent that the Italians did not
expect an air vice-marshal to attempt to escape. After much thought,
Boyd briefed Leeming on a plan that he had been working out.

'As you know, during the day the sentries are stationed outside the
garden,' said Boyd in his room that night. 'It is, of course, impossible for
anyone to pass unnoticed through the cordon of sentries in daylight.'

Leeming agreed, pointing out that the sentries were close together
and there was scant cover.

'We know that every evening the sentries close in, coming into
the garden and forming a cordon around the villa,' continued Boyd,
warming to his subject. 'Right now they are only a yard or so from
its walls.'[17]

'It does mean that at night anyone leaving the house *will* be seen
immediately, sir,' said Leeming, his brow furrowed in thought.

'Well, I've been thinking about that. As it's impossible to pass
through the line of sentries by day or by night, we need to let the
sentries do the passing.'

'Come again, sir?' said Leeming, nonplussed.

'Each evening we will walk in the garden, wearing our raincoats,'
said Boyd. 'We'll carry on like that for a couple of weeks, so that the

Eye-ties get used to us. We will always begin at dusk, just before the sentries march in to the garden and close in for the night.' Boyd paused and lit up his pipe.

'The scheme is simple, John,' said Boyd, puffing contentedly. 'One evening, instead of going as usual into the house at the end of our walk, we climb over the garden wall.' Leeming nodded, seeing where Boyd's thinking was going.

'Once over the wall, we won't attempt to go any further, otherwise we will run in to the line of sentries. Instead, we lie quite still beside the wall. I noticed a spot where there are quite a few shrubs. We probably won't be seen in the fading light.'[18]

'And then we wait for the sentries to march into the garden and take up their customary positions around the house,' said Leeming, nodding.

'Precisely,' replied Boyd, smiling. 'There will be no guards between us and open country.'

'It's *so* simple,' said Leeming. 'It *could* work.'

'Just think about it, John. The sentries will assume that we are back inside the villa. No one will be any the wiser until breakfast thirteen hours later. A thirteen-hour head start!'

It was decided that Boyd and Leeming would remain concealed in the shrubbery until it was fully dark, then walk to the local railway station about two miles away. Their 'escape dress' would consist of their blue RAF uniform trousers, black shoes, civilian raincoats and black fedora hats, the latter having already been kindly provided by the Italians since Boyd and Leeming had salvaged so little of their personal kit from the crashed Wellington on Sicily.

'The streets will be dark, and I'm positive that our escape get-ups will pass muster in the poor light,' said Boyd.

'There *is* the bother of purchasing tickets to consider, sir,' replied Leeming. 'I mean, we'd have to have a stab at the lingo.'

'*Due biglietti per Roma per favore,*' said Boyd in halting but reasonably passable Italian.

'So it's Rome?' said Leeming.

'Yes, Vatican City, the British Embassy there.'[19]

For the next two weeks Boyd and Leeming made their preparations. They exercised in the garden as agreed, lulling the sentries into a false sense of normality. Then, every night, Leeming would creep out on to the villa's roof and lie concealed, watching the sentries and taking note of the patches of cover and the light and darkness, watching the state of the Moon, monitoring wind and rain, and trying to work out the optimum time for their escape. Through seemingly innocent 'chats' with unwitting guards, Leeming also gained an idea of train times to Rome from Sulmona station, and even managed to persuade a guard to show him a map of Rome, whereupon he swiftly memorised a route to the neutral territory of Vatican City.[20]

Another consideration was money. They needed Italian lira, and began negotiations to obtain some during their fortnight's preparation. It was complicated, but the Italians permitted officer POWs to effectively draw a portion of their normal pay through the Italian government, which would then be reimbursed by London.[21] One day in April 1941 the lira finally arrived. It was a Monday. But that night Leeming judged that the position of the Moon was not right: there was too much light to make proper concealment successful. It would be a serious risk to ignore this important point. Boyd and Leeming reluctantly agreed to postpone the escape for one week. But both men remained upbeat – all that was needed was the correct light conditions and they would be away.

*

'What's this?' asked Adrian Carton de Wiart on being handed a glass by an officious Italian officer.

'Whisky and soda, General,' the officer replied. De Wiart glanced at the drink as though it were poisoned and banged it down on the table before him untouched.

'I thought all Englishmen drank whisky and soda, no?' said the officer, smiling unconvincingly.

'Well not this one,' replied De Wiart gruffly.[22]

Along with two Italian officers, a German field police captain was in attendance. Although De Wiart was an Italian prisoner, the Germans insisted on being present at his 'interrogation' in order to glean anything useful for the Reich.

If his interrogators were hoping that a pleasant drink might loosen the old general's tongue, they were sorely mistaken. 'I detest whisky,' wrote De Wiart of the encounter, '[and] it availed them nothing ...'[23]

The Italian and German officers conducting the questioning changed tack and tried to glean some idea of what De Wiart had been tasked with doing for the Allied war effort, though all their gambits were met with the same answer from their prickly subject.

'Carton de Wiart, Adrian, Major-General, British Army.'[24]

*

The interrogation of Brigadier Edward Todhunter was less confrontational, though no more successful. Remaining in Derna, Libya when Neame and O'Connor were taken on their abortive Berlin trip, he had been moved to a barrack block there along with several other senior officers, including Lieutenant-Colonel George Fanshawe, lately commanding officer of The Queen's Bays (2nd Dragoon Guards) and Brigadier 'Rudolph' Vaughan, who had commanded the 3rd Indian Motor Brigade under Gambier-Parry's 2nd Armoured Division. General Gambier-Parry and Colonel Younghusband were to join them later.[25] The prisoners slept on bunks and were well treated and fed.

On 12 April 1941 Brigadier Todhunter was collected by a German officer and driven to Benghazi. He was given a room at the Hotel Italiana before the next day boarding a *Luftwaffe* transport plane to Tripoli. Shortly after arrival he was hauled off for questioning 'by various people which ultimately resolved itself into an amiable discussion of world affairs over a whisky and soda.'[26] Like De Wiart, Todhunter gave the enemy no information. The Italian and German interrogators had accorded the British officers every courtesy according to their ranks and not pressed them too hard.

Todhunter was driven to the cavalry barracks where he met De Wiart for the first time. The two officers had much to talk about, and the Italians permitted them freedom of movement within the grounds of the barracks, their officers and men punctiliously saluting the two Britons as they wandered about trying to make sense of their predicament.[27] It was all slightly surreal. De Wiart and Todhunter were given rooms with a shared bathroom and they were to dine with the Italian officers twice daily. Because the Italians couldn't speak English, nor the prisoners Italian, everyone rubbed along with their schoolboy French – schoolboy, that is, except for De Wiart who, being half Belgian, was naturally fluent.

*

Edward Todhunter leaned on the ship's rail, his head turned away from the tall, spare figure of Carton de Wiart who stood beside him staring at the land. Behind Todhunter's glasses his eyes had misted up. The ship that was taking the two British POWs from Africa to Italy had steamed into the Bay of Naples on 21 April 1941 passing close by the town of Sorrento on the island of Capri. For Todhunter, who had honeymooned there years before, it was a poignant moment. 'I could see the Hotel Quisisana where we stayed, and all the places we went for such lovely walks,' wrote Todhunter to his wife Betty a few days later. 'I wished I could have put the clock back fourteen years, or else that I could have swum ashore and sent a cable for you to come and join me.'[28] At that moment, leaning on the ship's rail, staring across the sea, Todhunter felt so far from home and his loved ones that it almost physically hurt. He removed his spectacles, rubbed his eyes briefly and took a deep breath of clean, salty air that steadied him.

Todhunter and De Wiart's journey had begun on 16 April, when, after lunch at the cavalry barracks, they had been conveyed to Tripoli harbour and herded aboard a small, 5,000-ton steamer. A rather pompous Italian staff officer was assigned as their escort, but he soon relaxed once they were safely aboard ship as his duties meant that he could visit his home for a few days after delivering his charges safely ashore in Italy. De Wiart christened their new friend 'Tutti-Frutti'.[29]

The two Britons were each assigned a single cabin, but the ship didn't move for days. More British prisoners were loaded aboard, including several officers from the Rifle Brigade and the Royal Tank Regiment, and Todhunter and De Wiart, who was a physical fitness fanatic, took to walking and running about the confines of the ship in an effort to relieve the boredom of waiting.

De Wiart's morale was raised by an act of kindness from a visiting Italian general. He had been hatless throughout his captivity, his cap having gone down with his kit aboard the stricken Wellington, and the Italian general procured for him a British officer's cap, 'swathed it in a red band,' wrote De Wiart, 'and restored me my dignity'.[30]

The downside of remaining stationary inside an enemy harbour soon became apparent as the RAF put in an appearance. Bombs impacted around the harbour, but none landed closer to the prisoners than a quarter of a mile. Nonetheless, prisoners and Italians alike were eager to get away. The ship sailed on 19 April and tied up alongside the quay in Naples on the 21st after an uneventful crossing.[31] De Wiart had prayed for a British submarine, so that they might take their chances in the sea, but nary a periscope was spotted.

That evening Todhunter and De Wiart finally set foot on Italian soil. Tutti-Frutti escorted them on to a train and revealed their ultimate destination – Sulmona in the Abruzzi. Both men expected some kind of prison camp, but Tutti-Frutti didn't elaborate. The two British officers travelled in splendid isolation through the darkened Italian countryside in a first-class compartment. After leaving Rome, the train gradually climbed into the mountains, the air inside the carriage growing uncomfortably cold. The two prisoners felt the change in temperature, dressed as they were in desert uniforms.

*

On Thursday there erupted a commotion outside the Villa Orsini. Colonel Mazawattee was almost running as he came through the camp gates brandishing a piece of paper in one hand and his handkerchief in the other. 'Many, many, many!' he was yelling in English.

Air Vice-Marshal Boyd and Flight Lieutenant Leeming went into the courtyard to meet him along with Lieutenant Ricciardi.

Mazawattee was almost dancing on the spot, the buttons of his uniform straining to control his ample girth. He raced up to Boyd and waved the paper under his nose.

'Many, many!' shouted Mazawattee. 'All of the highest rank! See, I have their names here!'

'What on earth are you blithering about,' said Boyd, reaching for the paper, but Mazawattee snatched it away and began reading aloud in his heavily accented voice.

'See, Sir O'Connor; Sir Neame, Philip; Lord Carton de Wiart, Adrian. Look: others, plenty, *many* of them – Sir General Gambier-Parry, Colonels Combe, Todhunter, and Lord Younghusband. Plenty. The war is over. England cannot go on now. No, certainly, surely.'[32]

Boyd, his face like thunder, drew himself up to his full height, which wasn't very much, and glowered at the giddy colonel.

'You haven't got Churchill, have you?' boomed Boyd.

Mazawattee stopped moving, his face fell and he sloped off muttering about more prisoners, more guards, more barbed wire and more responsibilities.

Boyd turned to Leeming, shaking his head. 'I don't believe a word of it,' he said gravely. 'I bet they caught one colonel and imagined the rest.'[33] Leeming just nodded and wondered where all this left their carefully planned escape.

CHAPTER 4

Men of Honour

*'If the men we've got here are a fair sample of the
British Forces I don't see how we can lose the war!'*

Air Vice-Marshal Owen Boyd
Villa Orsini, 1941

When Flight Lieutenant Leeming first clapped eyes on the tall
and partially intact figure of Adrian Carton de Wiart hauling
himself out of an Italian military car at the villa's gates on 23 April
1941[1] he thought he was seeing things. He couldn't understand how
such an elderly and obviously incapacitated general had been anywhere near the front lines in the first place, let alone fallen into
enemy hands.

De Wiart had arrived from Sulmona station in company with
Brigadier Todhunter to discover that the villa was already stuffed full
of top brass. Since Colonel Mazawattee's extraordinary announce-
ment of the capture of so many senior Allied officers, the Villa Orsini
had been deluged by what Leeming teasingly described as 'generals
what-whating all over the place'. Leeming, as 'Mess Secretary', was
expected to organise everything for the new arrivals, from making
sure that enough food was brought up to the villa, to sufficient beds,
cutlery and linen. Mazawattee assisted Leeming by forgetting to
order half of the essentials.

The little camp had grown exponentially. Mazawattee had paid
another visit to *Campo 78* at Sulmona and collected additional men to
act as 'servants' at the villa, bringing the number of other ranks up to

ten. With the senior officers, the number of prisoners had suddenly mushroomed from five to 21.

Leeming strode forward and shook De Wiart's remaining hand, introducing himself. The black eye patch and empty sleeve were complemented, he later recalled, by a 'fierce-looking moustache and a "hang the devil on the yard-arm" sort of manner'.[2]

When Leeming learned of the circumstances of De Wiart's capture, he was astonished. The old general had been knocked unconscious when his Wellington had struck the water, had come to and managed to swim one-handed half a mile to shore dragging along a pilot a third of his age who'd broken his leg. 'You looked at him and thought immediately of a pirate with a cutlass in his teeth climbing up the side of some old-time merchantman,' Leeming would write.[3]

Sleeping arrangements immediately presented some problems. The villa was big, but it wasn't designed to hold so many men. This was compounded by the obvious point that the senior officers, men of certain rank and in some cases advanced years, each required their own rooms. Air Vice-Marshal Boyd gave up his room to General Neame, who by dint of seniority was made 'father of the camp'. Boyd moved into Leeming's room, meaning that the junior officer had to vacate as well. Leeming trooped up to the roof, where there was a sort of greenhouse, and settled in there.

All day long sweating and cursing Italian soldiers and British other ranks bustled about the villa, moving furniture, hauling supplies and generally trying to make the place habitable, while an increasingly harassed Leeming tried to control events and deal with a long list of demands and complaints from various generals and brigadiers.

When Leeming showed De Wiart into his small room, the camp's Italian medical officer lurked behind him. It had been reported to him that General De Wiart was suffering from concussion due to a plane crash. The doctor, who meant well, tried to give De Wiart a physical examination.

'Get your bloody hands off of me!' bellowed De Wiart, glaring down at the terrified doctor with his one eye. The doctor tried to protest, but De Wiart cut him off.

'Don't bother about me. Look after these other devils. They like it; I don't.'[4]

The medical officer admitted defeat and slunk away. De Wiart claimed to feel no ill effects from the plane crash whatsoever. 'Never felt better,' replied De Wiart when Leeming asked him about any side effects from the crash. 'Never had the vestige of a headache,' continued De Wiart, hooking his walking stick over his mangled arm. 'I imagine a few hours in a cold sea must be the perfect cure for unconsciousness.'[5] It was perhaps unsurprising that the British orderlies soon christened the indestructible General De Wiart 'Long John Silver'.

*

By the end of the day Mazawattee's gleeful list had become physical reality. The villa indeed contained some of the British Empire's greatest military leaders. Generals Neame, O'Connor, De Wiart and Gambier-Parry; Air Vice-Marshal Boyd; Brigadiers Todhunter and Combe; Colonel Younghusband and Lieutenant-Colonel Fanshawe. It made depressing reading for Leeming, and it was easy to understand the Italians' gloating attitude.

If Mazawattee felt that Boyd had been a burden, with his constant list of complaints and recommendations, General Neame soon showed himself to be considerably worse. Possessed of a mischievous sense of humour, Neame decided that constantly needling and winding up Mazawattee, and the Italians in general, was one way that he could contribute to ultimate Allied victory. To this end, 'Green Ink' penned notes to the commandant that led to long drawn-out disputes about this or that clause of the Geneva Convention, and general prisoner of war rights. Mazawattee, to his credit, instead of telling Neame to shut up and mind his own business, allowed himself to be led into the General's game, but never won any of the arguments. The

Italians, no matter their frustration and irritation, always remained perfectly correct and courteous, and Neame and some of the other prisoners used this against them. Neame was mentally just too quick for the commandant.

One of Neame's genuine peeves was the issue of overcrowding at the villa. The situation was, in his opinion, intolerable and the Italians needed to move the prisoners to a bigger property. Confronting Mazawattee over this, the commandant fell back on the old trick that he had used when dealing with Boyd of agreeing to everything the prisoners demanded without actually doing anything. Leeming had already fully briefed Neame on this tactic of Mazawattee's, but Neame couldn't help but push the point and expose Mazawattee by listening to the increasingly ridiculous answers that he gave.

'Certainly, certainly,' wheezed Mazawattee, when Neame demanded a bigger property, 'a large mansion *will* be provided. A *palazzo* is now being prepared.'

'A palace?' replied Neame, raising one eyebrow suspiciously.

'Surely, surely; a *palazzo* with *plenty* space in *great* park,' continued Mazawattee, tugging at his uniform collar, which suddenly appeared to be tighter than usual.

'Deer in the park?' asked Neame. Leeming, who was standing beside the general, turned away, a grin spreading across his face.

'But of course,' replied the commandant, spreading his palms before him. 'Plenty deers, *si*, plenty.'

'What about a swimming bath?' continued Neame.

'*Most* certainly,' replied Mazawattee confidently, his face increasingly sheened with perspiration.

'When?'

'*Perdono?*'

'When do we leave?' asked Neame impatiently.

'Oh, yes, I understand. You leave at once,' said Mazawattee, nodding triumphantly, '*well* ... within the next few days.'[6]

Whenever Neame raised the issue of moving with Mazawattee

over the ensuing weeks, he was met with the same empty promises. Discussing the issue with Lieutenant Ricciardi, the prisoners were assured that such a move was indeed planned. They were to be taken north, to either Lombardy or Piedmont. That would place the prisoners much closer to Switzerland. Boyd and Leeming agreed a week after the arrival of the other generals to postpone all of their escape attempts until they arrived at the new camp. It looked as though they would be 200 miles closer to a neutral country. Switzerland appeared a more appealing prospect than tiny and well-guarded Vatican City.

*

Early one summer morning Lieutenant Ricciardi opened his bedroom curtains and gasped in surprise. Dangling outside of the window was a Beretta automatic pistol, suspended in mid-air by a length of string tied to the trigger guard. Cursing, Ricciardi quickly searched his room, a horrible sinking feeling in the pit of his stomach. His own pistol was missing. Ricciardi opened his window and leaned out. The string led up to the bedroom above his. He quickly untied the weapon and examined it. It was his; of that there was no doubt. He extracted the magazine – still full. Shaking his head in disbelief, Ricciardi stood for some time bathed in early morning sunlight, the heavy pistol in his hand, trying to work out how he had lost it and why it was returned to him in such a strange manner. He never did discover who was responsible for this curious episode.

In fact, Ricciardi had lost his pistol a day earlier while he was out picnicking with the prisoners. The line between guards and prisoners had started to become blurred since the main batch of generals had arrived in April. With the prisoners having agreed among themselves to postpone any escape attempts until they reached their new home – whenever and wherever that might be – Boyd suggested that they instead put the Italians to sleep: lull them into a false sense of security by appearing to cooperate with them. Relations between guards and prisoners became ever more cordial, even friendly. This was demonstrated by the long walks and picnics that the prisoners were permitted to take in the vicinity of the villa. These helped to stave off the boredom that all of the prisoners felt keenly. They had had active, busy careers and great responsibilities, but now had little to do. Todhunter wrote to his mother outlining just how bad the boredom had become. The prisoners needed diversions, and that could come from books and 'any form of stupid game'.[7] They only had cards, draughts and backgammon to pass the evenings. The United States Embassy had promised badminton equipment and a ping-pong table, but they were still waiting for them.

The Italians permitted shopping trips to nearby Sulmona, much to De Wiart's delight, as apart from the clothes he stood up in and the bamboo cane he had salvaged from the crashed Wellington, all his kit had gone to the bottom of the Mediterranean. De Wiart's favourite shop was Unione Militare, an Italian version of the British NAAFI, where he was able to buy good-quality Italian army clothing and footwear.[8]

The weather mostly was perfect that summer, except a nasty patch in May. 'We have had a week of cold beastly weather which makes … life generally miserable,'[9] wrote Todhunter sourly to his father. But once the weather brightened again, the excursions resumed, the long walks which did so much to keep up the prisoners' morale. Though the prisoners were heavily guarded during these trips, it was apparent that the guards enjoyed the excursions as much as their prisoners. The Generals were old enough to be fathers, or even grandfathers, to many of the young Italian conscripts, and for their part most of the Italians seemed bemused and more than a little embarrassed to be guarding such nice old gentlemen. But when opportunities presented themselves, the British were not averse to taking advantage of them.

During one long walk Leeming shouldered Ricciardi's pack for him. The guards and the prisoners tended to muck in together, helping each other carry food and other supplies for the picnic. Ricciardi had earlier taken his pistol out of its holster and shoved it in his pack, forgetting all about it. Leeming noticed the weapon nestled among the cans of food that they planned to boil up when they made camp. When no one was looking, he quickly pulled the pistol from the pack and hid it under his shirt.

Later that evening, back at the villa, Leeming showed Boyd the Beretta. Boyd's face dropped.

'You'll have to return it,' he said.

'Return it? But why sir?' asked Leeming, slightly crestfallen.

'When Gussie finds he's lost it, he may start all sorts of inquiries. It would be a serious thing if they found you'd got it. You must hand it back at once,'[10] insisted Boyd.

Leeming understood Boyd's point. But he couldn't very well march up to Ricciardi and simply hand him back his weapon. Ricciardi would have to report the matter to Mazawattee and Leeming would be in serious trouble. After some thought, Leeming came up with the novel idea of suspending the pistol on a length of string outside Ricciardi's bedroom from the room above.

*

A high point for the prisoners was the sudden and unexpected delivery of a large consignment of Red Cross parcels to the villa on 4 May 1941. Brigadiers Todhunter and Combe were placed in charge of sorting them out. 'John Combe and I have given a lifelike display of two rather quarrelsome children sitting on the floor opening Christmas presents,'[11] wrote Todhunter to his mother. The contents of the parcels would be used to supplement the menu cooked up between Leeming and the two cooks, Sergeant Baxter and his assistant. But tensions already existed among the generals, cooped up together in the overcrowded villa.[12] 'You would have laughed a lot to see nine respectable middle-aged senior officers quarrelling as to whether John and I had shared out the chocolate fairly,' Todhunter went on.[13]

The supplies saw immediate service when the prisoners hosted a party the following evening to mark General De Wiart's birthday. Baxter managed to make a cake using some of their precious Red Cross chocolate, to which he then added the letters 'C de W' in spaghetti on top. The special dinner consisted of Red Cross tinned chicken and sausages.

The ten other ranks prisoners that Colonel Mazawattee had brought up to the villa from *Campo 78* took care of the housekeeping and cooking duties for the generals. This allowed the senior officers to take up a series of useful 'hobbies', some of them revealing hidden talents that could prove useful in escape attempts.

Air Vice-Marshal Boyd and Colonel Younghusband proved to be excellent carpenters, building hutches and pens for the rabbits that Brigadier Todhunter kept in an attempt to supplement the prisoners' supply of fresh meat, and for Brigadier Combe's chickens – which were intended to provide both meat and eggs.[14] The commandant allowed the prisoners to convert a small garage into a woodworking shop, and further permitted them to purchase a bench and tools. They were occasionally assisted by two tame guards, one who had been a cabinetmaker in Civvy Street and the other a French polisher.

General Neame, VC winner, Olympic champion, explorer and big game hunter, took up the needle and thread and started stitching attractive tapestries, manufacturing chair backs and seats. (His other 'hobby' was annoying the Italians, and he excelled at both pursuits.)

Todhunter proved incapable of breeding any rabbits, which was quite a feat considering their reproductive reputation. 'The feller would make a fortune in Australia,' quipped Boyd one evening in the mess. 'Why, the Australian Government would pay Todhunter anything he liked to ask.'[15]

Combe fussed over his sixteen laying hens with the devotion of a mother over her children. But, like Todhunter and his rabbits, producing eggs for the table proved difficult. Combe's hens were either 'not laying' or were 'eating their own eggs'.[16] The hens further annoyed Sergeant Baxter by covering the steps to the kitchen in excrement.

Some of the other prisoners took up gardening, trying to create order out of the tangled, weed-strewn mess that they had inherited, or took to laying out allotments to grow fresh vegetables for the table. Such physical labours, as well as being pleasant diversions from the routine of imprisonment, were also important in keeping the middle-aged generals fit and ready for whatever escaping opportunities were to present themselves. 'The first shock of capture had passed,' recalled Leeming, 'the excitement of settling down had died away; life had become monotonous. Day after day the same trivialities, the same people, the same voices, the same mannerisms. In our little community, cut off from the outside world, little bursts of irritability, of impatience, began to happen.'[17]

Keeping fit was taken very seriously, and not just by De Wiart, who owing to his injuries was unable to perform manual labour, but by everyone. 'Before lunch I walked round the garden 24 times as fast as I could, which I reckon to be about four miles,' wrote Todhunter one day, adding that his normal routine was more like eighteen times round in the morning, followed by 'a walk in the afternoon with one of the officers of the guard'.[18]

Brigadier Todhunter, like all of the prisoners except De Wiart, suddenly began learning Italian. Dick O'Connor took the studying very seriously, and was soon quite fluent. Its aid to escape was obvious. De Wiart, however, could not be persuaded. One day one of the Italian officers made the mistake of asking De Wiart if he wanted to take 'this golden opportunity' to learn the local tongue.

'I don't want to learn your bloody language!'[19] roared back De Wiart. Instead, 'Long John Silver' had taken to sunbathing on the terrace or studying the little lizards that inhabited the garden.

Brigadier Todhunter was one of several, including General O'Connor, who persevered with the language. 'To combat boredom I am learning Italian with marked lack of success,'[20] he wrote home. Todhunter also collected Italian newspapers and periodicals and painstakingly translated the news stories into English, producing a bulletin for the other prisoners.[21] He also began writing to family, friends and organisations asking for books, collecting them together into a small library as another aid in the continual fight against boredom. But the books they received seemed almost like a cruel joke to Todhunter and the others. 'We had a parcel of books from the Red Cross for which we are duly grateful but they are a pretty odd selection, collected I should think from various British Institutions in Rome which are now closed down,' wrote Todhunter. 'In this parcel there was Vol. 1 of a monumental work on Applied Sociology, Vol. 2 of *The Flora and Fauna of Sardinia*, a book of 1885 on the tombs of the Popes and a book of rather gloomy illustrations of Dartmoor taken in 1901. Beside these *A Bachelor Girl in Burma* and *The Work of the Church in the Malay Peninsula from 1900 to 1905* by the Bishop of Labuan and signed by the author gave us quite a thrill!'[22]

The one prisoner who was unable to work or even to enjoy Todhunter's expanding collection of eclectic volumes was General De Wiart. 'His one arm prevents him doing much like carpentering or gardening and his one eye prevents him doing very much reading or writing,' noted Todhunter. But his spirit was irrepressible: 'He really is the most gallant old sportsman though.'[23]

Mostly the prisoners thought about moving – moving away from the villa to a new camp, closer to Switzerland and with fresh escape opportunities. The months dragged by, but still nothing happened. 'There is still no definite news of our move,' wrote home Todhunter in despair in June 1941, 'though we hear that it will take place shortly.'[24] Mazawattee's repeated assurances on this subject sounded increasingly hollow as the prisoners sweated out the humid Abruzzo summer, when temperatures hit 100°F in the shade.[25] General Neame was, however, surprised when his old batman, Gunner Pickford from the Royal Horse Artillery, was located and sent up to the villa by the Italians.

Not every officer was happy with his batman. Mazawattee had drafted many of the officers' orderlies into the role at short notice and without any training. 'I have got a young sapper who was caught at Sollum last September,' wrote Todhunter. 'He is very willing but I suspect a better sapper than valet.'[26] But all of the generals were very happy with the new cook sent in to assist Sergeant Baxter. 'He is a pretty odd looking soldier but he was a cook at Claridge's before the war so he can be excused a lot.'[27]

Non-Fascist news from the outside world filtered into the villa by surreptitious means. The United States was not yet in the war, so the US Embassy in Rome continued to act as the 'Protecting Power', sending diplomats and a military attaché to the villa on occasion to check on the prisoners' welfare. The Italian government was paranoid about such contacts. Strict instructions were issued to Colonel Mazawattee that the Americans were to be treated correctly and courteously, but that they were not to be left alone with any of the prisoners lest they exchanged information about the progress of the war, or any other vital intelligence. Ricciardi detailed Warrant Officer Maresciallo and Sergeant Conti to closely shadow the visiting dignitaries and watch for any improprieties. But despite such precautions, the prisoners were usually able to get one of the diplomats alone for a few minutes through some ruse or other, during which the American would quickly fill them in on the latest news.[28]

One surprising visitor was a jolly and ebullient Irish priest who delighted in telling the prisoners rather risqué stories. Forty-three-year-old Hugh O'Flaherty, dressed in the scarlet and black cassock of a Roman Catholic monsignor, toured POW camps in Italy acting on behalf of the Pope. One of his tasks was to try to discover the fates of those who had been declared missing in action. If O'Flaherty discovered any of these soldiers alive in the camps he tried to reassure their families through Radio Vatican. With his thick brown hair, round spectacles and permanent half grin, O'Flaherty was very popular, and as a fellow native English speaker, the prisoners at the Villa Orsini took to him strongly.

General O'Connor had decided that it was imperative that they establish contact with the War Office in London, and had racked his brains as to how communication could be established. O'Connor, who had rapidly shown himself to be completely dedicated to the idea of escape, wanted the British government to smuggle maps, passports and other useful equipment into the villa to aid future escapes from their new camp. He also wanted the British to put the prisoners in contact with one of their agents in Italy. To this end, O'Connor wrote a letter to the War Office. When O'Flaherty visited, O'Connor managed to ask him whether he would pass the letter to the American defence attaché in Rome, Colonel Norman Fiske. O'Flaherty took the letter and hid it inside his cassock. In fact, O'Flaherty was part of a network involved in concealing people from Mussolini's authorities; he would become known to history as 'The Scarlet Pimpernel of the Vatican'. Pope Pius XII was aware that O'Flaherty was helping prisoners, and disagreed with his activities from the point of view of preserving Vatican neutrality, though he did not censure him as he accepted that he was doing God's work.

That Colonel Fiske accepted the letter from O'Flaherty and passed it to London via the diplomatic bag was also a violation of President Roosevelt's avowed isolationism from the war in Europe. The United States was officially neutral, but it appeared that there were already some who believed in the 'special relationship' with Great Britain.

When Fiske himself visited the Villa Orsini to check on the prisoners, O'Connor took the opportunity of smuggling out a long report on the Western Desert campaign to London. It was done via the toilet.

When Fiske shook hands with O'Connor, the General said in a quiet tone: 'Very good of you to come to see us. Look under the lavatory seat.'[29]

Fiske didn't bat an eyelid, but carried on chatting to O'Connor and the other officers as if he had heard nothing unusual. The Italian guards took no notice. After a while Fiske asked to use the toilet and was duly escorted to a latrine by one of the Italians. Locking himself inside, the American found a small packet of papers exactly where O'Connor had said, lodged under the lavatory seat.

Letters passed in this way ended up with MI9, the department of British Military Intelligence that dealt with prisoners of war, which was headed by the colourful Norman Crockatt in London. Crockatt was able to receive good information on what was happening at the Villa Orsini until the United States entered the war following Japan's attack on Pearl Harbor in early December 1941.

Importantly, the smuggled letter would lead to the setting up of a coded letter-writing operation between London and the generals in Italy. There was a code called HK, developed by Lieutenant-Colonel L. Winterbottom of MI9 in conjunction with a Foreign Office specialist named Hooker, that would allow the generals to communicate with MI9 through their regular mail, sent to the Metropole Hotel on Northumberland Avenue, London. Devised to enable servicemen to maintain contact with London from their camps if captured (RAF aircrew and commandos were among those trained in its use),[30] HK was fairly simple to use 'and in skilled hands unusually hard to detect. All the user had to do was to indicate by the fashion in which he wrote the date that the letter contained the message, show by his opening words which part of the code he was using, and then write an apparently normal chatty letter, from which an inner meaning could be unravelled with the code's help.'[31]

The establishment of the letter-writing operation was unwittingly assisted by Colonel Mazawattee when he allowed a young British officer to visit the villa one day from the local POW camp. These visits, though infrequent, were made by several other junior officers after General Neame petitioned the commandant, claiming that the generals needed some conversational stimulation and a change of faces once in a while.

The first visitor, an army commando taken prisoner during a raid on Sicily, succeeded in teaching O'Connor and some of the others the 'Winterbottom Code' during his few hours at the villa, and there-after the prisoners were able to communicate with British Military Intelligence by letter. The Italians were never to discover this secret link with the outside world.

O'Connor also received a letter directly from the War Office in reply to his requests for assistance, smuggled in to him at great personal risk once again by Colonel Fiske.[32]

*

As July gave way to August, and still with no confirmation of the move, morale in the Villa Orsini was falling steadily. General O'Connor sprained his ankle and was hobbling about for a couple of weeks in a bad temper, while Brigadier Todhunter had a bad run of health. He spent ten days in bed with lumbago and possible mild food poisoning. The temperature was still over 90 degrees in the shade.[33] Nothing was happening – the prisoners simply existed. All escape activity had been postponed till the great move, the heat and food was playing on everyone's patience and forbearance, and the monotony was broken only by the daily excursions to hike and picnic under guard. Some of the prisoners coped better than others. General De Wiart was like a caged tiger, while Gambier-Parry could be impulsive, 'flashing out, and saying exactly what he thought, yet sorry for his outbursts almost as soon as he had spoken.'[34] With so many strong personalities trapped inside a relatively small house, disagreements and arguments arose frequently during that hot summer, but nothing that was said in the heat of the moment was taken to heart by anyone. It was really just a collective case of mild cabin fever. 'One of the worst things about this type of life is having nothing definite to look forward to,' wrote Todhunter. 'After all, the ordinary criminal in the jug knows that if he behaves himself he will get out on a certain day but here it is a case of this year, next year etc.'[35] The only relief occurred in mid-August, when the temperature started to drop, which was considered a blessing by all of the prisoners. 'The weather is getting cooler and the flies are getting less,' wrote Todhunter. 'We have had some very good rain this week … the nights are cooler and I have gone back to a thin blanket instead of only a sheet.'[36]

The monotony of prison life was broken on 21 August by a joint birthday party held for Generals Gambier-Parry and O'Connor. 'Our cooks made a cake using as far as I can make out macaroni ground in a coffee grinder,' wrote Todhunter, 'and not only iced it (without any icing sugar) but put a fine Major Generals badge on it. In the evening we had a birthday dinner … fishcakes, tinned peaches, cheese and coffee.'[37]

By early September snow was visible on the surrounding hills, while the villa was lashed with rain. The thought in everyone's mind was the same: *when do we move?* It was rapidly becoming the only topic of conversation.

CHAPTER 5

Advance Party

*'The idea of a journey was a real thrill. For although we
had made the best of it, life at Sulmona had been terribly
boring. Most of us had accepted the unalterable, and
refused to admit even in our own minds how really sick
and tired we were of our existence at the Villa Orsini.'*

Flight Lieutenant John Leeming

'Chaps, the day has finally come,' announced an excited General
Neame as he entered the prisoners' sitting room on 19 September
1941. 'I've just spoken to Mazawattee. He's confirmed it.'

'They're finally getting rid of the idiot?' asked Boyd, looking up
from one of Todhunter's carefully translated news-sheets.

'No, old chap, much better news. The move north, it's on.' Neame
could barely disguise his excitement.

'Not that old chestnut again,' moaned Gambier-Parry, looking
up irritably from his book.

'We leave in five days,' announced Neame. The room erupted.
Generals and brigadiers jumped from their chairs as if electrocuted.
They crowded around Neame, demanding more details.

'Leeming's going ahead with an advance party to set things up
on the 23rd of September,' said Neame triumphantly. 'He's taking
Baxter and two of the other NCOs with him. We leave on the 24th.'[1]

'But where, old boy, *where* is he going?' demanded De Wiart,
his moustache appearing even more bristly than usual as he towered
over the little crowd.

'Well, it seems old Mazawattee wasn't pulling our legs when he mentioned a palace,' said Neame. 'We're going to a castle, chaps, 200 miles north of here outside Florence.'[2]

'Florence?' said G-P, perking up considerably, his artistic interests piqued by the possibility of close proximity to the famous Uffizi Gallery.

'That's what the commandant said,' replied Neame. 'The Castello di Vincigliata. Mazawattee just told me that it is a summer palace standing in a great park. Ricciardi confirmed what the commandant said. He says it's a lovely old place.'[3]

'Well, that's splendid news for us,' said Dick O'Connor, brightening up considerably. Florence was only 250 miles from the Swiss frontier, and O'Connor's mind was already considering this fact. Several of the other officers beamed, knowing that the chance for a serious escape attempt had suddenly materialised.

Neame, suddenly all business, started issuing orders concerning the gathering of kit for the move. He informed Todhunter and Combe that they would be taking their livestock with them as well.

'What about my workshop?' asked Boyd, referring to his carpentry equipment.

'That too. We're not leaving behind anything that might aid an escape in the new camp.'

'Sounds like a ruddy travelling circus to me,' muttered De Wiart under his breath as he strode off towards his room, a little more vim in his step now than when he had struggled down for breakfast an hour earlier.

*

For the several days before Flight Lieutenant Leeming left the Villa Orsini with the advance party on the 23rd, the big house was full of bustle and purpose. The generals and brigadiers packed, repacked and constantly discussed the impending move, chattering like excited holidaymakers who were about to leave on a pleasant vacation. After so many months of staring at the same walls and gardens, the same distant mountains and the same faces, it was almost as if they were being released, such was the level of frenetic excitement. There was so much to arrange, so much to sort out and pack, and so many lists and timetables to prepare. The other ranks prisoners hurried around assisting the senior officers, while Colonel Mazawattee for once did not interfere. The commandant was all smiles, for he was not to accompany the prisoners to the castle. Finally relieved of a responsibility that he had found both overbearing and loathsome from the start, Mazawattee was almost giddy with delight at the thought of bidding farewell to the difficult British prisoners, probably Boyd and Neame in particular, those two having proven to be exceptionally barbed spines in his side.

Everyone was happy to hear that Gussie Ricciardi would be accompanying the generals to the castle, where he would serve as adjutant to a new commandant. But in their enthusiasm and impatience to be gone from the overcrowded villa, the prisoners didn't take notice of the fact that two of their senior guards had in fact asked for transfers, unable to face the reality of where the prisoners were headed. It was an ominous sign that unfortunately was not noticed by the prisoners at the time.

*

Leeming sat in the back seat of an Italian army car alongside Sergeant Baxter. It had just driven through the gates of the Villa Orsini on its way to Sulmona station. Leeming turned and looked as the car passed through the portal. He couldn't see much. It was 3.30am on 23 September 1941 and still pitch dark. Beside the driver sat Second Lieutenant Ucelli, a rich young officer whose well-connected family had wangled him a transfer to guarding prisoners instead of fighting at the front in Libya. No one thought much of Ucelli, who was lazy and refused to live at the villa with the rest of the staff, instead having a taxi drive him up the hill to work each day from his rented digs in Sulmona town.

Motoring along behind Leeming's car was another identical khaki-coloured vehicle containing two more British other ranks – Sergeant Price, a Welshman from the Rhondda Valley, and Corporal Blackwell – escorted by the young and harmless Fascist ideologue Sergeant Conti.

Leeming felt overjoyed to be out of the villa. He would not be returning, for he was commanding the small advance party that was going to Vincigliata Castle one day earlier to prepare the building for the arrival of the senior officers and the rest of the men. He would remain at the castle to meet the generals and brigadiers and the orderlies, and hopefully would have managed to sort out their accommodation in the limited amount of time that had been afforded him by the Italians.

Leeming settled back in his seat. The roof racks of both vehicles were piled high with suitcases and boxes going to the castle, and the ever-vigilant Baxter held a neat clipboard containing an inventory of the prisoners' property across his knees, a stub of pencil tucked behind his right ear. Neither man spoke much, but both were thrilled to be going on such an adventure after so many months of imprisonment. There was also the added bonus of the possibility of a blitz escape, a lightning attempt, should the opportunity present itself. Although it had been decided that escape attempts would be put on hold until they were at the new location, the prisoners all accepted that if a golden opportunity were to arise they should seize it.

After a few minutes the two cars pulled into Sulmona station, where a detachment of steel-helmeted guards armed with Mannlicher-Carcano rifles stood waiting in the darkness. They stiffened to attention as Ucelli climbed out of his car. The prisoners and their baggage were loaded aboard a waiting steam train, Leeming and Ucelli in their own compartment, with Conti and the three British non-commissioned officers in an adjoining compartment. Armed guards patrolled the corridor outside the compartments to deter any thoughts of escape.

The sun rose, and Leeming and the others stared out of their carriage windows at the green countryside that flitted by. Their guards were also in high spirits, enjoying the journey and the break from the dull routine at the villa. In many ways, the guards were as isolated there as the prisoners, and as bored.

At 10.00am the train pulled slowly into Rome. After living in an isolated house in the country for so many months, the bustle of a big city was almost overwhelming, and the thrill of passing close by the Forum and Vatican City was palpable.

Leeming and the others disembarked, Baxter supervising various guards and porters as they offloaded the prisoners' baggage. Baxter carefully checked off each item on his clipboard before it was loaded on to trolleys. The Florence train was not due till after midday. Ucelli and Conti had both made arrangements to disappear to visit their fiancées in Rome, but, not trusting their conscript guards, Ucelli had the Britons locked in the station ticket office under the watchful eyes of several busy clerks.

Leeming saw immediately that there was a good chance of escaping. Though he was dressed in full RAF uniform, his pilot's wings above his left breast pocket, he thought it worth a try.

Leeming would aim for Vatican City. The distance to St Peter's Square from the station was just over two-and-a-half miles on foot. He would remove his cap and his tunic. If he wrapped his cap in his jacket, he could probably stroll through Rome with the most obvious parts of his uniform tucked under his arm, just wearing a shirt and his blue RAF trousers and braces. It wasn't much of a disguise, but he should only be on the road for less than an hour, taking into consideration finding his way in an unfamiliar city and avoiding any police guarding the approaches to Vatican City.

If he could make it, Leeming would almost certainly find sanctuary at the British Mission, led at the time by the Envoy Extraordinary and Minister Plenipotentiary Sir D'Arcy Osborne. The spry and trim 58-year-old Osborne, who would inherit his second cousin's title of

Duke of Leeds in 1943, was secretly involved with providing sanctuary to escaped Allied prisoners of war and Jews, using his own money to help finance these illicit activities. Osborne, codenamed 'Mount', was working closely with Irish Monsignor Hugh O'Flaherty, the 'Scarlet Pimpernel of the Vatican' who was already known to several of the generals from the Villa Orsini, and French diplomat François de Vial and between them they managed to conceal almost 4,000 people from the Italians and later the Nazis. Pope Pius XII, who in 1940 had publicly condemned German atrocities in Occupied Europe, largely turned a blind eye to such shenanigans. Vatican City had been recognised as a neutral state in 1939 and, though tiny (only measuring 110 acres), Mussolini left it alone, fearful of upsetting the Italian population by a direct assault on the heart of Roman Catholicism. Protected by a small military force consisting of the Noble Guard, Pontifical Swiss Guard, Palatine Guard and the Gendarmerie Corps, slipping into Vatican City was not difficult in 1941 as the Italian police lightly patrolled the borders, and St Peter's Square was easily accessible with just a white line painted on the ground marking the frontier. For Leeming, it represented a real chance, if he could shake off his guards and get clear of the station.

*

'*Gabinetto*?' said Leeming in Italian to one of the clerks, asking for the lavatory. The man nodded and escorted Leeming to the men's room beside the platform, waiting outside. Leeming quickly strode over to the stall that was beside a window set high in the wall. He felt excited. Italian military incompetence at leaving prisoners of war under the supervision of civilian railway workers had presented Leeming with an opportunity. He planned to simply climb through the lavatory window and walk off.

Locking the creaking wooden stall door behind him, he stepped up on to the toilet bowl, gingerly levered open the grimy window, and peered out. But at that moment his high hopes were cruelly dashed. Directly below Leeming bobbed the heads of two Italian workmen. They were sitting on a bench against the toilet wall, eating their lunch and chatting. He wouldn't get far climbing down in front of these men, who would report him immediately. He also couldn't hang about for too long in the lavatory before the ticket clerk started banging on the stall door. Cursing silently, Leeming pulled the window shut as quietly as he could and stepped down from the bowl. He stood in the stall for a few seconds, torn. There was nothing for it but to return to the ticket office. Perhaps another opportunity would present itself before they arrived at the castle. As a consolation, Leeming and his men took the opportunity to filch all the official-looking forms, notices and chits that they could manage under the noses of the clerks, who were mostly concerned with serving customers through iron grills. There was always the possibility that this material could be used for future escapes.

By now it was lunchtime and the prisoners had had nothing to eat since departing from Sulmona some time before dawn. Second Lieutenant Ucelli, who had by now returned to his duties, arranged for food to be provided for Sergeants Baxter and Price and Corporal Blackwell by the clerks, then turned to Leeming and asked him whether he would care to join him for lunch in the station restaurant. Leeming was genuinely taken aback, but happily agreed. It was a professional courtesy, one gentleman to another. It was all a little surreal, Leeming following Ucelli towards the restaurant through the crowds of travellers in the station. It was very strange to sit down and eat a proper meal, served by white-jacketed waiters, and to be surrounded by men, women and children all doing likewise.

'I was in Air Force uniform, the uniform of a country that had been at war with Italy for more than a year, yet we strolled into the crowded restaurant in Rome, and not one person showed the slightest distaste.'[4] Apart from a few embarrassed glances by fellow diners and the occasional nod or smile, Leeming and Ucelli were treated quite normally. In fact, his waiter was delighted to be serving an

Englishman again, and even apologised for the poor quality of the coffee that was served, secretly topping off Leeming's cup with some brandy. However, when he wrote about his adventures a few years later, Leeming was at pains to point out that all this occurred at a time when Italy was winning.[5] Such magnanimity cost Ucelli and the Italian Army nothing, and parading a captured British officer in full uniform through a very public place was in itself an exercise in demonstrating to the Italian people how well things were going.

*

Florence railway station was crowded with numerous officials waiting to meet the British party when the train juddered to a steamy halt on the platform after the journey from Rome. They seemed keen to get Leeming and his men on their way to the castle, but the unloading and itemising of the prisoners' baggage held up the proceedings, as Sergeant Baxter, armed with his trusty clipboard and pencil, dutifully checked everything off and safely aboard yet more cars. Ucelli's previously equitable mood now deteriorated and his spoiled and indulged nature, so familiar to the prisoners at the Villa Orsini, once more reasserted itself over the issue of the baggage. The stoical Baxter completely ignored the shouting, gesticulating Italian soldiers and officials who were deeply exasperated by the British NCO's methodical approach; nothing on earth would move him until he had finished.[6]

Baxter finally finished, tucked the clipboard under his left arm and marched smartly over to Leeming, slamming to attention before him. 'All present and correct, sir,' bellowed Baxter as he snapped out a parade-ground salute.

'Very good, Baxter,' replied Leeming, returning his salute. He turned to Second Lieutenant Ucelli.

'We're ready for you now, Mr Ucelli,' said Leeming, as if inviting him in for tea.

Ucelli, who had worked himself up into a red-faced rage shouting at Baxter and at his own men, glared at Leeming with ill-concealed loathing.

'*Avanti*, Flight Lieutenant, we go ... now!' Ucelli pointed at the two green-painted army Fiats that were now fully loaded.

Baxter got the passenger door open for Leeming before climbing in himself. Ucelli marched up to the car and stood by the passenger side door waiting for one of his men to open it for him. When no one did, he wrenched the door open and threw himself into the seat, his face by now a shade of puce. He slammed the door so violently that the window slipped and half opened on its own.

*

Within fifteen minutes the two cars had sped out of the pretty streets of Florence past churches and other impressive buildings – though the prisoners were unable to get their bearings or pause to admire the architecture – and begun to climb higher. They were soon in the coun-tryside, the drivers struggling to nurse the overladen cars up twisting mountain roads that led through a thick forest of tall cypress trees. Occasionally they passed by babbling brooks and giant rocks, the road growing ever more tortuous as the elevation continued to increase. They passed vineyards, then empty villas, whose British and American owners had fled or been dispossessed when Italy entered the war on the Axis side. Another belt of trees, this time olives, passed quickly by before the vehicles cut once more into cypress forest.[7] Then, suddenly, Leeming's car, which was leading, rounded another hairpin bend and he spotted something huge atop a tall hill further up. It was a castle, a huge menacing grey stone castle, its crenellated walls looking impos-sibly high from below. Two large towers, dotted with narrow archers' windows, rose high over the walls. Leeming leaned forward, trying to catch a better view as the car twisted around another bend in the road.

'Is that where we're going, Ucelli?' asked Leeming, tapping the young Italian on the shoulder. Ucelli turned slightly in his seat, his lip curling into a contemptuous smile.

'*Si*, that is where *you* are going,' he said, pointing at Leeming. 'It is the Castello di Vincigliata.'

'Stone the crows, sir,' muttered Baxter beside Leeming on the back seat. 'Looks like something out of a ruddy fairytale.'

'Or a nightmare, Sergeant,' added Leeming slowly, a knot of apprehension curling in the pit of his stomach as he stared at his forbidding new home.

CHAPTER 6

The Travelling Menagerie

*'From what we hear we are going to live in a medieval
castle, which luckily was inhabited until a short
time ago when the owner died. I believe it will be
comfortable and it is said to be in lovely country.'[1]*

Brigadier Edward Todhunter

A lion crouched on its haunches and stared at Flight Lieutenant
Leeming, its snarling mouth open, revealing rows of gleaming
teeth. Leeming, looking around with a feeling of dread worming its
way through his stomach, reached out and touched the lion's cold
head. The stone felt smooth beneath his hand, worn by many years
of use.

'Follow me,' said Second Lieutenant Ucelli curtly behind him,
the young Italian officer striding past Leeming towards a set of doors
beside a large stone staircase whose balustrade ended with the impressive stone lion. Leeming had a horrible feeling that he was entering
the lair of the beast as those metal banded and studded doors creaked
open before him.

*

Minutes earlier Leeming and the other three prisoners had arrived
before the main gate of the castle. Up close, the fortress was even
more forbidding then when viewed from the winding road below.
The two cars had driven over a bridge that crossed a dry moat in
front of the castle's massive entrance gates.[2] Stepping down, Leeming

glanced about. The castle's high walls stretched away on each side, the tops broken by crenellated battlements. The grey stone was worn and weathered and here and there tufts of vegetation clung tenaciously to its vertiginous sides. The main gates, as tall as cathedral doors, swung slowly inwards, creaking and protesting.

'Blimey!' exclaimed Sergeant Baxter at Leeming's side, 'Castle Dracula.' Leeming smiled thinly and without conviction. Baxter was making light of the situation, but all that was needed to complete the Gothic nightmare quality of the building were a few lightning bolts and the rumble of thunder. Sergeant Price and Corporal Blackwell dumped their kitbags at their feet and lit up cigarettes. Both eyed the gates suspiciously.

Several Italian soldiers armed with slung rifles struggled with the heavy studded doors, pushing them fully open. Ucelli led Leeming and the three British NCOs through the portal, Leeming noting grimly that the wall appeared to be about six feet thick, into a small inner courtyard. Facing them was the stone staircase and balcony with the stone lion at the end of the elaborate balustrade.

'Puts you in mind of Trafalgar Square, doesn't it?' murmured Blackwell, nodding towards the lion.

'Somebody's idea of a joke, if you ask me,' replied Sergeant Price in his broad Welsh accent.

Adjacent to the staircase, and below the balcony, was another set of armoured doors. These were drawn back and Leeming and the others walked into a gloomy compound between the castle's massive defensive walls and the tall inner keep. Leeming looked around, noting the narrow archers' windows set into the keep, its tall battlemented towers and broken statues and worn carvings. He glanced up at the outer wall, judging it to be at least fifteen feet high. Running around its top was a wooden walkway.

'Company, sir,' said Blackwell quietly, nodding towards the top of the perimeter wall.

'I see them, Corporal,' replied Leeming.

Several Italian sentries looked down at Leeming's party from their lofty position on the wooden walkway. The distance between the keep and the wall was only about twelve yards, meaning that anyone entering or leaving the castle's central bastion would be seen immediately by the sentries above.[3] The contrast between the gloomy, Gothic castle and the light and airy Villa Orsini was stark.

'Here comes the welcoming committee, sir,' said Blackwell, dropping his cigarette and stubbing it out with the toe of his boot.

'Welcome gentlemen,' said a voice behind Leeming. Leeming turned and watched a slim and very elegant Italian cavalry officer of medium height stride across the courtyard, a slight smile fixed to his face, his polished jackboots echoing on the stone floor. After the sloppy appearance of Colonel Mazawattee back at the Villa Orsini, this new officer looked like he had just stepped off a parade ground. His cap was worn at a slightly rakish angle, with a black belt and cross-strap worn over his grey-green service tunic from which was suspended a leather holster holding a Beretta automatic pistol.[4] The two rows of colourful medal ribbons above his left breast pocket indicated plenty of experience. On the cuffs of his uniform he wore the three yellow bars with a star beneath indicating the unique Italian army rank of First Captain. Three yellow stars with a bar beneath also adorned both of his collar patches. Far from the stereotypical Italian, his hair and eye colouring were almost fair, giving him an Anglo-Saxon appearance.[5]

Two other officers accompanied the captain. On their caps was the large silver exploding grenade badge of the *Carabinieri*, the Italian Military Police. Second Lieutenant Ucelli immediately stiffened to attention beside Leeming. He saluted the two more senior Italian officers, before turning to Leeming.

'The commandant,' he said, gesturing with one hand towards the first captain.

'Montalto,' said the commandant, extending his gloved hand to Leeming.

'Leeming,' replied the British officer.

'Flight Lieutenant Leeming, a pleasure to meet you,' said Captain the Duke of Montalto, Leeming noticing that his English was as flawless as his manner. Leeming was soon to discover that Montalto had attended Cheltenham College, an English public school. He had been selected for his position by Rome, which felt that because the castle was to hold notable British 'personages' the commandant also needed to be a 'somebody', and with Montalto's aristocratic lineage and understanding of the British, he seemed the perfect candidate. In contrast, Montalto considered the appointment to be something of an insult – he was a member of an elite cavalry regiment and had wanted to go to the front to fight.[6]

'And this is my security officer, Captain Pederneschi,' said Montalto, indicating the next senior officer beside him, who wore the three collar stars and three sleeve bars of an ordinary captain. Pederneschi nodded slightly but did not proffer his hand; Leeming noticing that his hard brown eyes looked the British prisoners over with barely disguised hostility.

'Lieutenant Visocchi,' continued Montalto, indicating the third officer, a young man in his early twenties.[7] Visocchi saluted Leeming, who returned his salute.

'This is Sergeant Baxter, who runs the mess,' said Leeming to Montalto, 'Sergeant Price and Corporal Blackwell.' The three British NCOs stood to attention and saluted. Montalto briefly nodded and returned their salutes.

'Now, you have much to do, is that not so, Mr Leeming?' asked the genial commandant.

'Yes, sir. My orders are to sort out the accommodation and make arrangements for the arrival of our main party tomorrow.'

'Yes, the generals. I am very much looking forward to making their acquaintances. Excellent. Pederneschi here will show you around and assist you.' Pederneschi's cold eyes fixed Leeming's, his face as stony as the lion that guarded the fortress's entrance.

Montalto made to take his leave, but then paused.

'Oh, I nearly forgot. Welcome to the Englishman's Castle,' he said, giving a slight bow before he strode off.

Leeming thought Montalto's comment exceedingly strange, but he said nothing. He glanced back at Pederneschi's glowering face and then up at the tall grey walls that claustrophobically rose up on all sides and the feeling of dread and helplessness that had taken hold of his stomach ever since he had first spied the castle from the car returned forcibly. How would they ever escape from such a place? 'We were, in truth, out of the frying-pan into the fire,' he later wrote.[8]

*

Leeming, Baxter and the others spent their first night in a collection of small rooms in the lower part of the castle's keep. Rising early the next morning, they set about the difficult task of preparing rooms for the arrival of the generals and brigadiers. It would prove to be a difficult task because there were so many rooms of different sizes spread across several different floors of the castle. Leeming considered the problem carefully and decided to allocate rooms according to the rank of the individual – meaning that the higher the rank, the larger the room the officer received. It seemed to Leeming to be a sensible solution that should avoid acrimony and debate. It turned out to cause the very confrontations that Leeming sought to avoid.

The rooms themselves were far from unappealing. Each was carpeted and furnished with great taste in the Florentine style. But dampness would make them cold, particularly those bedrooms on the higher levels. Radiators, electric heaters or brick wood-burning stoves provided heating for the rooms.[9] Officers shared bathrooms, and the other ranks were provided with 'shower-baths'.[10]

The lower part of the keep, as well as containing bedrooms, was given over to a series of public rooms that were to be made available to the senior officers.

On entering the keep, the first room was reserved for the eleven orderlies who would take care of the generals. It was a long room furnished with bunks, benches, stools and wooden tables. Lavatories and washrooms were located nearby. Lower down than the garden, between some medieval cloisters and the castle's ramparts, was the prisoners' kitchen, which was fully equipped and modern.[11] The kitchen actually consisted of two rooms, one containing an 'up-to-date range with wood firing' as well as a scullery, a water boiler and 'an adequate supply of dishes and kitchen accessories'.[12] The second room served as a pantry. Behind the kitchen were larders and store-rooms and the orderlies' dining room, all of which contributed to it resembling the below-stairs servants area of a great country house.

For the generals, the Italians had provided a vast dining hall, with old leather armchairs before a large and very heavy wooden table. Connected to this room was a common room decorated with frescoes and furniture, including a divan covered with cushions. This in turn led to the smoking room, with a stone fireplace big enough to roast a whole ox, then to rooms for reading and writing. These rooms, furnished with armchairs and art, created 'a very pleasant atmosphere for reading or meditation'.[13]

*

Back at the Villa Orsini, the rest of the prisoners were preparing to leave for the short journey to Sulmona station, where they would catch the train to Rome and thence to Florence. But the transfer was not proceeding smoothly.

Piled outside the villa was a veritable mountain of baggage and equipment that the senior British officers had managed to acquire or manufacture during their imprisonment. Fifteen large packing cases stood in one pile, beside eighteen suitcases and 27 cardboard boxes full of possessions. Next to this were an uncounted number of bundles tied up with string, beside Air Vice-Marshal Boyd's two large workbenches. Atop the workbenches were more boxes full of woodworking tools. Leaning against the side of the villa were piles of planks that Boyd had collected to manufacture furniture and shelves.

Brigadier Todhunter's rabbits sat impassively inside their wood and wire hutches, chewing reflectively on lettuce and carrots, while Brigadier Combe's hens clucked and pecked inside their wooden hen-houses. The great white dog Mickey sat on the kerb next to his large kennel, also preparing to leave, while his master Lieutenant Ricciardi did his best to calm down Colonel Mazawattee, who was running around and in between the great piles, simultaneously sweating and gesticulating at General Neame and the other senior officers.

Before the great piles stood one small Italian army truck, its driver standing beside the lowered tailgate, also gesticulating and arguing with any of the prisoners who cared to take notice. It was very clear to General Neame and his comrades that the truck was not big enough to accommodate all of the prisoners' possessions. Herein lay the rub.

'*Generale* Neame,' said Mazawattee, scampering up to the senior British officer. 'You must *only* take what the truck can hold, no?'

Neame, his arms folded across his chest, looked down at the commandant and shook his head.

'I've already told you, commandant. We are not leaving unless we take *all* of our luggage with us. I've been most emphatic on this point.'

'But *Generale*!' exclaimed Mazawattee, almost stamping one of his jackbooted feet on the road in frustration. 'It is *not* possible! You must only take what can be carried in this truck!'[14]

Neame, one eyebrow raised quizzically, was unmoved.

'It's a damned bad show, Colonel, a damned bad show, what?' said Neame archly. 'You must find *more* transport.'

'No, *Generale*, no, no, no! It is impossible,' Mazawattee's face was by now a deep shade of red. '*This* is the only truck that is available!' Then he changed tack, his tone suddenly becoming reasonable. 'It is no worry, *Generale*, no worry. I will *personally* ensure that *any* of your possessions that cannot be loaded on to this truck will be sent on to you tomorrow. You have my *word*.' Mazawattee's several chins jutted out in the style of Mussolini.

'No, commandant. I've made the position of the British prisoners perfectly clear. We're not leaving without our luggage – *all* of it,' replied Neame, the other officers standing near to him nodding or muttering in agreement.

'But *Generale*!' exclaimed Mazawattee, 'you will miss the train!'

And so the argument dragged on, as Mazawattee and Neame became more and more angry and frustrated.[15]

*

The last view General Neame and the other senior officers had of the Villa Orsini was of a crestfallen Colonel Mazawattee standing before the grand entrance sulking. His unhappy tenure in command of the awkward British generals was finally over, and Mazawattee should have felt elation. But he had been bested again. General Neame had completely overridden all of Mazawattee's arguments until more trucks had been procured to take *all* of the prisoners' belongings down to Sulmona station. Mazawattee had been forced to stand aside as Philip Neame, enjoying the responsibility, had busily set about overseeing the loading of the trucks, ordering around the Italian sentries that had been press-ganged into helping as if they were his own men rather than his jailors.[16] Mazawattee had been reduced to a pouting and unhappy spectator until the little convoy of overladen trucks and cars had finally departed, engines straining under the weight of so much equipment and baggage, and so many bodies. The Villa Orsini would remain empty for a while before fresh prisoners arrived.

*

Arriving at Sulmona station, the generals were pleased to see two junior British officers waiting for them. They had been sent up from the other officers' camp at Sulmona, and were to accompany the larger party to the castle.

'Ranfurly, *very* good to see you again,' said a beaming Neame, as he gripped Lieutenant the Earl of Ranfurly's hand. His old ADC had been returned to him at last, and would stay by his side for the duration of Neame's imprisonment. The other officer was Lieutenant Victor Smith, a Fleet Air Arm pilot who had occasionally visited the Villa Orsini to act as the prisoners' accountant. The older officers liked him very much.[17]

Lord Ranfurly had had a very tough time of it since he had last seen General Neame in North Africa. After the *Luftwaffe* had flown the senior officers to Italy, Ranfurly, along with hundreds of other British officers held by the Italians, had been loaded on to trucks and driven to Benghazi. There they had been crammed into huts – 40 or 50 officers to each small hut – and 'not allowed out for anything'.[18] There were no washing arrangements and the only rations were one 'dog biscuit' and a tin of bully beef between two a day. There was hardly any water and very soon dysentery broke out. 'The Italians would do nothing for us unless the Germans were around,'[19] wrote Ranfurly bitterly. After a week of this horrendous treatment, the British officers were loaded aboard Fiat trucks and driven for five days to POW cages at Subrato, twenty miles beyond Tripoli. During the journey through the desert the prisoners were only allowed off the trucks during night-time rest stops.[20]

At Subrato Ranfurly and the others were put on to starvation rations, receiving only two plates of soup each per day. The Italians also stole from them. 'I reported this,' wrote Ranfurly, 'and was sent to the orderly room. The Camp Commandant gave the thieves six months and me two packets of cigarettes; he delivered the sentence lying in bed.'[21]

The prisoners' sufferings were not yet over, for after ten days in the horrendous conditions at Subrato, the British officers were sent by train to Tripoli, locked inside airless freight wagons, 40 to each car. Then they were forced-marched five miles to the docks and put on board a ship. Incredibly, the British POWs were given first-class cabins, good food and deck exercise. This was probably because a German liaison officer came aboard every day to check on their welfare and distribute cigarettes.[22] There followed a three-day sea crossing to Naples and transit across the city by bus. Loaded aboard another train, Ranfurly himself fell ill during the slow journey to the main Sulmona POW camp, a final five-mile march almost finishing him off.[23] It was with great relief that Ranfurly discovered that the Italians had granted General Neame's request for his old ADC.

*

Baron Ricciardi shepherded the generals from the cars towards the long steam train that sat idling at the platform. A younger Italian officer, who was a good deal less friendly than Gussie, strutted about, yelling and gesticulating, while the guards and the British orderlies began to unload the small mountain of luggage from the accompanying trucks. Joining the Italian soldiers was the harassed station master, whose eyes widened as he watched the steady unloading of boxes, suitcases and bundles on to his platform.

It was clear to everyone that such a huge volume of luggage, animals and equipment could not easily be put aboard the train, which consisted of several carriages each divided into compartments with a side corridor. General Neame soon found himself dragged into another long argument with the Italians, until the station master, throwing up his hands in defeat, stalked off to find a goods van to attach to the rear of the train.

Once the goods van was hitched to the guards' van, the laborious process of transferring all of the prisoners' possessions aboard commenced.[24]

'All luggage must be loaded on the van,' stated the younger Italian officer to Neame, who was standing beside his travelling 'trunk'. This enormous piece of luggage had been specially purchased by Neame from Rome for just such a move. Its shape and dimensions were akin to those of a cupboard.

'Not this, Lieutenant,' replied Neame smoothly. 'This stays with me.'

'But *Generale*, it is not possible,' said the officer, raising his voice. 'It *must* go in the van.'

'Absolutely not, old boy,' replied Neame, his arms folded, eyes glaring. A fresh argument now erupted, as Neame dug in his heels and refused to allow anyone to move his trunk.[25] Eventually Gussie intervened and it was permitted that the trunk be loaded aboard Neame's compartment by several disgruntled guards. It was at this point that Brigadier Combe diverted the Italians' attention further along the platform.

'You know, I'm worried that my hens are suffering,'[26] said Combe to Brigadier Todhunter. Todhunter, who had been supervising the loading of his rabbit hutches and their precious contents, walked over to the nearest henhouse and peered inside.

'They do look at bit browned off,' he said in agreement.

Combe had caged his hens the evening before, and the length of time was concerning him.

'Think they might like to stretch their legs a bit,' muttered Combe, and before Todhunter could reply he had started opening the henhouse doors. Within seconds the platform was full of lively hens strutting around, flapping their wings and generally enjoying themselves. The other British prisoners dissolved into howls of laughter as Gussie's men ran around trying to recapture the hens while Combe ran after them, remonstrating with them to be careful and not injure his birds.

Meanwhile, the saga of Neame's gigantic trunk had not yet ended. Several sweating and cursing guards had managed with great difficulty to manoeuvre it into a compartment, wedging it between the overhead luggage racks. The guards stepped back, relieved that the job was over, and made to leave.

'Oh no, no, this won't do at all,' began General Neame to the young officer in charge. 'It's dangerous, you understand?' he said, pointing to the trunk above them. 'It could fall and kill someone.'[27]

The Italian, his eyes glancing towards the heavens in silent protest, took a deep breath. Then, with heavy heart, he turned and
ordered his men to take the trunk down. After some considerable
effort the great trunk was laid across the compartment's seats, creating a wall behind which General Neame sat silently by the carriage
window. The problem was obvious: the trunk blocked the escort
commander from seeing if Neame was still in the carriage. Another
argument erupted.

In the meantime, the Italians had managed to recapture all of
Combe's hens except for one stubborn layer called Victoria. The
hens and their houses were loaded aboard the goods van and Combe
was pushed on board the passenger carriage to join the other officers. Victoria was still free on the platform. A concerned Combe
leaned out of the window, trying to see his hen. At this point the
station master blew his whistle and the steam train lurched forward,
its bogeys and wheels squealing on the tracks, carriages jerking and
shuddering. Suddenly, Combe saw a figure run up to the window – it
was one of the station porters that had helped to load the prisoners'
luggage. He had Victoria in his hands, and quickly handed her up to
Combe as the train pulled away from the platform.

'Bless you, young man, bless you!' shouted Combe, as he was bundled into the compartment. Taking a length of string from his pocket,
Combe quickly tied Victoria's legs together and placed her in one of
the overhead luggage racks. By now, the compartment was filled by
the raised voices of Neame and the escort commander, who were
still arguing over the positioning of the general's travelling trunk.
Admitting defeat, the young Italian officer decided to clamber over
the obstacle and seat himself opposite Neame. As he passed beneath
Victoria on her lofty perch, the stressed hen gave vent to her feelings
and defecated all over the officer's cap and shoulder.[28]

'I told you my hens were unwell,' said Combe to the red-faced
officer.

'Never mind, old chap,' said General O'Connor to the Italian, a huge grin plastered across his face. 'It's a sign of good luck where I come from.'

The officer's eyes darted about the compartment before he abruptly stalked off in search of a damp cloth, followed down the corridor by gales of laughter from the generals and brigadiers, several of whom were holding on to each other and wiping tears from their eyes. It was, all in all, a fitting end to their imprisonment at Sulmona.

*

A few hours later the train pulled into Florence station, following a transfer at Rome. Everyone perked up, looking forward to seeing their new home, which the Italians continued to describe with such enchantment 'that I could well picture all the charms of *Decameron Nights*', wrote De Wiart, 'and was only wondering what I should do by day.'[29]

'Well, blow me down, it's old Tutti-Frutti,' declared Brigadier Todhunter to the compartment and General De Wiart in particular. Standing on the platform was indeed the genial Italian officer who had escorted Todhunter and De Wiart by ship from Libya to the Villa Orsini months before. Both men were quite touched that this officer should have taken the time to greet them again. It appeared to be another portent that their lot was improving.

The baggage and animals were unloaded on to several trucks sent down from the castle, and the British prisoners climbed into cars for the onward journey. Conversation ceased as the convoy, escorted by a motorcycle combination, began to climb out of Florence and into the countryside. The generals and brigadiers sat silently staring out of the car windows, evaluating the lay of the land, 'wondering whether or not it was going to be good 'escaping country'.[30] But then, like John Leeming the day before, they clapped eyes upon the Castello di Vincigliata and their hearts fell.

'You know, I have a bad feeling about this, chaps,' said Brigadier

Combe to the other officers in his car as he stared up at the castle's massive stone walls and battlemented towers.

'Abandon hope, all ye who enter here,' muttered General O'Connor next to Combe, quoting Dante. His eyes had taken on a hard, flinty expression as he stared through the car's windows at the castle. He had spoken for everyone in the party.

CHAPTER 7

The Eagles' Nest

*'Although Vincigliata itself was a bitter disappointment
to us with its impregnable and unrelenting appearance,
the actual move acted as a tremendous impetus and spur
to our escape plans. From the moment we arrived in
Vincigliata we never thought of anything else at all.'*

Major-General Adrian Carton de Wiart

Dick O'Connor's eyes darted everywhere as the cars and trucks carrying the generals and their luggage turned on to the castle's approach road. The surrounding country was gloomy and dense with cypresses. The grey-brown walls of the castle's outer perimeter were slick from a gentle rain that had begun to fall once the caravan had entered the hills above Florence.

'Some country club,' remarked O'Connor to no one in particular, Mazawattee's promises prominent in his mind. Like John Leeming the day before, O'Connor's eyes scanned the approach for any sign of a weakness in the castle's defences that could be exploited by the prisoners. But the structure appeared solid. It was a medieval Florentine fortress with five stories above ground and two below. As the vehicles passed into the castle's shadow, everyone noted the immense thickness of the walls, and the magnitude of the battlements: 15–30 feet high with towers in the northeast and northwest corners, enclosing a tall central keep.

There was little talking as the generals passed through several portals into the castle's gloomy inner sanctum on 24 September 1941.

'We were a silent, despondent bunch as we entered this vault of a prison,' described Carton de Wiart.[1] The only bright moment was seeing John Leeming again; he greeted them in front of the main accommodation area.

If Leeming was pleased to see the generals, his enthusiasm rapidly wore off as he started to show them to their rooms. Leeming's rationale of allocating rooms by the simple expedient of the higher a man's rank, the larger his room, had seemed sensible. But he had not taken into account the personal feelings of the generals, who he described, with commendable understatement, as being 'tired and overheated' on arrival.[2]

'Look here, Leeming, can't you give me a room better suited for escape?' said General O'Connor conspiratorially when shown his allocated room. Within ten minutes of the generals' arrival, Leeming's carefully worked-out accommodation plan was in tatters.

'It's a blasted dungeon, man!' growled De Wiart on being shown to his new subterranean digs. 'Winter's almost upon us. I shall freeze down here.'[3] General Neame, who had spent most of his life in tropical climes and consequently couldn't stand the cold, shared De Wiart's objection. 'I can't sleep in here, Leeming,' said Neame, scanning his new room, the largest bedroom in the castle, as befitted his position as 'father of the camp'. 'It's as big as a church, for goodness sake.' Both men demanded smaller, more easily heated rooms. De Wiart's problem was quickly solved by giving him a tiny room in the top of the central tower, General Gambier-Parry swapping with him. The uncomplaining Colonel Younghusband took Neame's 'church room', ironically pleased with the space after the overcrowding at the Villa Orsini.

Air Vice-Marshal Boyd was particularly fraught after the long journey. Never in great health since being taken prisoner, he looked all in as he approached Leeming. 'John, I don't give a damn where I sleep,' he said wearily. 'If it would be easier, I'll swap my room for one of the others.'[4]

'Is there nowhere better, old chap?'[5] asked Brigadier Combe on being presented with his room by Leeming, who was by now struggling to maintain his composure and feeling for all the world like the harassed manager of some third-rate hotel.

'I like to think that they were tired by the long journey from Sulmona,'[6] wrote Leeming charitably, having retired to his own small room with a considerable headache and the grumblings of the generals still ringing in his ears. The general consensus was that Leeming had made a mess of things.

*

The next morning, after a good night's rest, the prisoners began to explore their new home. It made for a depressing activity, for it appeared that their first impressions of the castle had been accurate.

'That damned Temple-Leader fellow has certainly made our lives difficult,' commented General De Wiart as he stood in the castle's courtyard and stared about him. 'What an absolutely wretched place.'[7]

The Duke of Montalto's intriguing comment to Leeming at their introduction, when he had described the Castello di Vincigliata as 'The Englishman's Castle' had been explained to Leeming by Baron Ricciardi. Leeming had then briefed the generals. It seemed that the castle was ancient, dating back to the 13th century. Originally, an important Florentine noble family had owned it, before it was passed to another family, the Usimbardi, famous for introducing glass manufacturing to Florence. It changed hands again before the Buonaccorsi banking family obtained the castle. In 1345, when the Florence banks crashed – caused, incidentally, by bad debts run up by King Edward III of England – the castle had been sold to the Albizi family of wealthy merchants. A branch of this family controlled the castle for over 300 years until by the mid-17th century it had been allowed to fall into disrepair.

In 1827 the castle and its lands were sold to Lorenzo da Rovezzano, and the ruin became a haunt of fashionable artists and writers who would travel up the eight miles from Florence to view it. The fortunes of the castle changed dramatically when an Englishman came upon the tranquil ruins one day and immediately seized upon the opportunity to create something striking and romantic.

John Temple-Leader had been born into a wealthy merchant family and entered the House of Commons young. A Liberal and a supporter of the Chartists, Temple-Leader's political career had not flourished, and though well connected and respected, the Commons did not hold him. He was a man who was fascinated by Europe and its history and was a personal friend of the exiled Louis-Napoleon, nephew of Napoleon I and the future Emperor of France. Temple-Leader also loved art and antiquities; numbered among his other acquaintances were the family of the painter Dante Gabriel Rossetti. In 1844, at the age of just 34, Temple-Leader abruptly left politics, and Britain, for the Continent, hardly ever to return.

After a brief stay in Cannes, Temple-Leader had settled in Florence where he bought several houses and villas and then carefully restored them to their former glory, filling them with his large collections of art and antiquities. The ruined Vincigliata Castle was purchased in 1855, and it would take Temple-Leader fifteen years to transform the mouldering old walls and collapsed towers into his vision of a fairytale castle, complete with two huge towers, crenellated battlements, dungeons and great gatehouses, surrounded by a moat and set on the side of a hill in 700 acres of grounds.[8]

In 1875 the celebrated American writer Henry James had visited the castle and admired Temple-Leader's massive folly. 'This elaborate piece of imitation has no superficial use,' wrote James, 'but, even if it were less complete, less successful, less brilliant, I should feel a reflective kindness for it. So handsome a piece of work is its own justification; it belongs to the heroics of culture.'[9]

With such a ringing endorsement from so famous a writer, it was little wonder that Temple-Leader's castle attracted many of the most famous and prominent personages making the Grand Tour across Europe, including royalty. In 1888 Queen Victoria signed the visitors' book and sketched in the grounds. Temple-Leader was rewarded by the Italian government for his preservation efforts in and around Florence, which had by the end of the 19th century a sizeable British expatriate community. King Victor Emmanuel I created Temple-Leader a Knight of the Order of the Crown of Italy.

But following Temple-Leader's death in 1903 his estates passed to his great-nephew Lord Westbury, who had no interest in the buildings or their contents. All were sold off. The castle once more entered a period of deterioration until it was loaned to the Italian government for use as a prisoner of war camp in 1941. By then, the building had been largely stripped of its artistic treasures, save for the stone lions that guarded the main gate, and its carvings and frescoes; the once immaculate formal gardens had been left to run to seed, and the whole place had taken on a look and feeling of faded grandeur and dusty irrelevance.

But Temple-Leader had effectively gifted the Italians the perfect prison. His careful rebuilding and remodelling work had been done using the best materials, resulting in a tremendously strong building that was, just like a real medieval castle, virtually impregnable, and therefore ideal for holding people inside.

'Imagine an old castle restored in the worst Victorian style,' wrote Lord Ranfurly to his wife, 'grey and featureless with enormous battlements and a tower in one corner.'[10]

The castle's walls, with an acre and a quarter of battlements, traced a rectangle 100 by 80 yards across the hilltop, with commanding views for several miles around, including down into Florence where the golden-roofed Duomo Cathedral could be seen on clear days.[11] Beyond the hill upon which the castle sat there was a slight hollow, then another hill, this one studded with villas formerly occupied by British expats, leading eventually to Monte Fano. To the west was a 'huge mass of rock several hundreds of feet higher than the castle',[12] which the prisoners would christen 'The Quarries'. Beyond this feature was the village of Fiesole, on a hill a little way out of Florence. To the east side of the castle lay the village of Settignano, with the Arno River flowing below towards Pisa and the Mediterranean Sea.

The castle itself consisted of a seven-storied keep (including, of course, two subterranean floors – De Wiart's 'blasted dungeon') the walls of which were two-and-a-half feet thick. Prisoner accommodation was on the southern side of the building, consisting of bedrooms and cloisters twenty feet below a formal interior garden with yew hedges,[13] with more bedrooms and the prisoners' public rooms in the keep proper. At the northwest corner of the keep was a bricked-up chapel and vestry. To the north of the keep was the gate tower, with two portals to enter the castle's courtyard, and another tower at the northeast corner of the massive outer walls, which stood 15–30 feet high depending on the elevation of the hill and which were fitted with a wooden inside walkway so that the sentries could patrol the perimeter between their guard boxes. The garrison lived in an area north of the keep, enclosed by its own internal ten-foot-high brick wall, known as 'The White Wall' because it was plastered.[14] Running parallel to the castle's western curtain wall was an outer garden enclosed by another wall with a gatehouse at its northern end leading out on to a public road.

There were no swimming pools, contrary to Colonel Mazawattee's vivid description given at Sulmona, and initially no walks were allowed and no playing areas provided, save for the odd cramped space. The gardens were a tangle of weeds. The only pleasant area for the prisoners to use was a terrace set above the cloisters on the castle's south side where they could sit or sunbathe with stunning views over the Florentine skyline. Perhaps the best thing the place had going for it was the modern plumbing, which Brigadier Todhunter was told had been installed by an American owner some years before.[15]

Two things about Temple-Leader's castle struck the prisoners. Firstly, the windows in the keep were small, making the place gloomy and chilly.[16] Secondly, the castle was a warren of passages and

96

odd-sized rooms, with many disused or closed-off areas. In contrast to Henry James's adoring description of the castle in 1875, Carton de Wiart was under no such illusions in 1941: 'Whether the Castello di Vincigliata is rococo or baroque I do not know, but I do know that Queen Victoria lunched there and Queen Elizabeth did not sleep there, and I know better still that I thought it was the most horrible looking place I had ever seen.'[17]

Being constantly observed soon took a toll on the prisoners' nerves. The castle appeared no more suitable to General Neame and the others than had the Villa Orsini. 'They consider themselves to be too cramped in their new residence,' commented a Red Cross inspection report, 'and in addition the walls and the surrounding road which dominate the Chateau garden and from which they are incessantly watched by sentries contribute considerably to their sense of imprisonment.'[18]

*

The prisoners soon noticed that the castle had a very different routine from that at the Villa Orsini. There was a roll call twice daily, where the entire complement of prisoners would assemble for counting in the courtyard; there were random inspections, and very strict black-out regulations. They were guarded by 200 heavily armed Italian *Carabinieri*. There was, however, widespread relief that their new commandant was a gentleman and clearly an Anglophile. General Neame was delighted to discover that the Duke of Montalto was an Old Cheltonian.[19] Lieutenant Ricciardi settled in to his new position on the staff at the castle alongside the ever-suspicious security officer Captain Pederneschi and the young Second Lieutenant Visocchi, who curiously spoke English with a strong Scottish accent, having studied in Glasgow before the war.[20]

*

The first escape committee meeting was convened within days of the prisoners' arrival. Now they were settled, planning for escapes could recommence, and this time in earnest.

'Well, gentlemen, we appear to be facing a much bigger challenge than that posed by the Villa Orsini,' said General Neame, chairing the meeting. 'I don't think any of us expected this,' he said, referring to the castle. The others nodded or grunted in agreement. Though they were nearly 200 miles closer to Switzerland, the castle presented any potential escapers with some very serious challenges.

'Clearly, the Eye-ties are determined to keep us under lock and key for the duration,' continued Neame grimly. Instructions were issued. Each prisoner was told to study the castle and the movements and habits of its guards. They must look for a chink in the castle's armour, some weakness in its defences, that might permit an escape attempt.

'We need ideas, gentlemen, and lots of them,' said Neame plainly.

*

Life at the castle took on much the same form as it had at the Villa Orsini. The orderlies dealt with the cooking, shopping and cleaning under Leeming's supervision, while General Neame assumed overall leadership of the camp, assisted by Brigadier Vaughan who acted as his right-hand man. Henhouses and rabbit cages were installed and the animals were tended by the senior officers. Air Vice-Marshal Boyd reopened his carpentry workshop. Brigadier Todhunter began accumulating books for what would one day be a 1,000-volume library, and General Gambier-Parry began instructing the others in art, including the dark art of forgery, as well as music, which was his other passion. He also took up poker in the evenings, but as Lord Ranfurly noted, 'plays extraordinarily badly and we all win his money'.[21] After the tedium of Sulmona, everyone at the castle felt buoyed up by their closer proximity to Switzerland, and this was soon reflected by a number of escape plans that were brought before Neame's secret committee.

*

'Right, Dick, tell us what you have,' said Neame to General O'Connor one evening in late September 1941. The officers were meeting once again in secret after dinner. For several weeks O'Connor and Carton de Wiart had been thrashing out the theory behind a new scheme. It was time to present their idea to Neame and the rest of the committee for their approval.

O'Connor and De Wiart had become fast friends, and were as thick as thieves plotting escapes. 'The ideas and the working out of the plans gave us a zest and a vital interest that nothing else could have done,' wrote De Wiart. 'Personally, without this one thought, I imagine I should have either have become disgruntled, irascible and peppery, or else have reached the state of apathy I slide into in hospital when, after a long illness, I start to dread the mere idea of recovering and am perfectly content to stay in bed, preferably for ever.'[22] Everyone coped with imprisonment in different ways, but the planning of escapes brought them together and gave them a defined purpose that none of the other activities they performed at the castle – from gardening, animal husbandry and music to carpentry and painting – would give them. Most importantly, it gave them hope.

'There is, in my opinion, every reason to think that four of us can get clean away,' said Dick O'Connor at the meeting, as he began to outline his and De Wiart's new scheme. 'Obviously, much preparation still remains to be made, but I'd like to run through what Carton and I have come up with.'

'Please do, Dick,' replied Neame, lighting a cigarette. The rest of the officer prisoners had gathered in the sitting room and were seated in comfortable armchairs. There was a certain faded grandeur to the castle's furnishings.[23] At this time of the evening, they all knew that the Italians rarely entered the castle. They would come at a certain time in the night to check that all of the prisoners were in their rooms asleep, but for now they shouldn't be disturbed.

'Carton and I propose an escape through the windows right behind you,' said O'Connor pointing. All heads turned to the darkened windows that were set along one side of the ground floor dining room. The dining room was located on the north side of the castle's central keep, facing the guards' compound and the two corner towers.

'The team will consist of six men. Four will form the escaping party, along with two assistants,' said O'Connor, turning back to the table. 'Once through one of those windows, the team will cross the garden to the white wall. The wall is, as you know, about ten feet tall, so they will carry a ladder. Once on top of the wall, the team will pull the ladder up after them and use it to descend into the Italian part of the castle. The team will then creep to the castle's outer wall and climb up to the battlements via the staircase near the gate tower.'[24] O'Connor paused, scanning the faces around him.

'Obviously, this sort of thing can only be done under the cover of darkness, and preferably a further layer of cover,' he added, running a finger along one corner of his white moustache.

'What sort of cover do you have in mind, Dick?' asked Neame.

'We'll wait until a windy and wet night. The noise of the wind will deaden the noise of our movements and the rain will hopefully keep the sentries in their boxes,'[25] replied O'Connor.

'How do you propose to get off the castle wall?' asked Neame.

'Well, this is where the two assistants come in to play,' replied O'Connor. 'We'll secure a rope to the battlements, and then each man can slide down to the dry moat outside. It's a drop of perhaps fifteen feet at that end of the castle. The assistants will then haul the rope back up and retrace their route back here, covering our tracks.'[26]

'Gosh, those chaps will be taking a big risk,' said Neame. 'They'll be making the journey twice.'

'That's right, Phil,' replied O'Connor. 'However, if done correctly, we could use this method more than once.'

'Well, I'd like to volunteer as one of the assistants, if you'll have me,' said Neame. 'This job is also going to require some muscle, so I think we should ask Sergeant Baxter to act as the second assistant. He's young and fit and probably the strongest man among us.'

'I was thinking along the same lines myself, Phil,' replied O'Connor. 'He's a grand type. I'll ask him later.'[27]

'Now, who do you have in mind for the escaping team, apart from yourself and Carton?' asked Neame.

'Hold on, sir,' piped up one of the generals. 'I don't mean to be indelicate, but surely Carton is in no shape for such a job?'

General De Wiart's head whipped round, his one eye flashing at this obvious remark. He was going, he thundered, and any so-and-so who thought otherwise 'could do this, that, and the other!' as Leeming later recounted.[28] His barrack-room language made even hardened soldiers blanch. 'He must hold the world record for bad language,'[29] wrote Lord Ranfurly to his wife. When it was pointed out, not unreasonably, that a one-armed man could not climb fifteen feet down a rope without assistance, O'Connor was ready with the answer.

'We'll tie the rope around Carton's waist, and General Neame, Baxter and myself can lower him to the ground. I, as the smallest and lightest, will be the last man over the wall.'[30]

'Quite so,' barked De Wiart, still fuming from the questioning of his ability.

'Who else will you be taking with you?' asked Neame.

'Boyd and Combe,' replied O'Connor. The other two escapers nodded silently, having already been let in on the plan several days before. The team was an eclectic mix. The redoubtable O'Connor lived and breathed escaping day and night. He thought about little else. De Wiart viewed the whole thing as essentially a game, and it appealed to his swashbuckling nature. Air Vice-Marshal Boyd was sober and serious. He was 'essentially a realist, and he wanted to have the answer ready for every situation that might arise.'[31] He believed that escaping was his duty, though he harboured serious reservations about their chances of actually getting out of Italy. Brigadier Combe, though a fusspot over his hens, was as solid as a rock when it came to escaping.

'What about the sentries on the battlements?' asked Brigadier Todhunter.

'Where we will climb up, the nearest sentry is about 50 yards away. As I mentioned before, the sentries will in all likelihood be inside their boxes because of the inclement weather. You may have noticed, gentlemen, that our guards at present are not as alert as they should be. I don't think they expect us bunch of old campaigners to try anything so foolish as escaping.'[32] The other officers guffawed.

'Well, gentlemen, we've a lot to think about,' said Neame matter-of-factly. 'I like your plan, Dick, and I think that with careful preparation you've every chance of pulling off a splendid show. The issues as I see them are as follows. The ground over which we will cross will need to be surveyed for cover, and noise tests conducted on windy nights.'

O'Connor and the others all nodded.

'Have you thought about disguises?'

'Actually, we've an excellent tailor among the orderlies, sir,' interjected Brigadier Combe. 'Private Dwyer. I think that he can help us put together escape outfits.'[33]

'We haven't yet spoken about the ultimate destination, which I take it will be the Swiss frontier,' said Neame.

'Carton and I have calculated that it will take the team about 21 days to march to the frontier,' said O'Connor. 'So we are making our ration packs up based on that duration. We've already started working out the correct weight-to-size ratios.'

'What about maps and compasses?' asked Neame.

'We're going to ask our tame doctor for some help on the maps side of things,' replied O'Connor, referring to the castle's Italian Army medical officer Dr Egon Bolaffio. Through his conversations with the prisoners, it was clear that Bolaffio was highly sympathetic to the Allied cause, and vocally anti-Fascist. He could probably be trusted. Due to his unique position, the doctor was able to come and go without unduly arousing interest from the guards, and, importantly, as an

Italian officer he wasn't searched. It was now a question of whether the good doctor was prepared to directly assist an escape. O'Connor and his conspirators were running a risk letting the doctor in on part of the plan, but it was a risk that they judged to be worth a stretch in solitary. The doctor, after all, would be playing for far higher stakes than any of the prisoners. If caught aiding an escape, Bolaffio could expect to be put up against the nearest wall and shot.[34]

'Once we have the necessary maps to hand, we'll be employing G-P's services to reproduce them.'

Gambier-Parry smiled and nodded. G-P's artistic skills were already widely appreciated by the other prisoners; they were skills that were easily turned to copying and forging.[35]

'Leeming has agreed to make the compasses,' said Boyd, turning to his ADC beside him.

'Good show, Leeming,' said Neame. Leeming knew that it was going to be a challenge, but he had already sketched out a preliminary design and thought about available materials.[36]

'So, we've much to do,' announced Neame at the end of the meeting. 'There's one more thing that I'd like to add before we break up. As you know, I favour any show that causes the Eye-ties maximum aggravation. Even if you don't get to Switzerland, simply getting our chaps beyond the walls will tie down inordinate Italian military resources that could be better employed elsewhere.' Everyone grunted their agreement. 'It will show *Il Duce* and his rabble that we are not prepared to sit out the rest of the show, as they undoubtedly expect.'

As the meeting broke up and the officers headed for their rooms, there was a feeling that a corner had at last been turned. They had a workable plan, and though there were many boxes yet to tick, the plan was sound. More than that, nearly everyone was to be involved in some way, whether or not they were on the actual escape team. Finally, after the months of lethargy and time-wasting at the Villa Orsini, they all had a defined goal to aim for. It rejuvenated them all, and gave purpose to their otherwise drab existences as prisoners.

It all looked so simple: how could they possibly fail?

*

In the event, Dr Bolaffio really came through for the prisoners. O'Connor managed to have a quiet word with the good doctor on one of his regular visits to the prisoners' rooms, normally made two or three times a week,[37] and Bolaffio was only too keen to help. A few days later he returned to O'Connor and ushered him into his room.

'Take these,' said the young Bolaffio, unbuttoning the top of his tunic and pulling out a flattened bundle of papers that he had secreted inside.

O'Connor quickly examined the 'papers' and was astonished to discover a complete set of Italian military maps for the region between the castle and the Swiss frontier.

'How in the hell did you get your hands on these, doctor?' asked a dumbfounded O'Connor.

'Headquarters in Florence,' replied Bolaffio. 'I "borrowed" them. But they must be returned soon, before they are missed. How long will you need to copy them, general?'

'Can you give us a week?' asked O'Connor, deeply impressed by the doctor's bravery and guile.

'A week would be too long,' replied Bolaffio, grimacing. 'Three days, general, then I will return for them.'[38]

Suddenly, the two conspirators heard footsteps in the corridor outside the room. O'Connor quickly stashed the maps under his bedding. Bolaffio started to 'examine' the general, just as Captain Pederneschi pushed the door, which was slightly ajar, wide open. Pederneschi stepped into O'Connor's room and stared at the two men, a pair of kid leather gloves held in one hand while the other rested on his leather pistol holster.

'Yes, that's nothing to worry about, General O'Connor,' said Bolaffio slowly, feeling O'Connor's glands in his neck. 'You will feel fine in a couple of days.'

'Are you ill, *Generale*?' enquired Pederneschi, his eyes boring into O'Connor's.

'Just a sore throat, Captain,' replied O'Connor hoarsely.

'Well, you should take better care of yourself … at *your* age,' replied Pederneschi, a slightly sarcastic tone entering his voice as he spoke.

*

'I'm too old for this nonsense,' complained a panting and sweating Owen Boyd as he hauled his short body up yet another flight of steps inside the castle's central keep.

'What about me, old boy,' asked a cheerful Carton de Wiart, who was right behind Boyd. 'I'm eight years older than you, you know!'

'Just think of the end goal, chaps,' gasped Brigadier Combe, behind De Wiart.

'The only … thing … I'm … thinking about,' managed Boyd, 'is my breakfast and … a … bloody … sit … down.'

'That's the trouble with you flyboys,' quipped De Wiart, 'you spend half your life sitting on your arses up in the wild blue yonder and the other half propping up one end of a bar!'

'Bloody … cheek!' gasped Air Vice-Marshal Boyd. 'But I'm too … tired … to argue with you.'

'How many steps to the top?' called out General O'Connor from the back of the queue of climbing men.

'One hundred … and fifty-seven,' announced De Wiart, grinning fiercely.

'You're loving this, aren't you Carton!' replied O'Connor.

'Nothing like a bracing climb in the morning, what!' bellowed De Wiart, barely breaking a sweat. 'I'll race you old farts to the top!' The endurance of the castle's most elderly resident was truly astonishing. He seemed hardly out of breath.

'God save us!' growled Boyd as De Wiart's tall frame elbowed past him up the stone steps. 'I do believe ... Carton ... will run ... all the way ... to Switzerland!'

Endurance training had begun shortly after General Neame had given the go-ahead for the white wall job. It had been calculated that the team of four escapers would need to hike cross-country for 21 days in order to bring them to the Swiss frontier and freedom. Each man would need to carry his kit, and rations to sustain him, in a rucksack, the weight of which was calculated at around 25lbs.[39] O'Connor and De Wiart quickly devised an exercise regime to bring the team to the peak of physical fitness for the trial ahead.

Dummy rucksacks were made, and were filled with old bricks to simulate the weight of the escape kit. Each morning O'Connor, De Wiart, Boyd and Combe rose at 5.30am and for one hour marched briskly up and down the tall stone staircases inside the central keep that rose seven floors from the dungeons to the top of the battlements. The other officers and men acted as lookouts to ensure that the calisthenics were not interrupted by the sudden appearance of an Italian guard.[40] It was a punishing routine for the middle-aged escapers. Combe, the youngest, was 48, while De Wiart was over 63 years old.

The generals also learned skills more appropriate to young commandos than middle-aged senior officers. Once on to the outer curtain wall of the castle during the night-time escape, the four-man team would be expected to climb down the fifteen-foot outside drop by rope. A quiet place was found where they could practise, and after several weeks the generals could shin up and down ropes like circus performers, with the exception of De Wiart. It had been agreed that Generals Neame and O'Connor, assisted by the burly Sergeant Baxter, would lower the one-handed hero to the ground. The technique for doing this was duly perfected. 'Baxter was an ardent weight-lifting devotee,' wrote De Wiart, 'performed every gymnastic, and let down my eleven stone and over six foot body as if I had been a baby in a blanket.'[41]

The window that would be used to exit the dining room was carefully prepared, its hinges oiled so that no sound would be made on the night of the escape. But much more involved efforts were under way to produce the escape equipment. Private Dwyer, the camp's tailor, worked for weeks recutting and dying pieces of uniform until all four men had a convincing suit of civilian clothes. Many experiments were made with the packing and repacking of the escapers' rucksacks, to find the correct load and size. Gambier-Parry excelled himself in the production of maps and route cards, hand-drawn from the maps that Dr Bolaffio had bravely 'borrowed' from Italian military headquarters in Florence. Mounted on linen, the maps could be folded out to show particular districts that the escapers would pass through on their way to Switzerland, and were completely waterproof.[42]

One of the most important pieces of kit that each escaper required was a compass, without which the maps would be next to useless. Flight Lieutenant Leeming was given the task of manufacturing four small compasses. He found that the small, round Bakelite boxes that held boot polish were ideal. Leeming fitted each emptied box with a magnetised needle, the tip marked with a small piece of luminous paint from a broken wristwatch to show north in the darkness. The compasses were waterproofed with glass lids made from carefully ground and shaped pieces of glass that Leeming stole from small windows in out-of-the-way parts of the castle. He shaped the glass on the castle's rough stone walls, a tedious job that required weeks of careful work. Once complete, each compass was immersed in a tank of water for 24 hours to test the waterproofing.[43]

Neame had set Zero Day, the day of the escape, provisionally for sometime in the autumn of 1941. By 7 November winter had 'set in with very cold weather,' noted Todhunter, 'which makes me and everyone else hungry.'[44] The supply of Red Cross parcels had been intermittent into the winter, and Todhunter noted dramatic weight loss. He had shed 21lbs since April.[45] The weather and food shortages conspired to make life rather grim for the prisoners. 'Our castle is pretty cold … and almost impossible to keep warm,' Todhunter wrote.[46]

The escape preparations took so long that it was Christmas before the civilian outfits, rope, compasses and maps were finally ready. It was now much too late in the year to contemplate an escape. The weather in Northern Italy was snowy and often very wet during the winter, and the four escapers would not have been able to survive outside for the best part of a month. There was nothing for it but to await the spring.

*

Christmas became a time of reflection for the prisoners, with their thoughts naturally turning to home and family. 'Somehow ordinary days are easy to bear and it is only on a day like yesterday that one really feels what it is like to be a prisoner,' wrote Lord Ranfurly to his wife on Boxing Day 1941. 'Luckily I was fairly busy preparing our rather ersatz celebrations and didn't have time to think too much.'[47]

The generals managed a fair Christmas, made easier by a healthy stock of wine and spirits. Presents arrived in the shape of gifts from the YMCA – board games, musical instruments and two complete badminton sets. Red Cross parcels had been sent, but unfortunately they arrived too late for the festivities. Mail did come, and Ranfurly was not alone in being outraged at how their imprisonment was being perceived back home by friends and family. 'So many people write to us in all seriousness and say, "How nice for you to see the art galleries, etc., in Florence." Are we indignant! I've only seen Florence from the railway station. This is a prison.'[48]

The prisoners had managed to fatten a few turkeys for Christmas and these had been slain and cooked. 'Our cooks excelled themselves and even contrived to make very passable imitations of mince pies and plum pudding, but they were very sensitive about the ingredients,' noted Todhunter. 'I strongly suspect coloured tripe of doing duty as candied peel!'[49] Entertainment was left up to the prisoners. 'After dinner you would have laughed to see our rather staid selection of old gentlemen playing charades,' wrote Todhunter to his father. 'It finally resolved itself into a series of lightning sketches mainly from the Old Testament all of which were very funny but would not have been a great success at a W.I. party!'[50]

*

A big shock came just after Christmas 1941 when the Duke of Montalto announced that he was being posted to Libya. The prisoners had grown close to the Italian aristocrat in the first three months of their imprisonment at the castle, Neame describing him as 'a first class officer ... who treated us in the best possible way'.[51] This had reached its zenith when Neame had extended an invitation to Montalto to join the senior officers for Christmas dinner. Montalto had accepted and dined pleasantly with the generals. But word had subsequently leaked out among the other Italian officers and guards of an incident at the dinner party. Neame had stood and proposed a toast to the king, the *British* king, and Montalto, undoubtedly deciding not to give offence, had duly stood along with everyone else around the table and drunk to George VI's health. A pro-Fascist member of the staff had leaked the news to the authorities in Rome, who had decided, not unreasonably, that Montalto had to go. He was packed off to the front line where he was (ironically) captured by the British and became a POW. His place was taken on 3 February 1942 by a man of more humble origins, an Anglophobic hardline Fascist, First Captain Tranquille of the *Bersaglieri*,[52] an elite corps of riflemen that in combat wore as their emblem a burst of black cockerel feathers on the right side of the helmet.

Tranquille was instantly disliked by most of the British prisoners, General Gambier-Parry describing him as being 'like one of those slugs that you find under a stone'. A thin man with sharp aquiline features and a pronounced stoop, Tranquille wore a permanent scowl and was to prove to be an assiduous commandant who had been sent to watch the prisoners very carefully indeed. He more than complemented his Fascist security officer, Captain Pederneschi, in this regard. General Neame was less harsh in his assessment of Tranquille, calling him 'an efficient and correct officer who organised and ran the castle well',[53] which was true, but he was not well liked. As for Pederneschi, Neame wasn't the only prisoner who had soon taken the measure of the man, noting that although he was 'outwardly affable' he could quickly lose his temper when crossed.[54] The prisoners intended that Captain Pederneschi should have plenty to lose his temper about over the following weeks and months.

CHAPTER 8

Trial and Error

*'If one of the first duties of a prisoner of war is to incite his guards
to mount more and more sentries and so dissipate his energies
away from the battlefield, then we were doing our duty.'*

Brigadier James Hargest

'Generale Neame, I am to inform you that more prisoners are to
arrive at the Castello on the 13th of March,' said First Captain
Tranquille in a bored tone on 9 March 1942.

'More prisoners? Do you know their names?' replied Neame,
standing before Tranquille's wooden office desk.

'They are all brigadiers,' said Tranquille, ignoring the question.
'Two British, two from New Zealand. You may meet them at the gate
when they arrive. I will have Lieutenant Visocchi inform you of the
time. Colonels Younghusband and Fanshawe are to be transferred to
another camp to make space.[1] That is all, *Generale*.' The grim-faced
Tranquille saluted the hatless Neame then slowly slumped into his
desk chair, his thin, slope-shouldered frame resembling a morose
vulture.

Neame left the commandant's office filled with excitement. Four
new faces would do much to improve the quality of conversation
among the prisoners, which after months together was becoming rather stale, though it was regrettable that Younghusband and
Fanshawe would be going. Both men would be sorely missed.[2]

The new arrivals would hopefully bring fresh news of the war and
its progress, as well as hoped-for skills and expertise that the escape

committee could use to its advantage. When Neame told the others, that evening in the mess, there was much excited chattering. The 13th would be an interesting day.

*

The new prisoners arrived from Florence station in two cars escorted by a single motorcycle. They emerged from the cars with undisguised looks of horror and fascination etched into their faces as they viewed the castle up close for the first time, a distinctly familiar reaction to the old boys who had arrived the year before. It was immediately evident that the guards were conducting a search prior to booking the prisoners into the camp. Brigadier James Hargest was still sitting in the back seat of the Italian army car, his window rolled down, when Brigadier Douglas 'Pip' Stirling, British 1st Armoured Brigade, walked past from the other car.

'They got my blasted field glasses,' Stirling hissed in a fierce whisper. Hargest was worried. He had concealed a stash of forbidden banknotes and a completely illegal army compass in an old bully beef tin that he had rigged to look unopened.

Fifty-year-old James Hargest would be unique among the prisoners at the castle in that as well as being a highly decorated combat soldier he was also an elected politician. Born in New Zealand in 1891, Hargest had been severely wounded at Gallipoli in 1915, winning a Military Cross, before commanding a battalion on the Western Front, bringing him the first of his eventual three DSOs. In 1931 he had been elected Member of Parliament for Invercargill, and when war broke out in September 1939 he had volunteered for active service once again. He was turned down on medical grounds and it was only through the personal intervention of the New Zealand Prime Minister that Hargest was appointed to command 5th Infantry Brigade, part of the 2nd New Zealand Infantry Division that went to Greece. Hargest had come in for some criticism over his handling of his brigade during the vital Battle for Maleme Airfield during the

German invasion of Crete, but he was subsequently awarded a Bar to his DSO. He had then taken his brigade to North Africa, where he was captured.

Hargest entered a small outer room of the castle where another door led through into staff quarters. A table and chair had been placed before the entrance, and Tranquille slouched behind it, waiting for the prisoners. Several burly guards stood around waiting to frisk the prisoners.

'I am going to search you, Brigadier Hargest,' announced Tranquille grandly. Hargest watched as his travelling bags were placed on the table before him by his batman, Private Howes. Hargest reached into his pocket and handed over the keys.

'Do you wish me to undress?' asked Hargest.

'Si, remove your coat,' replied Tranquille. Hargest quickly shrugged off his army greatcoat, extracting his precious tin from one pocket and also placing it on the table.

'My men will now search you,' said Tranquille. Several sentries expertly frisked Hargest, who raised his arms in reluctant cooperation. Tranquille suddenly ordered his men to stop.

'If you will give me your word that you do not have on your person any weapons, compasses, glasses or, how you say, files, I will stop the search.'

Hargest fixed Tranquille's brown eyes with his. 'I have nothing like that on my person, Captain, but I can't answer for my kit.'[3]

Tranquille ordered Hargest's bags searched. No contraband was discovered. Hargest suddenly reached forward and picked up the can of bully beef. 'I thought you might object to this,' he said, as cool as a cucumber. Tranquille barely glanced at the fake can, for he had seen hundreds in the Red Cross parcels that were delivered to the castle. The prisoners received 60 parcels every fortnight.[4]

'No, Brigadier, that's all right.'[5]

Hargest picked up his greatcoat and slid the can into a pocket. He was shown through a side door and into the back of the main gate where a small reception committee stood waiting for him. Pip Stirling was already deep in conversation with General De Wiart, while Neame, O'Connor and Lord Ranfurly each shook his hand in welcome.

'Jim Hargest, 5th New Zealand Infantry Brigade. And this is Reg Miles, another Kiwi,' said Hargest, introducing the rangy, tough-looking man beside him.

'Bert Armstrong, 5th South African Infantry Brigade,' announced the last officer to emerge from the office, a large, jolly-looking fellow who limped slightly when he walked. 'Everyone calls me "O Bass",' said Armstrong in his strong South African accent.

'When did you chaps go into the bag?' asked O'Connor.

'They got me at Tobruk, December '41. Reg at Belhamed,' said Hargest.

'Sidi Rezeg, November '41,' said Armstrong, rubbing his game leg.

'Tobruk for me also – bloody Rommel!' said Stirling.

Lord Ranfurly was particularly pleased to meet the New Zealanders. His grandfather had been Governor-General of New Zealand between 1897 and 1904, and Ranfurly's father had acted as ADC to the Governor-General. Dan Ranfurly had visited New Zealand himself before the war.[6]

'Welcome to the asylum, chaps,' said Neame. 'Let's show you to your quarters. It must have been a hellish journey. You'll probably want to freshen up a bit before the rest of the inmates chew your ears off. We're a bit short of visitors or news of late.'

*

The two New Zealand brigadiers, Hargest and Miles, were allocated small rooms in the top of the castle's tall keep, in what had been the servants' quarters during Temple-Leader's day. Hargest soon fell into conversation with General O'Connor.

'Miles and I are absolutely determined to escape by some

means, sir,' said Hargest, as he unpacked a few of his things in his brick-floored bedroom. O'Connor stood by the small window. 'Obviously, we don't want to embarrass any of the others who have already made preparations. Their plans must take priority.'

'Well, Hargest, we do have a scheme under way at the moment. It involves myself, General De Wiart, Air Vice-Marshal Boyd and Brigadier Combe and it's been in the works for months,' said O'Connor. 'In fact, we're rather hoping to get away in the next night or two.'[7]

O'Connor filled Hargest in on the details of the planned white wall job. Hargest was impressed. It seemed that the old generals knew their stuff. He and Miles would agree to lay off even elementary planning for their own job until after O'Connor's show had taken place. Instead, they offered their services to the existing scheme. Miles soon found employment. Gambier-Parry was overworked trying to produce maps for everyone, and Miles was an excellent copyist. He was set to work reproducing a map that was to be used during the white wall escape.

*

One week after the arrival of Hargest and Miles, General Neame announced that Zero Day, the day of the escape, was upon them. In the morning it had started raining hard, and the buzz among the generals was that today must be the day. All day various officers could be found peering through rain-streaked windows at the heavens or standing just inside doorways leading to the cloisters or terrace, smoking pipes or cigarettes, eyes narrowed as they contemplated the weather. A constant stream of amateur meteorological reports filtered back to the sitting room and smoking room, keeping everyone on edge. Dinner was served and it continued to rain steadily throughout. Many continued their routine of strolling to the doorways to check as the light faded from the grey, overcast sky and the night came on. The wait was agonising. At 9.00pm Generals Neame and O'Connor, the last pair to have gone outside, returned to the sitting room, where the rest of the generals were gathered before the fireplace on sofas and armchairs.

'Well, is it on?' asked Carton de Wiart without ceremony.

Neame slowly shook his head despairingly. 'I'm sorry chaps, but the wind has dropped and the rain is petering out.'[8]

'Damn it!' exclaimed Brigadier Combe loudly, thumping his fist down against the arm of his chair in frustration. Everyone in the room shared his passionate disappointment. There was nothing that Neame could do except postpone the attempt until more favourable weather conditions prevailed. It was back to waiting.

*

A few days later the friendly Italian medical officer, Dr Bolaffio, was performing one of his regular visits to the castle. The castle lacked an infirmary and, the authorities perhaps being mindful not only of the elevated ranks of their prisoners but also their ages, Bolaffio had been assigned to visit the camp regularly to check on all of the prisoners. For emergencies, Bolaffio had been issued with an army motorcycle combination so that he could take a sick patient straight down to hospital in Florence.[9] Bolaffio was often alone with the prisoners. On this visit he was particularly nervous.

'General Neame, I have heard that the castle is to be searched,' said the doctor in a fierce whisper.

'Searched?' exclaimed Neame in surprise. 'When?'

'I do not know for sure, but probably next week. Orders have arrived at our headquarters in Florence from Rome. Special experts are to be sent to search the castle.'

'Have you heard the reason for this sudden search?' asked Neame, his mind already turning to the caches of food, documents and civilian clothing that were hidden all over the castle in preparation for the white wall escape attempt.

'Don't worry, General, Rome does not suspect anything from you prisoners. It is just a new routine we must obey. It is also the same in the other prison camps in Italy. So if you have anything dangerous you burn it quick – especially any papers.'[10]

'Thank you for the warning, doctor,' said Neame, shaking Bolaffio's hand warmly. 'You are a good friend to us.'

Neame called a meeting of the escape committee later that day, and it was agreed to check all the hiding places to ensure that the searchers, when they came, didn't locate any of the compromising escape materials. Once that had been completed it was simply a waiting game until Rome's bloodhounds arrived.

*

'*Generale* Neame,' said Major Bacci, saluting smartly. Bacci was the *Carabinieri* officer who oversaw all of the POW camps in the Florence region since 24 September 1941.[11] He had arrived at the castle a few moments before with three truckloads of his men to begin the snap search. Bacci appeared slightly embarrassed by the task that Rome had set him.

The senior British officers were all inside their big sitting room. First Captain Tranquille had given orders earlier that they were to remain in this room while the search of the castle was conducted, and had posted several guards to back up his order.[12] Bacci had then arrived, immediately paying his compliments to the Senior British Officer.

'I am sorry, *Generale*,' began Bacci, a good-looking middle-aged officer with a pencil-thin black moustache and superbly tailored uniform. 'I hope that you will understand that it is nothing to do with me,' he said, spreading his palms outward. 'I should never have thought of such a thing. But I have definite orders from Rome. I have explained that such a thing is unnecessary with the high-ranking officers, but Rome, it does not understand that.' As Bacci spoke, Neame and the other Britons made appropriate noises of agreement.

'Forgive me, gentlemen,' said Bacci, concluding his explanation.

'I have my orders. You will permit me to carry them out?'[13] Neame nodded gravely.

'I shall call out each of you one at a time when my men search your rooms. After the search has been completed, you will wait in the courtyard,' said Bacci. '*Generale* Neame, if you please, sir.'

Neame went first, escorted up to his room, which was diligently searched by several of Bacci's men. No contraband was found and Neame was led down to the courtyard to wait.

When Neame was led from the room, Dick O'Connor turned to the others, his face as white as a ghost.

'Oh God,' muttered O'Connor.

'Dick, what's the matter?' asked Gambier-Parry.

'My room,' muttered O'Connor, as if to himself, before breaking his reverie and grasping G-P's forearm fiercely. 'My room ... I've left some papers in my room.'

'What papers?' asked Brigadier Todhunter, a sinking feeling in the pit of his stomach.

'An appreciation of the escape,' said O'Connor sickly. 'I left it in my bedside table drawer.'

'Oh my God,' exclaimed Todhunter and Combe simultaneously.

'What can we do?' asked G-P. 'We are not allowed to leave this room, and the door is guarded.'

'The next person who is taken out, he must warn Phil,' said O'Connor, coming to his senses. 'Phil will have to go up to my room, retrieve the papers and hide them.'[14]

'We'd all better hope that this Bacci fellow doesn't pick you next, Dick,' said De Wiart ominously.

'I also have some letters in my room,' piped up Brigadier Combe.

'What letters?' demanded De Wiart.

'Farewell letters,' said Combe, almost wincing as he spoke.

'Farewell letters? Who in the hell to?' snapped De Wiart.

'Ricciardi and another friendly officer,' said Combe. The rest looked at him with amazement or bewilderment. 'Well, they've been damned good sports and it didn't seem right to not bid them a proper farewell,'[15] said Combe defensively. The officers were permitted to write two letters and two postcards per week to relatives and friends.[16] Combe's unusual take on the regulations was astonishing.

'Mad as a March hare!' barked De Wiart, shaking his head in disbelief.

'Well, never mind all that,' interjected Air Vice-Marshal Boyd. 'What are we going to do about it, that's the more pressing concern?'

'The same as for Connor's papers,' said De Wiart. 'The next man out of this room will bloody well have to warn Phil.'

'Er … I also have a problem,' piped up Brigadier Miles.

'Don't tell me you've been writing letters as well?' asked De Wiart.

'No, sir. It's a map … I was helping G-P to copy a map. It's in my tunic pocket on the back of my desk chair.'

'Anyone else?' said De Wiart ominously, his one eye flashing around the room in disgust.

Brigadier Armstrong reached into his tunic and pulled out a bundle of banknotes.

'I've 5,000 Egyptian piastres here,'[17] he said, holding up the cash.

'Well get rid of it, man!' boomed De Wiart furiously. 'That goes for the rest of you. Hide anything incriminating.' Moving quickly, the officers checked their pockets and within a minute or two various papers and quantities of money were stashed in crannies around the large room, even inside the pile of ashes in the fireplace.[18]

The generals had hardly finished when the door to the sitting room was thrown open and Major Bacci entered. He scanned the assembled faces, his eyes settling briefly on General O'Connor. Everyone froze. The only sound was the ticking of the large mantle clock over the fireplace. Then Bacci's eyes moved on. They swung across to Combe's face, which was the colour of putty.

'Brigadier Combe,' said Bacci. Combe's eyes met Bacci's. His stomach turned over as he bent to place his pipe in an ashtray.

'Are you not well?' asked Bacci.

'Well? Yes … I mean no … I mean, it's very … very stuffy in here,' stumbled Combe. Bacci raised one eyebrow.

'Please sit down, Brigadier. *Generale* Gambier-Parry, if you will follow me please,' said Bacci casually. Combe collapsed into the nearest armchair in relief. As G-P was led from the room he turned back and briefly nodded to O'Connor. The whole escape plan, honed and refined over months of hard work, now hung in the balance. The generals had one chance to stop Bacci and his hounds from uncovering the whole show.

*

'Phil, we have a problem,' said Gambier-Parry quietly as he strode over to where General Neame was standing in the courtyard. G-P had just been brought down from his room, which had been satisfactorily searched by Major Bacci's men without result.

'The chaps are going potty in the sitting room,' continued G-P. 'Seems that Dick has left some escape papers in his bedside drawer.'[19]

'Come again?' exclaimed Neame, desperately trying to disguise his shock from a nearby Italian guard who glanced over at the two generals.

'Dick asks whether you'd mind popping up to his room and moving them to somewhere safer,' continued G-P.

Neame immediately grasped the situation, but also the difficulty of what G-P and O'Connor were asking him to do. But doing nothing was not an option – immediate action was the order of the day.

'Right, stay here, G-P,' said Neame, now recovered from his shock. Neame strode off towards the door that led to the bedrooms. As he approached, the sentry stiffened and looked at him sharply. The Italian soldier unhitched his rifle from his shoulder and prepared to challenge Neame.

'*Gabinetto* … *gabinetto*,' said Neame loudly, pointing towards the accommodation, asking to use the lavatory. The guard understood and relaxed, indicating with one hand for Neame to go ahead.

Gambier-Parry watched Neame disappear inside. His nerves were on edge, naturally enough given the serious repercussions that would follow if Neame were caught, or if he failed to retrieve the papers. But there was something else troubling G-P. Had he forgotten something?

Neame quickly slipped into the accommodation area. It was dead quiet. Then Neame heard muffled voices coming down the stone staircase that he was about to climb to reach O'Connor's room. Major Bacci and his searchers must be on the same floor as O'Connor's bedroom. Neame realised that he'd have to chance running into them. With his heart in his mouth he started to climb on tiptoe, trying not to make any noise until he reached the next landing.

Pressing himself against the corner, Neame tentatively peeked around and down the corridor that led to several of the generals' bedrooms, including O'Connor's. There was no one in the passageway, but he could hear Italian voices and the sound of furniture being moved in one of the rooms at the far end. He'd have to chance it. Neame could see O'Connor's bedroom door not far away – just a few quick steps and he could be inside. Moving as fast as he dared, Neame tiptoed down the corridor to O'Connor's bedroom, placing his hand on the door handle. Just at that moment, an Italian soldier appeared in the doorway of the bedroom at the end. He had his back to Neame and was talking loudly to someone else. Neame froze. If the soldier turned, he would be caught. Gingerly, Neame turned O'Connor's door handle, which squeaked alarmingly, and then quickly darted into the bedroom, pushing the door shut behind him. He waited for a few seconds, listening for approaching footsteps but there were none – he'd got away with it.

Neame went at once to the bedside table. He pulled out the packet of papers and stuffed them in the waistband of his trousers, pulling his sweater down over them. His mind racing, he made a snap decision. He would hide them on the roof, under a loose tile. Moving quickly, he walked over to the door and listened. He could hear the Italian soldiers talking again at the end of the corridor. Opening the door a fraction, Neame peered out. Everything appeared to be as before. He stuck his head out into the corridor – it was empty, the soldier having returned to the bedroom. Neame gently closed O'Connor's door then crept across to the staircase and headed upstairs. Once on the roof, Neame quickly hid O'Connor's papers beneath a loose tile before returning the way he had come. Although expecting to run into a soldier on the stairs at every turn, Neame was lucky. He successfully emerged back into the courtyard and wandered over to G-P, whose pensive face spelled trouble.

'I forgot to tell you,' said G-P, 'Combe left some papers in his room. Two letters. He wrote two letters …'[20] Neame slowly shook his head in disbelief.

'I won't get away with it again,' said Neame. G-P's facial expression agreed, but there was no choice. 'Right,' said Neame stoutly, 'here goes nothing.'

Neame immediately walked over to the guarded door again, holding one hand to his stomach.

'*Disinteria! Gabinetto! Presto!*'[21] The guard was horrified at the thought of dysentery and immediately allowed Neame to pass. Moving fast, Neame made his way carefully to Combe's room, again without being detected, snatched up the letters and headed once again for the battlements on the roof. Once again, Bacci and his men were busy in the other bedrooms and Neame encountered no one on the stairs.

Back safely once again in the courtyard, though by now red-faced and sweating from his two climbs up to the top of the keep, Neame met several of the other generals whose rooms had been searched. They were standing around looking pensive.

'Looks as though we've got away with it,' murmured Boyd. 'Splendid show, by the way.'

But the search went on.

Brigadier Hargest was called before his friend Miles. He

determined that he would somehow retrieve the half-finished map from Miles' tunic pocket. But the question was how? Bacci's men finished searching Hargest's room and Bacci started to escort the New Zealander towards the staircase that led all the way back down to the courtyard. As they walked, Hargest engaged Bacci in polite conversation, his mind racing. Suddenly, the solution to the problem occurred to him. Both Hargest and Miles had gone down to lunch dressed in shirtsleeves, having left their service tunics in their rooms. They were both about the same size and even had a similar array of medal ribbons above their tunics' left breast pockets. As Hargest and Bacci started to make their way down the stone steps, Hargest acted.

'It's turning cold, don't you think, Major?' asked Hargest, stopping. Before Bacci had time to reply Hargest started quickly back up the steps. 'I'm going for my jacket,'[22] said Hargest as he disappeared around the corner. Bacci muttered something, but didn't order him to stop. Hargest strode quickly down the corridor and darted into Miles's room, struggling into his friend's khaki tunic before hurrying back down to where Major Bacci was waiting for him impatiently. The switch wasn't noticed.

The castle was a big place, and after searching the senior officers' bedrooms, Bacci and his men turned their attention to the other ranks and the dining room, sitting rooms and kitchen. As the hours dragged by, and not one item of incriminating material was uncovered, Bacci and his men began to flag. By evening Bacci needed a break, and so he climbed up to the battlements for some fresh air and a smoke.[23]

Bacci strolled about in the twilight, enjoying a few moments of peace and solitude. Suddenly, he caught sight of something that didn't look right. A tile on one of the roof spaces beside the open battlements was not quite flat. Bacci walked over, tossing his cigarette to one side, and lifted the heavy terracotta tile. Beneath, bundled together, were General O'Connor's papers. Bacci gave them a cursory examination.

He couldn't quite believe what he held in his hands – a detailed plan for an escape attempt using six men via the Italian area of the camp. Bacci was elated at his discovery, but also deeply disappointed. The British generals had been deceiving him – pretending to be honourable gentlemen but all the while plotting an escape. Bacci said a silent prayer of thanks for having made this discovery – had the escape plot succeeded and a gaggle of British generals broken free into the Italian countryside Major Bacci would have been one of those held responsible by Rome.

Bacci now ordered a thorough search of the keep's roof. He soon turned up Brigadier Combe's two farewell letters, which made for very interesting reading for the authorities.[24] By the time they left the castle that night, the Italian searchers had 'the flush of triumph on their faces'.[25]

As well as revealing that the middle-aged British generals were plotting an escape, the cache of papers discovered by Bacci also indicated that Lieutenant Ricciardi and Dr Bolaffio were undoubtedly sympathetic to these prisoners. Action was taken at once. Ricciardi, though he had not aided the escape attempt in any way, was transferred to North Africa. His going was to be keenly felt by the generals, for they all considered Gussie to be a close friend.[26] Combe in particular felt dreadful about the whole thing. The only consolation was that Mickey, Gussie's giant white dog, would remain at the castle. Dr Bolaffio also left under a cloud of official suspicion. Neame was moved to write in 1943 that after the war Bolaffio should receive official British recognition for his brave aid rendered to the prisoners' escape plans.[27]

Of more serious concern were the months of careful preparation and training for the white wall job, now irrevocably blown to the enemy. 'It was a tragedy that any written notes should have been made at all,'[28] wrote Neame with commendable understatement. It was decided that from then on, regardless of how complex an escape operation was planned to be, nothing would be committed to paper.[29]

Major Bacci now redoubled his efforts at searching the castle.

What had been merely a formality and an embarrassing inconvenience to both sides now became a determined effort by the Italians to discover escape equipment. The castle would be taken apart if necessary. The number of sentries, with bayonets fixed to their rifles, increased considerably. Further searches turned up some Italian money and more documents. Bacci was so thorough that he had Italian workmen brought to the castle to carefully remove every roof tile so the space beneath could be inspected; the tiles were then replaced.

Neame and the others realised that this interminable search would continue until Bacci found something else of real value, so it was decided to let him find some of Private Dwyer's fake civilian clothes in the hope that this would satisfy him.[30] A few easily replaceable items of clothing were gathered together and hidden in a cavity below one of the staircases. Two of the generals mentioned this stash within earshot of one of the Italian officers, who quickly searched and found the items. 'After that interest in the hunt began to die away,'[31] wrote Leeming of the sorry episode.

*

The next day a staff car pulled up at the castle. First Captain Tranquille ordered a roll call and the entire British contingent was assembled in the courtyard. The Italian War Ministry in Rome had decided that the generals required an official warning concerning their behaviour as guests of Mussolini. To this end the Florence corps commander, Major-General Chiappe, had been dispatched to the castle to upbraid the POWs.[32]

The commandant had requested that the prisoners parade in full uniform, due to the presence of Chiappe and his staff officers. At 11.00am the British were drawn up in ranks before the general and his staff. General Neame turned to the POWs.

'British contingent, attention!'

The generals and other ranks snapped to attention. Neame

about-turned smartly and faced the Italian officers, who saluted, Neame returning their salute.

'You may stand your men at ease, *Generale*,' said First Captain Tranquille.

'British contingent, stand at ease!' bellowed Neame.

Chiappe's aide-de-camp handed Chiappe the 'official reprimand'[33] and he began to read. After first describing the heinous and under-handed plans the POWs had hatched, the reprimand pointed out the hopelessness and regrettable nature of those plans.

'The Italian Government regrets the severity of making an offi-cial reprimand,' read Chiappe, 'but it has to be pointed out that the conduct of the British senior officers has been very bad, and that they have brought disgrace upon themselves by their wicked actions. You are hereby told to desist from all escape attempts and to abandon all such shameful ideas immediately.'[34] Chiappe stopped, sighed, and handed the paper to his aide. Commandant Tranquille stared at the prisoners, a slight smile creasing his thin lips. Smoothing down his tunic, General Chiappe spoke again.

'I would like to say, gentlemen, that in the same circumstances I hope I would have done the same.' Tranquille's face dropped. 'Would it be possible for you to have a glass of wine with me?'[35] said Chiappe, smiling broadly.

*

The Italians were taking no further chances with their illustrious captives. Within days of the discovery of the white wall plot, electri-cians came up from Florence to install new lights on the castle walls and on the white wall. Holes were drilled into the top of the white wall and iron posts cemented into place. Eleven strands of barbed wire were then strung through the posts, and an extra sentry posted to watch the wall like a hawk.

From now on, anytime the prisoners left the castle for escorted walks through the local countryside, they would have to wear full uniform rather than their usual casual attire, again to prevent any escape attempts.[36]

The sentries became jumpy. A few nights after the escape plot was discovered, one of the guards on the castle wall fired two shots at someone or something outside the moat, perhaps thinking that it was an escaper. No dead body was ever produced from this incident and Tranquille gave the guard a severe dressing-down.

CHAPTER 9

Going Underground

'Dick O'Connor was the most enthusiastic plotter of all,
with Jim Hargest and Reg Miles as close runners-up.'

Lieutenant-General Sir Philip Neame

'Can you help me, Bain?' asked John Leeming, as he concluded his story of an amazing discovery in the bottom of the castle well. RAF Sergeant Ronald Bain, a red-headed Irishman who assisted with housekeeping, was the camp's qualified electrician and was able to procure or manufacture many things, making him invaluable when it came to assisting escapes.

All castles require a source of fresh water, and the Castello di Vincigliata was no exception. Though no longer of any practical use now that indoor plumbing and electricity had been introduced to the ancient building, the castle still retained its deep well in the prisoners' courtyard area. It was a dingy affair, with mossy, slimy walls, and the bottom was very hard to make out.

'How did you find it, sir?' asked Bain of Leeming's amazing new discovery.

'I was leaning over the top, just peering down, and the light caught what looks like a stone or brick opening just above the level of the stagnant water in the bottom.'

'Are you sure your eyes aren't playing tricks on you, sir?' asked the Irishman seriously.

'To begin with, I thought they might have been. But, no, I'm absolutely sure the opening is there, Bain.'

'How big do you think it is?'

'It looks like a small doorway ... certainly big enough for a man,' replied Leeming, still excited from his initial discovery.

'And you want me to help you to take a closer look, right?' said Bain, rubbing his chin reflectively.

'That's right. Any ideas?'

'Well, first we need to take a good look at the thing,' said Bain. 'How deep is the well, would you say?'

'About 40 feet,' said Leeming.

Bain accompanied Leeming to the well head and peered downwards, letting his eyes slowly adjust to the gloom. After a few seconds he turned to Leeming.

'You're right, sir, there's definitely an opening just above the waterline.'[1]

'Question is, how to confirm what we suspect we see?' asked Leeming.

'How about we lower a candle down the well shaft?' suggested Bain. 'Then we can take a closer look at this doorway of yours. I can rig up something simple and we could have a go when the castle is quieter late this afternoon.'

'Top man,' said Leeming. 'I'd like to confirm what I think before I take this before the escape committee.'

It was decided. Sergeant Bain attached a large candle and its holder to a string harness, and late that afternoon, when no Italian guards were about, he and Leeming carefully lowered the rudimentary light down into the well.

'I see it,' whispered Bain fiercely as the candlelight wobbled about, illuminating black depthless water and mossy walls. 'I'd say the opening is about three feet high and a couple of feet wide, sir.'[2] Leeming confirmed Bain's observations. The implication was obvious: an opening must lead to a passage ... but a passage to where?

*

As soon as Leeming had confirmed the existence of the well passage-way, he immediately informed General Neame and Air Vice-Marshal Boyd. Neame decided to put together a team to conduct a reconnaissance of the shaft. As well as himself and Boyd, the team was made up of Leeming, Sergeants Baxter and Bain, General O'Connor and the irrepressible Sergeant Price.[3] This last man was brought on to the team as it was felt by Neame that hailing from the Rhondda Valley in South Wales, Price must know something about mining, and would be invaluable for such subterranean work.

Sitting above the well head was an extremely old ornamental iron pulley, originally used to raise buckets of water from the well deep below. Everyone was a little wary of the pulley arrangement, which clearly hadn't been used in decades. The compact Boyd would be the first man down. One morning, just before dawn, when the castle was dead quiet, the team crept over to the well head with a long length of rope that had been hidden since the abortive white wall attempt, and wound it on to the ancient pulley. One end of the rope had been fitted with several 'holdfasts', or loops, where the person being lowered could put their feet.

'Right, away you go, John,' whispered Neame to Boyd, his breath steaming in the bitterly cold air. 'And good luck.'

Boyd nodded, his face set in a determined expression. He climbed over the well head and attached himself to the rope. Sergeant Baxter and several of the young orderlies took the strain on the other end, ready to pay it out through the pulley as Boyd was lowered.

'Okay, lower away,' hissed Neame, and Baxter's team started to let out the rope. Boyd disappeared jerkily into the gloomy well shaft, the others crowding around the opening, monitoring his descent.

'I'm … spinning!' came Boyd's startled cry after he had been lowered ten feet. Unable to let go of the rope to touch the walls, Boyd had started to rotate out of control on the rope.[4]

'Bring him back up,' said O'Connor urgently to Neame. Neame gave the order and a rather dizzy Boyd was hauled back to the surface.

'Try again?' asked Neame a few minutes later.

'Of course,' replied Boyd stoutly. 'If someone gives me a stick, I can hold it as I hold the rope and stop this confounded spinning by touching the sides.' A stick was quickly fetched and Boyd was lowered once more.

'Good grief!' hissed O'Connor at the sudden banshee scream that had started to emanate from the ancient pulley as Boyd passed twenty feet.

'Stop!' whispered Neame to Baxter. Neame leaned over the well head and hissed at the dangling Air Vice-Marshal: 'Just hang on, Boyd, and we'll try again.'

'Right, lower away,' Neame said to Baxter. Sergeant Price was operating the old iron wheel attached to the pulley, but each half-revolution produced a squeaking noise loud enough to wake the dead.

'Stop!' ordered Neame again. There was a hurried discussion as Boyd, whose arms were beginning to ache from the effort of clinging on to the rope, dangled twenty feet above the pool of black water in the bottom of the well.

'I'll fetch some oil, sir,' said Sergeant Bain. 'Just hold on a minute.' He dashed off indoors and returned a few moments later with a bottle of hair oil to be applied to the well's moving parts.[5] However, by this time the reconnaissance attempt had already gone on longer than expected.

'Pull him back up!' ordered Neame, and an exhausted Boyd was brought back to the surface. Round one had definitely gone to the ancient well, but, determined not to be beaten, the team agreed to have another go at dawn the next morning.

*

Attempt number two was much more successful. The offending well pulley had been carefully overhauled by Sergeant Bain to prevent any repetition of the appalling caterwauling of the previous morning.

This time, General O'Connor was selected for the operation. He was an ideal choice, being small and wiry and full of guts.

O'Connor was lowered without incident. The rest of the party couldn't see him reach the bottom, for it was dawn, with little light. But after some swaying the rope suddenly went slack. A very tense ten minutes dragged by, as Neame and the rest of the ground level team waited in virtual silence. No Italian appeared, but it was growing lighter and soon the castle would come alive. Suddenly, the rope coming taut broke everyone's silent reverie. O'Connor was back on. Neame gave the order to haul him up.

'It's more than we could have hoped for,' said a sweaty and grimy O'Connor, as he clambered over the edge of the well head. 'Leeming was right. There is indeed a doorway. It's ancient, and I'd say about five feet high and three feet wide.'

'Is there a passage, sir?' asked Leeming excitedly.

'Yes,' replied O'Connor, grinning. 'It runs straight out from the well in the direction of the garden for between twenty and thirty feet. But there's a snag.'

The others all grimaced or glanced at each other.

'The passage is blocked by a brick wall,' said O'Connor. 'It looks quite new compared with the ancient stonework in the passage. But the good news is that the wall looks to be only a single brick thickness. I think we could break through without too much trouble.'[6]

Neame turned to Leeming, his face beaming.

'Because of you, John, we may have a way out to freedom. Bloody good show!'

Neame grasped Leeming's hand fiercely in his and shook it vigorously. What lay beyond that damp red-brick wall was anyone's guess, but Neame and his team were determined to find out.

*

'John, can I have a word,' said General Neame casually to Leeming, after the well team had dispersed and the castle had come alive.

'Do you know that large cupboard built into an alcove in the dungeons?' asked Neame. The accommodation quarters in the below-ground part of the castle had naturally enough been given this name by the POWs. Leeming knew exactly which cupboard the general was referring to, as he, like all the other prisoners, had carefully explored every inch of the building in the search for possible escape routes. The cupboard was built into an alcove along one of the corridors that led to bedrooms.[7]

'There's something a bit queer about that cupboard,' said Neame. As their resident Royal Engineer, Neame's opinion about such things was widely respected.

'How so, sir?' replied Leeming, whose mind was still filled with the well passage and wall.

'Well, I don't know whether you've noticed, but the back of the cupboard is plastered.'

'Yes, sir, so I recall,' said Leeming distractedly.

'Doesn't that strike you as a bit odd?' asked Neame. 'After all, the alcove and ceiling are both stone.'

'Come to think of it, it does seem a bit strange,' replied Leeming, his mind starting to focus on this new issue.

'I'm thinking that we should have a look at what's beneath that plasterwork,' said Neame. 'How would you like to do it?'

Leeming was a little taken aback.

'I thought I was to go with the well team, sir?' he asked, slightly crestfallen.

'I've detailed Air Marshal Boyd and Sergeants Price and Bain for the next descent tomorrow morning,' replied Neame without explanation. 'I'd like you, Bain and Sergeant Baxter to examine the cupboard wall this afternoon, when most of us are out on our daily walk and the castle will be quiet. Think you can manage?'

'If you say so, sir,' said Leeming, who thought the whole thing sounded like something of a sideshow. But the old boy must know what he's doing, thought Leeming.

'Jolly good show,' said Neame, touching his index finger to the side of his nose. 'I think that there's more to that plaster wall than meets the eye.'

*

Later that afternoon, when the generals had left on their escorted constitutional, Leeming, Bain and Baxter slipped down to the dungeons to begin their exploration. Leeming ran the flat of his hand over the white, plastered surface of the cupboard's back wall and then tapped it with a knuckle. It sounded solid enough.

Sergeant Baxter produced a small hammer and, working fast, he knocked out a small section of plaster revealing a red-brick wall beneath. With some improvised tools the three prisoners worked at the mortar that held one of the bricks in place, until, after much sweating and whispering, they prised it loose. Leeming pressed his face to the gap. He could only see a dark void, but he could feel a slight movement of air.

'Right, chaps, let's widen the hole so that I can climb through,' said Leeming to the two sergeants. After another half-hour of chipping away at the hard mortar and pulling aside loosened bricks the hole looked just wide enough for Leeming – who was not the smallest prisoner in the castle – to slip through.

'Good luck, sir,' said Baxter, before the two NCOs hoisted Leeming up and through the hole. Leeming became stuck halfway, the gap not quite wide enough, but a hefty shove from the two muscular sergeants dislodged another brick and Leeming landed in a sweaty pile on the other side.

Leeming stood, letting his eyes adjust to the half-light. He was inside a stone passageway. 'Battered but wildly excited … I crawled down the passage,' he later recounted. 'Ahead I could see daylight, the silhouette of an opening, a doorway.'[8]

Leeming reached the doorway and daylight, but for a few seconds he couldn't process what he was seeing. Before him was a long shaft rising up high above him, while below the doorway was a pool of dark water. Then it dawned on him – he was at the bottom of the castle's well! 'The passage from the well led to the alcove in the dungeons.'[9] It was a truly crushing moment – at a stroke two potential escape routes out of the castle had proved to be dead ends.

Leeming crawled dispiritedly back down the passage to the brick wall and struggled through into the dungeons. He told Bain and Baxter what he had found, and they commiserated with him.

'So what are we going to do about this?' asked Leeming, gesturing towards the large hole in the alcove wall. 'If the Eye-ties find this, we'll all be for it.' Since the discovery of the white wall escape plans, the Italians were keeping a closer watch over both the prisoners and the integrity of their castle.[10]

Leeming's party managed to replace the bricks, but that still left the damaged plaster to contend with. For an hour they experimented with various camouflage, including mixing powdered plaster with water, even 'painting the bricks with mud.' The result of these experiments was merely to make the ugly hole even more obvious to any Italian searchers. 'Suddenly, just as we were getting desperate, Bain raced off to the kitchen and, in spite of the protests of Horsey, our cook, grabbed a large rice-pudding that stood ready for our dinner,' recalled Leeming. 'Back at the plaster wall, he slopped the rice-pudding on to the brickwork, then, scraping and smoothing the mixture flat, blended it to the ragged edges of the plaster round the hole.'[11] As a final touch, the three men picked up bits of broken plaster from the floor, ground them to powder and chucked this on to the drying rice pudding. Incredibly, the Italians never discovered the hole.

*

Three escapes had now been explored, and all three had come to naught. The failure of the first attempt, the white wall job, had only led to a drastic tightening of security by the Italians, which would make subsequent escapes even more difficult. Major Bacci's discovery of General O'Connor's written appreciation and plans for the white wall escape had removed from the minds of the Italians the notion that the British generals were simply a kindly bunch of old duffers who were seeing out the duration in genteel comfort. Instead, they were now viewed as troublemakers who could, at any time of the day or night, launch a diabolical escape plan. For Commandant Tranquille and Area Commandant Bacci, not to mention General Chiappe in Florence, any successful escape by such high-profile and important prisoners would bring serious repercussions from Mussolini himself in Rome. But the British took no notice of Chiappe's exhortation to behave themselves, and planning was soon under way for a fresh escape scheme.

*

Brigadiers Hargest and Miles, as latecomers to the castle, had a lot of catching up to do regarding amassing escape equipment. Although no definite scheme had been decided upon or worked out, it was thought wise by all of the prisoners to continue collecting civilian clothing, food and maps for the time when they would inevitably try.

Hargest and Miles had arrived at the castle with only their army uniforms and a couple of British army blankets. The Italians had stopped the practice of allowing prisoners to purchase items of clothing from the local town, so unlike the rest of the POWs who had bought every piece of civilian attire they could get away with at Sulmona, Hargest and Miles would have to make everything that they would need – apart from an old pair of navy blue RAF trousers that Air Vice-Marshal Boyd gifted to Miles.

The two New Zealanders decided to make coats out of their blankets. Pyjamas were used as a template, and the blankets were slowly transformed into passable jackets. Workmen's caps were also fashioned from the remaining blanket material, complete with cardboard peaks taken from chocolate box lids. How well such ersatz items would stand up to inclement weather was anyone's guess.[12]

Hargest lacked any civilian trousers, so he experimented in his bathtub with dyeing a pair of old battledress trousers to an unmilitary hue. He eventually succeeded using some boot polish mixed with a bottle of ink. The downside was that his hands were so stained afterwards that he was forced to wear a pair of woollen gloves to all parades for several days.[13]

Stashing food in a drain inspection hole beneath the other ranks' dining room, Hargest and Miles accumulated a couple of tins of bully beef, some soup cubes and eventually five pounds of Red Cross chocolate.

The New Zealanders, like everyone else in the castle, also began to discuss and examine where to go should they succeed in escaping. The obvious choice was Switzerland. Hargest and Miles decided that they would make for the nearest point of Switzerland, the border town of Chiasso near Lake Como. The distance was roughly 230 miles. Hargest hit upon a novel way of discovering more about the region they would aim for. The Italians understood that the New Zealanders came from a mountainous country, so 'it was natural that we discussed this type of scenery with the Italian officers, who were easily induced to talk'.[14] Much valuable intelligence was thus gleaned during these innocent chats. But what Hargest and Miles really required were proper maps of the routes to Switzerland, particularly since many of G-P's carefully made copies had been seized by Major Bacci and his men. Hargest recalled that years before he had read *Garibaldi and the Thousand*, about the formation of modern Italy, and that the book had contained several maps of the frontier region. 'As we were studying the language I asked if I might have a copy of it in Italian,'[15] wrote Hargest, whose ruse worked. A few weeks later an Italian-language version of the book arrived, complete with maps of the frontier. The book was passed to Gambier-Parry, who set to work producing new hand-drawn maps from the illustrations.

*

Like the Britons, Hargest and Miles spent weeks carefully exploring every nook and cranny in the castle, trying to find a weakness that they could exploit. Air Vice-Marshal Boyd often joined them. They noticed that there were some rooms in the castle that were closed off from the prisoners. Working on the idea that there must be a lower level than the subterranean rooms accessible to the POWs – proper dungeons – and that one of the closed-off rooms might be connected to those hidden levels, several exploratory excavations were made.

Miles, Hargest and Boyd first targeted a bricked-up doorway in the banqueting hall, which was in use as a dormitory. A large stack of deckchairs was used to cover the hole being cut in the wall.

As with all escape attempts, it was important that lookouts, known in prisoner parlance as 'stooges', be used to warn of the approach of any guards. To this end Sergeant Howes and some of the orderlies formed a system of stooges to protect the excavation. Hargest and Boyd, using woodworking tools and a meat knife, made a hole in the wall's plaster before slowly and carefully excavating a hole in the skin of red bricks beneath. Behind the wall was a solid oak door that had been reinforced with steel. The excavation stopped and the men returned to their rooms 'to ponder on this apparently insuperable difficulty'.[16]

The next morning, the excavation recommenced. Knocking a hole through the door, which turned out to be four inches thick, was difficult and time-consuming. The prisoners bored a series of holes close together, and then used a hacksaw to join up the holes to create a space big enough for a man to climb through.[17] It took several days to complete, and Boyd's woodworking tools took a terrible beating cutting through the door's steel supports. When the hole was large enough, the smallest and slimmest of their orderlies was lifted through to clear some furniture that was blocking the way. Then the others clambered through. What Hargest and Boyd discovered on the other side of the door 'was a most elaborately fitted-up old kitchen, complete with a giant roasting pit; but no stairway'.[18] The operation was another bust. The castle seemed impregnable. The bricks and plaster were replaced and the disappointing news relayed to General Neame and the others.

*

With the failure of two subterranean potential avenues of escape, thoughts turned back to the castle's walls. Though the Italians had blown the white wall escalade attempt even before it was tried, the theory of somehow vaulting over the walls remained in some of the prisoners' minds. One of those was Dick O'Connor, one of the original conceivers of the white wall job. In his opinion, an escape over the perimeter wall was still possible, regardless of how much the Italians had beefed up the defences. The million-dollar question was how. O'Connor spent weeks contemplating this problem, and began to formulate a novel solution to that thorny question.

In the meantime, some of the other prisoners were also looking at the wall, but rather than considering going *over* it, some were considering going *through* it to freedom. The keys to success, in their opinion, were rabbits.

Jim Hargest spotted an opportunity when he was in the lower cloisters outside the prisoners' accommodation one day. The castle's curtain wall, which was about three feet thick at this point, had been pierced, probably during Temple-Leader's tenure, presumably to provide people in the lower cloisters with a splendid view of distant Florence. During the conversion of the castle to a POW camp these two windows had been filled in with cemented rocks and the mortar plastered so as to fit in with the surrounding ancient stone.

Rabbits came into the equation because the rabbit-keeper, Brigadier Pip Stirling (who had taken over this duty from Brigadier Todhunter) kept a line of wooden hutches against the wall in front of one of the bricked-up windows. Hargest decided to work with just two other officers for this escape attempt – Boyd and Hargest's fellow countryman Reg Miles.

Hargest asked Stirling to stack some empty hutches on top of the occupied ones, so creating a wooden wall three feet tall, with a sufficient gap behind to allow a man to work in secret. The only downside to Hargest's plan was the Italian sentries on the wooden walkway fitted to the inside of the castle battlements. Every few minutes a sentry would stroll along the walkway, arriving at a position high above the spot where Hargest would be interfering with the wall; Hargest needed to know when this occurred so he could cease work and be silent till the sentry reversed his beat and moved out of earshot. Sergeant Howes volunteered to act as a stooge. He spent all day sitting under the blazing sun sketching, and giving Hargest a surreptitious signal at the approach of the sentry.[19]

Hargest, armed with a large meat knife that Boyd had fitted with a stout wooden handle, slipped behind the barrier of hutches, his movement shielded by Stirling as he tended to his rabbits. Working quickly, Hargest scraped off the plaster that covered the mortar holding two of the rocks together. It was all looking too simple.

Later that evening Neame popped into Hargest's room to talk to him.

'Word is, Hargest, that you are working on an escape plan concerning the wall?' asked Neame casually. Neame was actually quite angry that Hargest and his associates had decided not to share the details with the other prisoners. The reason for their reticence was that Boyd believed that earlier plans had come to naught partly because of too many people knowing about them, leading to careless talk or slip-ups. Neame, though, thought that everyone should share with everyone else – that the castle's POWs were too few in number not to cooperate on every escape scheme.

'I don't approve of such secrecy, Hargest,' said Neame plainly. 'I hope that you will share your plan with us all. In the meantime, can you give me the basics now?'

Hargest understood Neame's position, but he also agreed with Boyd's point about careless talk or actions.

'Once we've made a hole through the window space we'll pass through it feet foremost, holding on by a rope fastened to a cross-stick on the inside,' replied Hargest. 'Once through, we'll be about twelve feet above the ground on the outside. We can lower ourselves by means of the rope.'

'Have you ever tried going through a hole backside foremost and ending up twelve feet above ground and doing it without noise?' asked Neame in a concerned voice.

'No, I haven't,' replied Hargest, 'but it seems easy.'

'Well,' said Neame wearily, 'just try it to make sure.'[20]

Privately, Neame didn't think that Hargest's plan had much chance of success,[21] but by this stage, and with a long string of failed attempts behind them, anything was worth a try. Boyd rigged up a wooden box of the approximate dimensions of the hole that they would have to squeeze through and the three of them spent time perfecting the feet-first escape. After some initial difficulties, the technique was mastered.

Meanwhile, work continued on the wall. After two weeks of careful excavations Hargest, Miles and Boyd had managed to loosen several of the large stones by scraping away the mortar that bound them together. The stones were left *in situ* – they would only be fully removed from the wall when the moment came for the escape. But then disaster struck.

In the evening, Hargest and the others, at Neame's urging, out-lined the plan to the rest of the prisoners. The following morning some of the prisoners were taken outside the castle for a walk in the grounds. As they passed the place where Hargest and his team were excavating, a couple of the prisoners paused and glanced at the wall. Though it was almost involuntary, the guards noticed. Major Bacci was informed.[22]

Early the following morning Bacci and a platoon of *Carabinieri* marched into the castle and headed straight for the cloister wall. Fortunately, Hargest and friends had not yet begun work. Conferring with First Captain Tranquille, Bacci ordered Brigadier Stirling and some of the orderlies to immediately remove the stack of rabbit hutches close to the wall. Bacci and Tranquille probably assumed that the hutches were to be used by the prisoners to climb the wall. Bacci inspected the wall behind the hutches carefully. He quickly noted that several of the rocks in the filled-in window were loose, but he didn't seem to realise that the prisoners had worked them loose.[23] Bacci gave orders that they be cemented back into place. Even worse, Tranquille posted a new sentry at night below the outer wall and put up more searchlights on the battlements.[24]

CHAPTER 10

Six Seconds

'In spite of the difficulties it seemed that the plan was a possibility, although it contained a large number of "ifs".'

Lieutenant-General Sir Richard O'Connor

'If we can't escape by night, then we should try to escape by day,'[1] stated Dick O'Connor to the gathered escape committee. 'I still maintain that the theory behind the white wall plan was sound. While sterling efforts have been made by several of the officers around this table to get under or through the castle's walls, the fact remains that none have succeeded.' The others all nodded their heads. The run of bad luck since the white wall job had been blown had been unremitting, with every possible escape avenue that they had explored ending in a dead end or near-discovery by the Italians. Morale was low, and worse, the Italians were suspicious.[2]

'The wall, gentlemen, still remains our best chance of getting out of here,' said O'Connor, '*and* I think I've found the way.'

The others were intrigued. O'Connor's reputation for dogged determination concerning escape planning was respected by everyone. The man was relentless in his scheming and the recent reverses had not soured him one bit.

'Our illustrious commandant doesn't think that escaping in broad daylight is possible, so he reduces the day sentries while increasing the number of sentries posted at night,'[3] said O'Connor conspiratorially.

'I'm sorry, Dick, but I think the man may have a point,' piped up General Gambier-Parry from the end of the dining room table.

'Nonsense, G-P,' replied O'Connor, 'I think that his over-confidence is actually a weakness, so let me outline to you my plan.'[4]

O'Connor reached inside his tunic as he sat at the big dining room table with the rest of the escape committee and pulled out a piece of notepaper on which he had traced a basic map of the castle, with the guards' various sentry boxes marked on it. He continued to outline his new escape scheme.

'The sentries on the walls cover their beats in their own time, in no regular routine, so one cannot predict where they will be at any given time, right?'[5] asked O'Connor to the group.

'Agreed,' said General Neame at O'Connor's elbow.

'Wrong,' said O'Connor. 'There is a time during the day when we can know exactly where every man jack of them will be: relief time.' This was when the sentries were changed, timed to occur every even hour. 'During the relief every sentry is at his box.' O'Connor pointed with a pencil to 'Tower A' on his diagram. 'Starting here, the relief moves clockwise along the sentry platform, finally descending into the area on the far side of the white wall near Tower B. The relief consists of a corporal and four privates. As you've all seen, they have a short handover ceremony at each box immediately after which the party, with the corporal at the head and the latest relieved sentry in rear, continues marching in quick time towards the next sentry to be relieved.'[6] O'Connor paused.

'It goes without saying that no ladder can be used to reach the top of the wall without a sentry seeing it, and the height up to the wooden walkway is too high to climb up unassisted.' The others studied the drawing or watched O'Connor's face closely. A plan was starting to take form before them.

'The escape I have in mind is initially just for myself,' said O'Connor lightly, 'though I will need help. I think that if successful we can get out two more men on the same day. I've given the scheme a great deal of thought, and I think that the best place for me to be hoisted up on to the battlements walkway is this stone bench here,' said O'Connor, indicating with his pencil.

'I'll need two men to hoist me up,' said O'Connor.

Brigadiers Combe and Miles quickly volunteered.

'You chaps will have to stand *on* the bench, which is about eighteen inches high, and hoist me right up.' Fortunately for everyone, General Dick was a small, wiry man.

'I've picked this bench for another reason,' continued O'Connor. 'It's quite close to the main door to the courtyard, so we can smuggle out the necessary escape kit quickly and stash it without much risk of being seen. I've also noticed that the projection of the wall in this part of the castle completely masks the sentry's view from Box 3 here,' said O'Connor, pointing with his pencil, 'provided the chap remains immediately outside the box and does not move in the direction of Sentry Box 2 here.'[7]

'I see where you are going with this, Dick,' said Neame. 'You're going to make the attempt during the relief?'

'That's right, Phil. It's the only time when the sentries are all at their boxes. This means that my attempt to scale the wall is restricted to that special moment,' said O'Connor.

'You won't have long, old chap,' said General De Wiart. 'The relief is normally pretty quick.'

'I've taken that into account in my calculations, Carton,' replied O'Connor.

O'Connor had chosen to use the marching guards as a screen between himself and the sentry at Box 2. He planned to make his climb up the wall just at the instant when the guards had passed; in this way the marching guards would be between Sentry No. 2 and himself. The guards would block the sentry's view and it was unlikely that they would look back. The noise of the soldiers' heavy boots would provide O'Connor with further cover.[8]

'What about the sentry at Box 3?' asked Neame.

'He *could* be a problem. If he moves so much as five feet towards Box 2, any movement on the platform or wall above the bench will be visible to him. Also, it goes without saying that Sentry No. 1 has to be prevented from moving towards the end of his beat at Box 2, where he would be in a position to see what was going on.'[9]

'So you manage to get past the sentries without being seen,' said Gambier-Parry, 'but how do you get off the wall without being spotted?'

'Obviously I'll be using a rope, but it has to be fixed in such a manner that it cannot be seen from the inside of the wall,' said O'Connor. 'I've decided upon the following method. If you look on my diagram I've marked these points on the wall X, Y and Z.' O'Connor pointed with his pencil as everyone strained to see. It became apparent that Dick planned to head for one of the embrasures on the far side of the walkway, and make his way down from there. 'These points were once loopholes,' he continued. 'You may have noticed that Temple-Leader had some of them filled with red-brick boxes that are about six inches wide at the inside of the wall and four inches high, about twelve inches long, and tapering to about four inches wide at the outer face of the wall.'[10] It was this eye for detail that marked O'Connor out as such a serious escaper.

'The loophole at 'Z' is empty. I was thinking that it might be possible to make a block of wood of the same shape and size as the flower box, paint the side that faces inside red, and fix a strong hook at the outside end of the block, sufficiently strong to bear the weight of the rope and myself.'[11]

'Brilliant, Dick, absolutely brilliant,' said Neame, grinning.

'If I can push the block in the aperture and fix a rope on the hook, I should be able to slip down to the ground. The chances of being discovered are very unlikely because the back of the block will perfectly blend with the other flower boxes. And it's equally unlikely that the rope will be seen hanging from the outside as any ground sentries only come on at night and few people pass by the walls during the day. I further suggest that the rope should be camouflaged to resemble the colour of the castle's wall.'[12]

'How do you propose to get the rope and block up to the wall in the first place?' asked Brigadier Combe.

'I shall wear the rope coiled over my left shoulder and under my right arm. The block will be attached by its hook to a strong belt of string round my waist,'[13] replied O'Connor. 'I shall also be taking a small valise that I shall strap to my back like a rucksack during the descent.'

'What about clothing?' asked Brigadier Miles. 'I mean, you can't come swanning into the courtyard in mufti.'

'Quite,' replied O'Connor. 'I'll have to walk out dressed in uniform then slip my uniform off while sitting on the bench. I'll wear civilian clothes under my uniform and the tunic can be stowed under the bench.'

'Well, Dick, it's a fantastic plan,' said Neame, 'but it does contain quite a lot of "ifs".'

'What about rope?' asked Brigadier Todhunter. 'We lost some in those damned searches after the white wall fiasco.'

'My servant Stones and Able Seaman Cunningham have already started helping me make the necessary rope. Lord Ranfurly has kindly donated his bed sheets. We're making it in sections of seven feet, up to 49 feet in total. I estimate that at least 28 feet will be required to cover the drop on the other side of the wall, and the less rope that I have to carry the better.'[14]

'So, the arrangements that need to be made are some practice sessions for Combe and Miles hoisting me up from a bench,' said O'Connor. 'We've got a few seconds to play with, so we have to work as a well-oiled team. I'd appreciate some suggestions as to how we can prevent Sentry No. 3 from moving towards Box 2.'[15]

'Well, I'd like to have a try at distracting around Box 2,' volunteered Pip Stirling.

A fair discussion of everything O'Connor had placed before them followed. It was decided that O'Connor would attempt to escape at 2.00pm on a day yet to be chosen. Brigadier Combe would go at 4.00pm (another officer taking over hoisting duties) and Air Vice-Marshal Boyd at 6.00pm. The advantage for Combe and Boyd was that O'Connor's block and rope would already be in place, so they would have less to worry about. All they would need to do was have themselves hoisted up to the battlements and then climb down the outside of the wall.[16]

*

The first order of business was manufacturing sufficient rope for the attempt. Ranfurly had donated some bed sheets, and these were being made into rope by O'Connor's batman Trooper Stones, who was from Brigadier Combe's old regiment, the 11th Hussars, and Able Seaman Cunningham, who had been sent to the castle to act as a barber.[17] Cunningham's training in shipboard knots and rope work proved particularly useful. He cut the sheets into narrow strips about seven feet long and two inches wide and then plaited them together. The resulting rope was strong, light and very flexible.[18] The only problem was the rope's cream colouring – something would have to be done about it before the escape.

O'Connor, Miles and Combe started immediate practice sessions. It was estimated that O'Connor would have about six seconds in which to be hoisted up on to the battlement walkway and disappear into the embrasure. That was an incredibly tight schedule, but O'Connor felt that if he, Combe and Miles could perfect the hoist from the bench it was workable. Obviously, such training sessions had to be concealed from the Italians, so O'Connor's room was used. Against one wall was a high wardrobe that would double as the castle's outer wall, the top acting as the guards' walkway. A wooden bench was brought into O'Connor's room and placed below the wardrobe. The three men sat on the bench and then, at the given signal, O'Connor would stand on the bench facing the wardrobe, legs stiff, on tiptoe. Miles on the left and Combe on the right would immediately bend down and seize O'Connor under his insteps, then push him up to the full length of their arms above their heads, ending with O'Connor clambering on to the top of the wardrobe. Later, the three practised with O'Connor wearing his valise and rope coiled across his trunk, with the wooden block hooked to his waist. After exhaustive practice,

O'Connor knew that he could make it within the six-second window of opportunity.[19] Practice sessions were also held where fresh hoisters were brought in ready to allow Combe and Boyd to attempt the same escape at two-hour intervals following O'Connor. If everything went according to plan, three senior British officers would be free in the Italian countryside before the enemy discovered their absence.

*

The issue of the rope's colour was solved one evening by O'Connor, who managed to stain the material a darker hue in a bath full of coffee. He then hung the long rope in coils all about his bathroom ceiling to dry. He intended to hide it once it had dried out and went down for supper as usual. O'Connor was tired from his training programme and the usual boisterous conversation in the mess tired him out further. Every night it was the same: noisy games of backgammon at which De Wiart excelled; Neame and Boyd arguing about which was better, the army or the air force; G-P chattering away about art or music while Combe and Miles contradicted each other. Lots of strong personalities locked up together in a small space made for a lively and frequently cantankerous social scene. O'Connor excused himself and headed for bed. He had a nagging feeling that something was off, out of kilter, but he couldn't think what it was. He closed his eyes and drifted off to sleep.

O'Connor's eyes flew open. It was very dark – the middle of the night. Someone was in his bathroom making a hell of a row, crashing around and shouting. Then it dawned upon him with awful certainty. The rope! He'd forgotten to hide the rope that was drying in the bathroom. A figure blundered from the bathroom door past his bed and out into the corridor. Second Lieutenant Visocchi was beside himself and shouting for help.

Lights started to come on all over the castle, and within minutes the sounds of hobnailed boots clattering up the stone steps inside the prisoners' part of the castle heralded the arrival of Italian soldiers, bayonets fixed to their rifles. O'Connor stood by his bed as Commandant Tranquille, hastily buttoning his tunic, burst into his room followed by Captain Pederneschi and several guards. The rope was quickly hauled down and taken away.

O'Connor had completely forgotten about the 'night check', when an Italian officer did the rounds in the middle of the night, checking that all of the prisoners were in their beds and everything was in order. Second Lieutenant Visocchi had been detailed the duty and had quietly looked in on a sleeping General O'Connor, before tip-toeing into O'Connor's bathroom to make his routine check. When Visocchi walked into O'Connor's darkened bathroom he hadn't seen the rope hanging all around the room. A coil had gone around his neck, and in the darkness Visocchi had struggled, the coil becoming tight. He thought he was being strangled till he unhitched himself and ran shouting from the room.[20]

Major Bacci was immediately summoned from Florence, and when he arrived a search was being made of the castle. All of the prisoners were roughly awakened by their lights being switched on and *Carabinieri* opening drawers, looking under beds and conducting rough searches. Jim Hargest had taken to drawing maps, though he lacked the artistic talents of Gambier-Parry. Some of these were found in his room by Bacci's men and confiscated. When Bacci entered G-P's room, he found the general sitting up in bed with a thunderous expression on his face while Bacci's men searched. Hoping to calm G-P down, he brought up the subject of maps.

'Ah, my *Generale*, you must forgive us, yes,' said Bacci in a sooth-ing voice, 'but what have we found in the room of *Generale* Hargest but a set of those so beautiful maps you make?'

'Then all I can say,' thundered G-P, his face red with rage, 'is you're no judge! How dare you suggest that I'd draw things like that! If you had the slightest knowledge of art …' But an alarmed Bacci retreated out into the corridor before G-P could finish. When he saw Flight Lieutenant Leeming, Bacci was still shocked by G-P's strong reaction. 'He is so unreasonable!' said Bacci excitedly. 'Fancy talking of art at a time like this!'[21]

A full search of the castle was conducted under Bacci's supervision, but apart from O'Connor's rope and Hargest's maps, nothing further was discovered. The prisoners received another visit from Major-General Chiappe, Florence Corps Commander, who reminded them again of the futility of escape, and it was decided to postpone O'Connor's attempt for a month until everything settled down again.

*

General Neame decided to counter the notion that the prisoners were troublemakers by explaining why O'Connor and some of the others had been discovered with escape equipment. Letters had reached two of the prisoners from old friends in India that contained reference to a lunch party at Dehra Dun that had been attended by two Italian generals being held prisoner nearby.[22] The fact that Italian generals were being entertained and allowed to socialise outside of their camp struck Neame and the others as unfair. Neame took the opportunity to compare and contrast the prisoners' lot at Vincigliata in a strongly worded report to the Swiss Legation in Rome.

'We are fettered by petty restrictions,' wrote Neame indignantly, 'and live surrounded by immense battlements, which are alive with sentries, notwithstanding which our bedrooms are invaded, and we are disturbed nightly by visiting rounds. Our only exits from this prison are walks along set routes under heavy escort, often more numerous than the prisoners themselves.' A particular bone of contention was the close proximity of Florence. 'We are denied any form of alleviation to the monotony of prison life, such as visits to places in the famous city of Florence, so renowned for its art, or any contact with, or view of civilisation.'[23] Neame compared and contrasted the castle with the Villa Orsini. 'The deterioration of our treatment since we left Sulmona and came to Florence has been most marked. At Sulmona we had far more liberty, which we did not abuse, and were treated far more courteously, and due attention was always paid to my requests to the Senior Officer.'[24]

It was little wonder, according to Neame, that men living under such conditions would be driven to attempt to escape. The prisoners, 'goaded into action by intolerable conditions of restraint, were planning escape, being ready to accept any risk, rather than continue to endure the irksome conditions here'.[25]

*

Reg Miles had been looking depressed lately, and his friend Hargest realised that it had been two years since Miles's only son Reginald, a pilot with the Fleet Air Arm, had been lost when the aircraft carrier HMS *Glorious* was sunk. It was important to try to keep busy, for the largely pointless and goalless life of a prisoner of war could wear down a man's morale and leave him open to depression and too much contemplation. So the burly Miles, with Combe, returned to hoisting O'Connor on to the top of his wardrobe, keeping their edge when it came to the escape operation. No one could afford to relax if an escape requiring such exquisite timing was to come off.

Commandant Tranquille ordered that spare sheets were no longer to be issued to the prisoners, and that the officer conducting the 'night check' was to be accompanied by two *Carabinieri*. Nevertheless, a number of sheets already in the prisoners' possession were donated to the cause and Able Seaman Cunningham used the one-month hiatus to manufacture fresh lengths of rope.

After several false starts, a new date for the operation was set. Zero Day was to be 24 July 1942.[26] The tension among those taking part grew as the date approached. Everyone knew that they were playing for higher stakes now. The Italians knew that the prisoners were actively engaged in planning escape attempts. And everyone knew that the guards had been given orders to fire at anyone who crossed the walls. That made O'Connor's attempt life-threatening. It also meant that if the timing was slightly off, even if only by two or three seconds, someone could get hurt or even killed. There was absolutely no margin for error.

*

The Italian government was stung by General Neame's complaints about the treatment of the British and Commonwealth senior officers. While O'Connor and his team readied themselves for Zero Day, the Italian Ministry of Foreign Affairs wrote to the Protecting Power with their side of the story. 'General Neame is interned with his comrades in a fortress, he enjoys all the comforts appertaining to his high rank (bath adjacent to bedroom, suitable dining room, another room for leisure, etc.) beside sufficient liberty of movement compatible however with the exigencies of supervision, which has become the more necessary following a recent attempt to escape …'[27]

The Italians were particularly offended by the idea that senior Italian officers in British hands were being treated with greater leniency than that shown to Neame and his friends. 'Italian generals who are prisoners of war in the British Empire … had frequently had to complain of treatment, both moral and material, inadequate to their rank and age …'[28] Neame's missives certainly caused a useful bureaucratic distraction while Dick O'Connor's scheme was prepared.

The British government was dragged into the dispute, and complained directly to the Swiss on Neame's behalf. 'The absence of privacy accorded the British Generals, their walks under heavy guard and the lack of visits to towns compare unfavourably with the accommodation of Italian Generals in their own quarters in detached buildings in which they enjoy a full degree of privacy,' thundered the War Office's Directorate of Prisoners of War, '[in particular] the Italian Generals cooperative freedom of movement and the permission which they enjoy of being permitted to enter shops and purchase their requirements.'[29] If this war of words was intended by Neame to force the Italian authorities to relax some of the guarding arrangements around the prisoners at the castle, it did not succeed.

*

Dick O'Connor picked at his lunch on Zero Day, 24 July 1942. He wasn't very hungry. Several of the other officers taking part in the escape were equally nervous. O'Connor glanced at his watch: 1.30pm. The escape was to be made at 2.00pm. He headed up to his room to prepare. First he donned his civilian clothes, pulling his uniform on over them. It was a hot summer's day, and O'Connor was soon sweating. The valise containing his supplies was handed to Hargest, who took it down to the courtyard and concealed it in a bucket of earth. The rope, coiled, was similarly concealed, Hargest taking the buckets over to the bench and pushing them out of sight beneath. If any guard noticed them, they could be explained away as earth for the flower boxes which were dotted about the courtyard, and which the prisoners tended. Hargest then sat down on another bench, from which he would be able to see when the relief had passed over the heads of O'Connor, Miles and Combe on the stone bench and give them the signal. In the meantime, Pip Stirling had sauntered over to the corner of the wall beneath where a sentry patrolled, and had started to build a small bonfire from leaves, twigs and rubbish to act as a diversion.

At precisely 1.58pm O'Connor sauntered out from the keep and strolled over to the bench, sitting down between Miles and Combe.[30] No one said a word. O'Connor's eyes were fixed on Hargest, while Stirling fiddled with his little bonfire, not lighting it just yet. The minutes ticked by. A striking figure started moving along the terrace, whirling his arms in circular movements while jogging. Adrian Carton de Wiart – dressed, incongruously given the warmth of the day, in several layers of khaki sweaters – adjusted his black eye patch with his one remaining hand and continued with his calisthenics, his one good eye taking everything in. Over by the gate that led into the castle's lower quadrant, where the Italian garrison lived, Dan

Ranfurly with two enlisted men began to slowly sort firewood into piles ready for issue. Philip Neame sat high up on the battlements quietly stitching his tapestry, watching the escape unfold. Suddenly, the Italian relief appeared noisily and, led by a corporal, started to progress around the battlements in a clockwise direction changing the guards. O'Connor's heart rate increased as he listened to the tramp of the reliefs' boots growing louder on the walkway above.

Reaching the southwest corner of the terrace, the Italian soldiers briefly paused to change the sentry at Box No. 1 before continuing. They wore smart green open-necked field service uniforms with green shirts and ties, their trousers encased in woollen puttees up to the knee, with steel helmets on their heads. They marched on along the wall, passing over O'Connor's position on the bench, towards Sentry Box No. 2. O'Connor quickly divested himself of his army tunic and pulled on his valise and rope.

The escape team knew that if the new sentry at Box No. 1 stayed at his box or walked along the western wall to the foot of the terrace stairway, his angle of sight would be blocked by the top of the stairs. This would leave Dick in a perfect blind area.[31] But if the sentry went back along the south wall he would on his third pace come into view of the prisoners beneath the wall. The escape attempt would then be impossible. Dick's chances depended entirely on the vagaries of the Italian sentry. The corporal and the relief had reached Sentry Box No. 2 and had their backs to where O'Connor intended to cross the wall. Everyone tensed and watched.

Hargest in particular watched Sentry No. 1 like a hawk. With a sinking feeling in his stomach he saw the static Sentry No. 1 suddenly start to stroll the 'wrong' way. Hargest briefly raised his hand to Dick's party on the bench, the signal to hold fast. Pip Stirling also saw what was happening and reacted quickly. He patted his pockets, then turned and shouted up to the guard passing above: '*Avete un fiammifero?*' Asking a guard for a match was a pretty cheeky gambit on Stirling's part, but the bluff worked. A matchbox was tossed down to him. Throwing the guard a casual salute, Stirling struck a match and crouched down to light his little bonfire. He then threw the box of matches up on to the sentry walk, calling out a cheerful '*Grazie*!' The sentry strolled over and retrieved his matches and then stood looking down at the fire as Stirling bustled about, feeding more bits of wood into the growing flames. He was right where Hargest wanted him.

'Go ahead, sir,'[32] said Hargest in a low voice in Dick's direction. Dick O'Connor's eyes were wide, his forehead slicked with sweat as he stared back at Hargest. He nodded and then quickly stepped up on to the bench, just as he had practised so many times in his room, tensing his legs and straining on tiptoe. Miles and Combe stood up on the bench with Dick between them. In a couple of seconds they had hoisted Dick up to the wooden sentry's platform. It was higher than in training, and Dick struggled for a second or two to make it, the valise and rope weighing him down. As he kicked and pulled, the block with its metal hook around his waist became twisted. In two steps he was across the walkway and clambered into the embrasure. To his right, Sentry No. 2 had just been relieved. O'Connor had to struggle to release the cord that had become twisted around the block.[33] For five vital seconds he struggled with the cord. 'It came off in the end, and I very hastily placed it in the aperture, took the rope off my shoulder and threw it down over the wall, holding one end in my left hand.'[34]

O'Connor struggled for several more seconds to position the block, his ears cocked for a warning shout; none came. Quickly wiping sweat from his face, Dick O'Connor took a strong hold of Cunningham's bed-sheet rope and pushed his body out of the embrasure. He could see the ground 30 feet below him. O'Connor looked both ways along the castle's rough stone walls. All was quiet. He leaned back, holding the rope tightly with both hands, his feet pressed against the wall, and began awkwardly to descend. A feeling of exhilaration rose inside him – just a few more seconds and he would be down and free.

CHAPTER 11

The Ghost Goes West

*'I don't believe any party of would-be escapers ever worked
harder or more consistently than ours, and this included
all those grand fellows who helped for the sake of helping
with no hope of participating in the final break-out.'*

Brigadier James Hargest

'He's away!'[1] hissed Jim Hargest in a fierce whisper to Miles
and Combe, who had resumed sitting on the stone bench.
Hargest looked to his left. Sentry No. 1 was still lingering above
Pip Stirling's bonfire, looking down at the flames. Hargest glanced
along the battlement walkway to his right. Sentry No. 2 was looking
to his right, the 40 paces back to where Dick O'Connor had entered
the embrasure. Something was wrong.[2] The guard started to walk
towards Dick's position, unslinging his Mannlicher-Carcano 6.5mm
rifle. Hargest knew in that instant that the sentry had seen something.
Hargest realised he had to be stopped, and fast.

Hargest turned back and whispered to Miles: 'Sentry No. 2 has
seen something. Go quickly and intercept him and for goodness sake
keep his attention.'[3] Miles immediately tried to catch the guard's
attention, but the sentry was completely focused on the flash of white
he had seen by the embrasure and ignored the big South African.

What the sentry had seen out of the corner of his eye was a flash
of one of O'Connor's hands or a piece of his clothing as the General
had struggled for those extra few seconds with the wooden block
and its twisted rope.[4] The sentry went to the nearest embrasure and

leaned out, gasping in surprise. A small figure dressed in nondescript clothing and carrying a leather suitcase strapped to his back like a rucksack was most of the way down a brown rope.

The guard, in a considerable state of surprise, leaned out of the embrasure and levelled his rifle at the figure below, cycling the weapon's bolt with a harsh metallic click.

O'Connor, who was deep in concentration as he clumsily abseiled down the side of the castle, realised that the game was up when he heard a loud cry from above. Gripping the rope for dear life, O'Connor looked up and saw the head and shoulders of the Italian guard leaning out from an embrasure some distance away. His rifle was pointed squarely at O'Connor's dangling form.[5]

'*Arresto, arresto!*' yelled the Italian, ordering O'Connor to halt. '*Fermati o sparo!*' O'Connor, who had studied Italian assiduously since being made a prisoner, knew exactly what the guard was yelling: 'don't move or I fire'. He needed no further warning. The rope creaked and a slight warm breeze wafted up from below the castle.

The alarm had been raised and below him O'Connor soon saw a mass of helmeted and heavily armed Italian soldiers running to the place where the end of his rope lay coiled in the grass. They pointed rifles with fixed bayonets at him and seemed to all be shouting at once.[6] From their frantic gestures it was clear that they wanted him to climb down immediately. For a second or two O'Connor didn't move, just hung on the rope, his two feet planted firmly against the castle's rough stone wall, his arms aching badly from the effort to remain upright. A riot of emotions ran through his head. He had been foiled once again. But this experience would not in any way put him off having another go. While he remained a prisoner of the Italians, he would keep trying to escape.

Swallowing his disappointment, O'Connor clambered awkwardly down to the ground where the red-faced and excited Italians immediately accosted him.[7] Stripped of his pack and roughly searched, the crowd of Italian soldiers around O'Connor suddenly fell silent and parted. O'Connor turned and watched as Captain Pederneschi, his Beretta pistol drawn, strode up, his black jackboots polished like mirrors. He fixed O'Connor with his keen brown eyes. Beneath the visor of his cap his face carried a truly malevolent expression.

*

It was generally agreed that Captain Pederneschi completely lost his cool following General O'Connor's attempted escape. Neame wrote that Pederneschi went 'half mad with excitement'[8]; doubtless as security officer he was humiliated by O'Connor's successful vaulting of the castle wall. As well as yelling at O'Connor in an unintelligible stream of English and Italian, language for which General Neame complained to the commandant (the Italian officer, he said, had impugned the gentlemanly values of British officers),[9] Pederneschi reserved his greatest wrath for the hapless sentry who had foiled the escape. The security officer 'became almost hysterical, venting his rage on the poor sentry, calling him vile names and locking him up for the night.'[10]

O'Connor was bundled off to the commandant's office for questioning shortly after being recaptured, before being locked in his bedroom while the wheels of Italian military bureaucracy swung into action.[11]

The next day, 25 July, General Chiappe made yet another visit to the Castle, this time with orders from Rome to dispense punishments. The sentry locked up by Captain Pederneschi was released, Chiappe rewarding him with 500 lire for very sensibly not firing on the escaping British general.[12] Once more, the whole camp, including Dick O'Connor, was assembled for an official dressing-down.

'Gentlemen,' said Chiappe in a loud voice that echoed off the fortress's walls. 'There is no use attempting to escape. The castle is too strong; you will not escape from it alive. And even if you do, there is no chance of reaching the Swiss frontier.'[13] Chiappe looked directly at O'Connor.

'*Generale*, your punishment for attempting to escape is 30 days' solitary confinement, to be served in a different fortress.' O'Connor said nothing – he had expected nothing less than the regulation prison time for such an escapade.

'*Generale* Miles, *Generale* Combe and *Generale* Stirling, for helping the prisoner to escape you are each sentenced to ten days' solitary confinement, to be served in your rooms.'[14]

*

General O'Connor was to serve his sentence at *Campo* 5 at Gavi-Serravalle Scrivia in Piedmont, twenty miles north of the port of Genoa. The distance from Vincigliata was 165 miles. Tantalisingly, the new fortress was only 100 miles from Lake Como and the Swiss frontier. O'Connor was escorted from the castle to *Campo* 5 by an infantry colonel on Major-General Chiappe's staff, accompanied by two *Carabinieri*.[15] The strange vagaries of war showed themselves when O'Connor noticed that among the Italian colonel's medal ribbons was the British Military Cross.[16] He had been awarded it during the First World War, when the two countries were allies. The colonel pointed to the several rows of ribbons on O'Connor's tunic, touching one in particular. It was the Italian Silver Medal of Military Valor, awarded to O'Connor by Italy in October 1918 during an offensive on the Piave River. Two old allies were now deadly enemies – in theory at least.

At *Campo* 5 General O'Connor was placed in a gloomy cell that would be his home for a month. It was furnished with a small bed, table, chair and two chamber pots. Little light entered through the two small, barred windows. He was permitted two hours of exercise each day on the fortress's battlements, and his food was sent up from the main camp, where many British prisoners were housed. Forbidden to communicate with anyone, O'Connor overcame this ban by writing messages to the POW cooks on the inside of the mess tin that contained his hot food.[17]

*

While O'Connor languished in a jail cell, security at Vincigliata Castle was tightened further. The number of day sentries was increased and the sentries' platform that ran around the inside of the battlements was wired in. This was done by placing eleven strands of barbed wire around the platform, effectively creating a wire box for the sentries to patrol inside and making it impossible to climb up on to the platform.

A single strand of wire was fixed to little metal poles positioned five feet inside the castle's curtain wall.[18] Captain Pederneschi explained its purpose to the prisoners when the work was completed.

'This is the line of death,' said Pederneschi darkly, pointing with one gloved hand at the wire. 'No prisoner is allowed to cross it. If you do, you *will* be shot!'

The commandant instituted a series of rigorous room and kit searches, but due to the prisoners' ingenuity at hiding illicit escape gear, nothing of any significance was found.[19]

*

On 3 August a new officer arrived at the castle. Surgeon-Captain Ernest Vaughan of the Indian Medical Service had been captured at Tobruk. General Neame had applied for a British doctor for the camp, and the request had finally been granted. Vaughan proved to be a first-class supporter of escapes as well as a fantastic doctor.[20] He was assigned a dispensary within the castle but soon complained that the number of Red Cross sanitary parcels containing medical supplies and drugs was not sufficient.[21]

*

By late August the leaves had started to turn and would soon fall from many of the trees around the castle. The prisoners greeted this sight with consternation. As summer gave way to autumn, the natural cover that was essential for escapers hiking cross-country was disappearing. Such a time marked the end of the effective escape season until spring 1943. But planning, at least, could continue – the question was what means the next escape attempt should take. Everything thus far had been a complete bust.

*

General De Wiart had long been urging that the escape effort should be redirected away from the castle's walls. He had grown increasingly interested in the bricked-up chapel adjoining the large dining room on the keep's ground floor. Various prisoners had speculated that there must be underground vaults or rooms beneath the castle that could be used for escape. It seemed a perfectly sensible idea considering the great age of the fortress and its many rebuilds down the centuries. One lucky find had been a dusty old Italian book about Vincigliata Castle that was discovered mouldering in the corner of a closed-up room. It was studied carefully, in the hope that more of the castle's secrets would be revealed.[22]

Soon after O'Connor was sent away, De Wiart approached Neame urging him to formulate a plan to get into the chapel and explore. 'The castello with its crazy planning ought to have been a labyrinth of secret passages,' wrote De Wiart, 'leading straight to the top of the highest mountain or into a lovely lady's boudoir in a neighbouring villa.'[23] But the castle's design had proved extremely frustrating. 'All the passages led stupidly into one another, like a dog chasing its tail,'[24] wrote De Wiart. Many dark words were passed concerning the Englishman's Castle and the infernal Englishman who had rebuilt it.

'As now attempts have been made over the wall, by day and by night, there only remains *under* the wall,'[25] stated De Wiart. Neame agreed and called a meeting consisting of De Wiart, Boyd, Combe, Miles, Hargest and Stirling, with himself as chairman. Boyd and Miles had already examined the outside walls of the chapel, which was located on the northwest corner of the great keep, and made tentative sketches of its ground plan.[26]

'I have no idea how on earth we are going to break into the damn

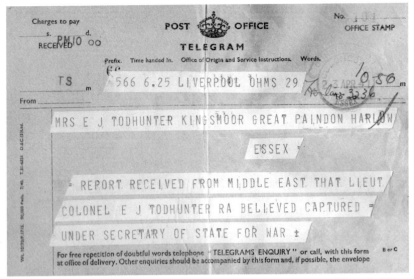

The telegram that Temporary Brigadier Edward Todhunter's wife received from the War Office in April 1941 informing her of her husband's suspected capture by the Germans in North Africa. An agonising wait ensued until confirmation was received that Todhunter was alive and well, albeit as a POW.

The first senior officers camp established by the Italians was at the Villa Orsini, a small stately home located outside the town of Sulmona in the Abruzzi. The British prisoners were held here from 1940 until their transfer to Vincigliata Castle outside Florence in September 1941 due to overcrowding and security fears.

Some of the senior officer prisoners, photographed at the Villa Orsini in 1941. From left to right: Brigadier John Combe, Major-General Adrian Carton de Wiart, Brigadier Ted Todhunter, and Major-General Michael Gambier-Parry, shown holding Baron Ricciardi's puppy, Mickey.

More prisoners at the Villa Orsini, pictured with a representative of the Italian Red Cross, Count Morro. From left to right: Flight Lieutenant John Leeming, Count Morro, Lieutenant-General Sir Richard O'Connor, Brigadier Todhunter, Air Vice-Marshal John Boyd, Brigadier Combe.

Vincigliata Castle in all its medieval glory. This view of the castle's south face shows its high curtain wall, central keep and towers, all largely the creation of 19th-century English owner John Temple-Leader.

The first close-up view the prisoners had of Vincigliata Castle – its imposing main gate. Beneath the driveway was a wide dry moat. Huge studded metal doors gave access to the castle.

(LEFT) The central keep of Vincigliata Castle, photographed when abandoned just after the war. It can be seen that the Italian guards' wooden walkway, suspended along the inside of the battlements, has partly collapsed through neglect.

(BELOW) This area of Vincigliata Castle was called 'The Cloisters' and was much used by the prisoners. During the war the generals kept the formal garden immaculate. The keep behind contained their bedrooms, orderlies' quarters and public rooms.

A tantalising view of freedom from Brigadier Todhunter's bedroom window. A sentry box can be seen in the left foreground.

Among the later arrivals at Vincigliata Castle were New Zealanders James Hargest (right) and Reg Miles, pictured here in 1941 while still at liberty. They would prove to be dedicated and resourceful escapers.

Photograph showing the wooden walkway erected by the Italian Army so that sentries could patrol Vincigliata Castle's battlements and look down on the prisoners contained within. In the top middle can be seen a surviving spotlight that illuminated the wall at night. Above the wooden handrail are metal poles supporting strands of barbed wire bent outwards. This was installed after General O'Connor's escape attempt in 1942 to make climbing on to the sentries' walkway impossible from below.

This photograph, taken just after the war, shows Vincigliata Castle's inner curtain wall beside the garden area used by prisoners for recreation. This area was the site of Lieutenant-General Sir Richard O'Connor's famous wall escalade attempt in 1942, when he climbed on to the raised wooden sentry platform (shown here in a dilapidated state) and out through one of the battlements. The close proximity of a wooden sentry box is obvious, necessitating a clever diversion plan by the other prisoners.

(ABOVE) An excellent view of the corner of the garden where General O'Connor launched his escalade escape in 1942. Though the guards' walkway and sentry box have deteriorated badly in this post-war photograph, they demonstrate how risky O'Connor's attempt was.

One of the many Italian identity cards carefully hand-forged by Major-General Gambier-Parry at Vincigliata Castle for use by escaping officers. This example was for Brigadier Edward Todhunter.

(ABOVE) Brigadier Combe (left) and Lieutenant-General Sir Philip Neame (second left) after their eventual escape from Vincigliata Castle after Italy changed sides in September 1943. The officers are pictured with two Italian partisans who aided their escape from Italy.

(LEFT) Photographed at the same time as the above, from left to right: Brigadier Combe, Lord Ranfurly and Brigadier Todhunter.

place,' said Air Vice-Marshal Boyd. 'The bricked-up doorway opens straight into the main courtyard, so we couldn't open it up without being observed.'

'Then the only way in would be through the wall of the keep,' said Miles.

'But we've no idea how thick the keep wall is,' said Combe. 'Judging by the rest of the castle, it's bound to be bally substantial.'

'I suggest we make a detailed reconnaissance first,' said Neame, calmly, his engineer's mind already starting to tick over. 'We can at least get a look inside through that little grille above the door. We'll try tomorrow afternoon, when most of the Italians are having their *siesta*.'[27] Regardless of any potential problems, 'hope rose strongly within us at once,' wrote Jim Hargest, 'and almost without discussion we were agreed to give it a try.'[28]

The next afternoon, out of sight of the sentries patrolling the high walls, Neame and the 'Tunnel Committee' mounted their first detailed exploration of the chapel. Taking a table from one of the rooms, Neame climbed up to the grille that was set about eight feet off the ground. The opaque glass shutter was open and, cupping his hands around his face, he peered through the grille, allowing his eyes to adjust to the gloom inside.

'I can see a small lobby,' said Neame slowly. 'Then there's an archway leading through to the chapel.'[29] Neame strained his eyes, his engineering training taking over. 'Wait … the lobby is *outside* the keep wall … the archway has been cut *through* the main keep wall. Interesting.' Neame jumped down from the table, and the others quickly took it back inside.

'Let's have a look at the dining room that adjoins the chapel,' said Neame, striding off with the others following him. In between the chapel wall and the dining room was a narrow service area that was dominated by a service lift and shaft. Neame peered up into the lift shaft. He saw that at the top of the shaft was a dummy archway in the wall, where he estimated the wall was about nine inches thinner than elsewhere. It was not the main keep wall. 'If we're going to break into the chapel, then that's the only place I can think we'd stand any chance of success,'[30] said Neame seriously.

A new meeting of the Tunnel Committee was called for the following day, once Neame had had a chance to think about the engineering overnight.

'When the lift is in the "up" position,' said Neame, 'the place where we will make a hole is completely concealed. Even with the lift down the closed doors of the lift shaft hide the area we're interested in. The light in the shaft is also dim – any way we could make it dimmer?'

'I can paste some paper over the small window in the service lobby,' said Miles. 'That should help.'

'Splendid,' said Neame smiling. 'What I suggest is sinking a shaft and tunnel through the chapel floor if we don't find any hidden vaults. I think we should commence work on breaking into the chapel at once. I suggest we work in reliefs of two.'[31]

Neame placed Boyd in charge of the operation to break into the chapel. More manpower was brought in in the form of Brigadier Todhunter. The teams were Boyd/Miles, Combe/Todhunter and Stirling/Hargest.[32] Others, including some of the younger orderlies, would support as and when needed.

Most importantly, a system of lookouts was necessary to ensure that those breaking into the chapel would not be discovered in the event of a surprise visitation by the Italians. A team of watchers led by General De Wiart, who due to his disabilities could not excavate, was arranged from a bedroom overlooking the white wall that led into the Italian sector of the castle. If any Italians were to enter the POW area through the white wall gate, the excavators could be warned at once.[33]

It was decided to fit the excavations in around the camp's usual routine, so as not to arouse suspicion. The Italians conducted twice-daily inspections and a head count, the prisoners were served meals at set times, and walks in the castle grounds and the local countryside were scheduled in the afternoons, weather permitting. Attendance was voluntary, so the workers on shift would not be missed provided they turned up every so often for an excursion. The excavators could work safely, under the cover of the watchers, twice a day: at 7.30–9.30am and 2.00–4.00pm.

The wall into the chapel, even though substantially thinner than the keep wall, proved very tough to break through. It was, the men would discover, two feet six inches thick, and was composed of solid masonry. It was essential that those doing the work made as little noise as possible, as the nearest sentries on the battlements were only ten to twenty yards away.

The prisoners lacked the right tools – all that could be sourced were some improvised short iron crowbars, a carpenter's chisel and mallet, and a shovel.[34] The crowbars were simply iron bars sharpened by Sergeant Baxter using the kitchen range as a furnace. Lord Ranfurly manufactured the shovel out of a piece of sheet iron, fixing a wooden handle to it. An old kitchen knife was also used, Boyd fitting it with a new wooden handle. The spoil was initially removed using garden buckets, but later the teams switched to canvas pails to cut down on noise.[35]

It took the team five days to cut a small hole through the wall. The hole was slowly widened until a person could wriggle through into the chapel. Boyd was commissioned to manufacture a three-ply wooden cover for the hole, disguised to look like plaster.[36] Lord Ranfurly manufactured a contraption to hold the board in place within the carefully cut square in the original plaster. He used a bottle of water as a weight inside a hollow tube of wood attached to the panel with a cord. 'To open the door,' recalled Hargest, 'one had merely to pull the panel out and lower it down the lift well out of the way, while to replace it one raised it and fitted it in – the bottle did the rest.'[37]

Noise *was* a problem. The two-man teams would stand on top of the lift that was normally used to bring food up to the generals' dining room from the servants' kitchen below.[38] As they chipped and cut away at the plaster and then the mortar that held the wall together, pieces clattered into the top of the metal lift, making a terrible noise that was greatly magnified by the narrow lift shaft. Any movement by the men atop the lift caused it to sway and crash into the sides of the shaft with a loud boom. A further problem was the constant cloud of plaster dust – it soon fouled up the lift's electric mechanism. Brigadier Hargest's gammy hip started playing up, leaving him often unable to work, but Miles and Stirling made particularly excellent progress.[39]

*

Once inside, the men found the chapel to be quite large, with windows set very high in the walls– so high, in fact, that nobody could look in from outside. The room was about twenty feet by twenty feet by fifteen feet,[40] with an altar, and the lobby or porch was about seven feet square and lower than the chapel itself by three steps. It was dark and gloomy inside, making it ideal for concealment.[41]

The chapel was crammed full of old boxes, dusty furniture and gloomy oil paintings. The room clearly hadn't been touched for years. They even discovered a case of good champagne and a single bottle of whisky. The alcohol wasn't touched. If the Italians discovered the excavation the last thing any of the prisoners needed was a further charge of petty theft.

The camp's master electrician, Sergeant Bain, was brought in to 'fix' the lift – he altered the mechanism so that it could only be lowered by pressing the button at the bottom, located in the servants' pantry. This was a further attempt at concealment should any nosy sentry peer into the lift shaft. Bain also removed the light at the top of the shaft.[42]

*

The question now was where to begin the tunnel. Neame ruled out the chapel, as it would involve moving the altar. Instead, the obvious place was the lobby. The tunnel would pass beneath the courtyard wall rather than under the main keep wall (as would be necessary if the tunnel were dug from the chapel itself) and Neame suspected that the courtyard wall had shallower foundations. Boyd would remain in charge of the actual excavation, with Neame acting as tunnel designer and engineer. The first task was to survey the land under which the tunnel would pass and decide upon the dimensions of the proposed tunnel.

After a heated debate with the other members of the Tunnel Committee, Neame settled upon his final plan.

'So, we are agreed,' said Neame to the group. 'The initial shaft will be ten feet straight down from the floor of the chapel lobby. Then a tunnel, of four feet by two feet, will open out from the shaft, driving straight across and under the driveway towards the outer wall.'[43]

Neame conducted a secret survey, which had to be done very carefully lest the sentries got wind. The distances were checked and rechecked, and Neame's calculations proved extremely accurate. Measuring the difference in level was far more difficult, 'as dead ground outside the castle, and the rising shaft in the end was two feet six inches deeper than I anticipated,' wrote Neame. 'Seven feet instead of four feet six inches – owing to a raised flower-bed held up by the stone revetment outside the wall.'[44] After several rounds of calculation, the tunnel would be dug on a downward slope of 1-in-8, 'so as to be fourteen feet deep on reaching the outer wall.' Neame's intention was to connect with the curtain wall's foundations, leaving two options: either cut through the foundation of the wall, or burrow under it leaving a rising shaft to the outside. 'It was also essential to touch and identify the base of the outer wall, so as to know where we were, for it was intended to come out immediately outside the wall, for concealment's sake.'[45] This might help the escapers as the only way sentries on the high wall above could see the base of the wall was by leaning out of a battlement – an unlikely proposition unless the escapers made any noise. In total, the tunnel would extend for 35 feet.[46]

How all this was worked out was truly remarkable, considering that Neame had no proper instruments. But Sergeant Bain, who Neame noted would have been commissioned if he hadn't been captured, made a series of survey instruments from protractors for Neame to use, and they also had a prismatic compass to carefully check all bearings.[47]

*

The tunnel broke ground on 18 September 1942. The honour of starting was given to Combe and Hargest. Brigadiers Todhunter and Stirling cleared a space by moving furniture and paintings out of the way. Breaking ground actually proved to be much more difficult than anticipated. The craftsmen that John Temple-Leader had employed to rebuild the castle half a century earlier had known their business. It took Combe and Hargest the entire first work session just to lever up two close-fitting tiles in the chapel porch floor. The noise was excessive, and the watchers that De Wiart had placed above could hear quite clearly the sounds which echoed through the building.

One watcher was placed in the dining room to watch the two gateways into the prisoners' part of the castle from the Italian quarters, with another in Brigadier Vaughan's bedroom on the keep's first floor to watch the sentries. But the routine was exhausting and inefficient, so De Wiart altered the arrangements. One man in Vaughan's bedroom would watch the gateways, while another was placed in De Wiart's bathroom with an excellent view of the sentries on the wall. The shutters in both rooms were carefully arranged so that the watchers could fulfil their duty without being observed from outside. A rotating system saw watchers work shifts of twenty minutes before being relieved, thereby maintaining their edge.[48]

But the system of watchers could still be improved. Sergeant Bain rigged up an electric bell system using buzzers and bits of wiring that the prisoners salvaged or pinched from all over the castle. Buttons were secretly installed in Vaughan's bedroom and De Wiart's bathroom that were connected to a buzzer in the chapel porch.[49] A simple series of signals was worked out that enabled the watchers to alert the digging team to approaching trouble.

One buzz meant 'stop temporarily'. Two buzzes meant 'carry on again'. Three buzzes signalled 'alarm – come to surface and prepare to evacuate', while four buzzes was the most serious, warning, 'really serious – be prepared for anything'.[50]

*

On 1 October 1942 Dick O'Connor returned from *Campo* 5. He had been held longer than his sentence, probably due to some administrative mix-up. His bout of solitary hadn't dampened his escaping spirit at all; in fact, his recent failure had made him even more determined to get out. 'I was delighted to see my friends again,' wrote O'Connor, 'and was also pleased to find that they were already well on with another escape project.'[51]

*

Air Vice-Marshal Boyd told Neame that he no longer wanted command of the digging operation following some bickering with the other men, and he reverted to an ordinary worker for the duration. Dick O'Connor joined, replacing Brigadier Todhunter, who dropped out, and Neame asked the charismatic O'Connor to take command of the working parties. General De Wiart would continue to organise and command the lookouts. As usual, General Dick was raring to go.

*

In early October Brigadier Todhunter celebrated his birthday and, as was now customary, a party was thrown in his honour. It was a pleasant diversion from the serious business of tunnelling. 'The kitchen staff managed to make an iced cake with chocolate with the Arms of Essex on it,' wrote home Todhunter proudly. 'For dinner we had *hors d'oeuvres* in which the *pièce de résistance* was tinned *pâté de fois gras*: "Viener Schnitzel" made of rabbit with fried onions and potatoes and a savoury of tinned bangers on toast.'[52] But Todhunter had pause for reflection over what occurred next. 'I took my cake down for the batmen to finish and it made me feel a bit old,' he wrote. The batmen evidently had the measure of Todhunter as a hunting, fishing, country gentleman of the old school and were discussing appropriate decorations for him: as he approached the messroom he heard a booming voice say, 'The poor old bloke might have had a gun on his cake!'[53] It was Todhunter's 42nd birthday; he was one of the youngest of the senior officer prisoners in the castle.

*

One morning in late October 1942 Owen Boyd had just come off a digging shift in the tunnel. Progress was exceptionally slow. Between opening the shaft in the chapel porch on 18 September and O'Connor's arrival back at the castle, the vertical shaft had progressed just three feet. The need to work as silently as possible, and the two short excavation periods each day slowed the work. The dimensions of the hole also meant that only one man could work, while his partner stood by to relieve him.[54] The soil was hard-packed clay with horizontal strata of rock. Working through the rock bands was very difficult with the basic tools that were available and the other limitations. Boyd was exhausted. It was 8.00am, and he clambered back through the hole in the chapel wall on to the lift, before emerging from the shaft in the pantry beside the orderlies' kitchen. Like everyone else, he wore an old pair of woollen pyjamas when digging, and these were filthy and encrusted with dirt and clay.[55] One day, when General Neame had been so dressed, and clambering awkwardly through the chapel wall hole from the lift, one of the other diggers had facetiously remarked, 'the ghost goes west'.[56] It was a more appropriate remark than many realised at the time, for they were like wraiths, surreptitiously flitting about the great castle at all hours and disappearing through apparently solid walls.

Boyd wore long socks pulled up over his pyjama bottoms to keep the worst of the dirt from accumulating on his shins. The socks had been stripped off and stuffed into his greatcoat pockets, and a pair of unlaced shoes hastily slipped on. Boyd didn't feel worried about moving around at this time – Carton de Wiart's screen of watchers had given no alarm on the tunnel's warning buzzer.

Boyd started back up the stairs towards his room. As he turned a corner he ran straight into Captain Pederneschi. Boyd took a step back in silent horror, his heart hammering in his chest. No Italian officer should have entered the keep without a warning sounding from one of the two watchers on the first floor. What the hell the castle's chief watchdog was doing prowling around at this time of the day immediately put Boyd in mind of a search or the discovery of their escape plot. Pederneschi stared at Boyd, his eyes looking him up and down, evidently intrigued by Boyd's unusual sartorial arrangement.

'Air Marshal Boyd,' said Pederneschi, 'where are you going?'

Boyd, involuntarily thrusting his dirty hands into his pockets, thought quickly.

'A book, Captain,' he said. 'I was looking for a book.'[57]

'I see,' replied Pederneschi flatly. His eyes glanced down at Boyd's pockets. 'And where is your book?'

'Couldn't find the blessed thing,' spluttered Boyd. 'Must've left it in my room after all.' Pederneschi didn't look convinced, and he kept looking Boyd up and down with his sharp brown eyes.

'I'm getting old I guess,' said Boyd, adding a nervous laugh. 'Forgetful.'

Pederneschi relaxed and smiled.

'Ah yes, getting old is a terrible thing, no?'

'Indeed,' muttered Boyd. 'Well, if you'll excuse me, Captain, I must get dressed for breakfast.' Boyd pushed past Pederneschi and rapidly climbed up the stairs, the slightly grubby legs of a pair of white long johns sticking out from under his coat as he climbed.

Pederneschi watched him go. The security officer stood for a few seconds, staring up the now empty staircase, as if deep in thought, his dark eyes slightly narrowed and blank. Then he turned, shrugging his shoulders, before he resumed climbing down to the ground floor.

CHAPTER 12

Under the Dome

*'Neame with his sapper's knowledge gave us the lay-out
for our labours, and with such a degree of accuracy
that at the end we were hardly a centimetre out.'*

Major-General Adrian Carton de Wiart

The Virgin Mary, her face calm and composed in the dim light of the chapel, her hands pressed together in silent prayer, swayed slightly, the rope around her waist coming taut. Then, out from the hole in front of the large heavy marble statue, holding on to the rope, crawled a man so filthy that his clothes were indistinguishable from his head and hands. Brigadier James Hargest lay for a moment on the cold floor of the chapel, waiting for his breath to return. He was exhausted.

'Okay, Reg,' said Hargest breathlessly to his digging partner Brigadier Miles, who waited by the small hole in the floor of the chapel porch, 'away you go.'

Several buckets were neatly stacked beside the hole ready to be lowered down and then hauled back to the surface full of spoil from the tunnel. The soil and rocks were progressively filling the floor space inside the chapel, a great mountain of dirt held back by bits of furniture and coconut matting. The whole room smelled musty with spoil. Looming over the tunnel entrance in silent repose was the great heavy statue of Our Lady, pressed into service as an ersatz bollard, the attached rope enabling the diggers to climb their way out. Hargest propped his back against the cold of the statue's marble and listened. He soon heard Miles scratching and digging away at the rocks and hard clay ten feet below where he sat resting. Within minutes came the familiar command 'bucket!', muffled and distant inside the tunnel. Hargest wearily hitched a canvas pail to a second rope and lowered it down through the floor.

*

The first big challenge for the excavators had begun when they had managed to sink the vertical tunnel access shaft six feet below the floor of the chapel porch. They struck hard, unyielding granite.

'We'll never get through that,' declared Brigadier Combe, tapping the handle of his trowel on the great rock that was slowly being uncovered with each fresh scrape.

General Neame, the tunnel's designer, shared Combe's pessimism. Normally, such a blockage could only be cleared with explosives.[1] It was decided to excavate further, to determine the dimensions of the granite plug.

After several more days digging the rock revealed itself to be dome-shaped and very large. It didn't bode well for the tunnel. It was soon christened 'The Dome of St Paul', for it looked as immovable and as huge as a cathedral.

'We'll have to try to undermine it somehow,' said Neame, his grimy face creased in concentration. After some discussion, a method was worked out. They decided to excavate horizontally to see just how large the thing was. If it extended for several feet in all directions, then it was game over for the tunnel.

The diggers went at the dome with the homemade iron bars, eventually finding the edges of the object. Using the bars was difficult because every thump and bang of iron on rock reverberated up through the keep. The watchers on duty on the first floor exchanged concerned looks – how could the sentries not hear the row coming from underground? Nervous fingers hovered over buzzers, ready to immediately call a halt to the operation if a sentry so much as looked in the direction of the chapel.

After several days of furious activity, the Dome of St Paul was revealed as a large granite plug surrounded by what Hargest termed 'rotten rock'. This flaky rock was hacked and dug away until two stout ropes could be passed around the solid central plug. It took four sweating, straining and cursing men to haul the granite boulder out of the shaft and into the chapel.

*

Air Vice-Marshal Boyd's early morning encounter with Captain Pederneschi, along with some other near-misses, had led Dick O'Connor to conclude 'there is no doubt that Generals as a class do not make good sentries!'.[2] Nevertheless, General De Wiart continued to perfect his screen of watchers. Each morning Trooper Collins, O'Connor's batman, would make a quick sweep of the castle to check that no Italians were in the POW areas. The emergency buzzers would also be tested before the first shift of the day came on. Collins would report on the status of the castle to De Wiart, who would buzz the diggers to commence excavating.

The Italian garrison worked to set timetables, so by careful observation De Wiart's team knew what was normal behaviour from their captors and what was not. At 7.30am the watchers would see a small gate open in the white wall, and an Italian NCO would step through to extinguish the light above the cloister steps. He would then open the door to the courtyard. Fifteen minutes later came a changing of the guard in the Italian courtyard beyond the white wall. Special attention was paid to this, as sometimes the officer of the day would wander into the prisoners' area afterwards. At 9.00am an Italian private would walk over to the prisoners' kitchen with the day's fresh milk. Because he was close to the chapel, a watcher always gave a one-buzz warning to the diggers in the tunnel. They would immediately cease work, and inevitably one would turn to the other and mutter 'milkman' with a grin. On some days laundry would be taken out or returned.

At weekends there were some changes. On Saturdays at 8.30am the 'shopping sergeant' brought the weekly flowers to Brigadier Stirling. These were to be used at the religious service that General Neame presided over in the dining room on Sunday morning. At 7.45am on Sundays the three or four Roman Catholics among the prisoners would be escorted to a local church for a service.[3]

The prisoners observed their 200 guards very closely, and came to know many of their habits and eccentricities. The guards never knew that several pairs of eyes were watching their every move throughout the day when they were on duty. Each sentry was different. Some were very alert and suspicious; others were lazy, spending their time chatting to other sentries, reading letters or even dozing in the sun.[4] Captain Pederneschi remained a wild card, often appearing in the keep suddenly and without warning; he would prowl around like a cat, looking for signs of illicit behaviour. Searches were made every night, with Pederneschi instructing guards to pick over the prisoners' garden or rubbish piles. They found nothing. There were no more concealed maps, coils of homemade rope or civilian clothes stashed under tiles or beneath flowerpots. Perhaps the Italians thought that they had finally defeated the British since O'Connor's failed wall escalade. The strengthened defences on the perimeter wall and more rigorous guarding routine appeared to be working. But the Italians, though they never realised it, were being purposely lulled into a false sense of security while below their boots the prisoners sweated and dug.

*

Neame had determined that the entrance shaft to the tunnel must reach ten feet deep, and he had set a provisional date of 31 October 1942 to achieve this. But once the Dome of St Paul had been removed, the going downwards improved, and the required depth was reached a few days ahead of schedule. Now the direction changed, with the actual tunnel begun at right angles to the keep wall. The soil was even tougher than in the vertical shaft, and was ribboned with frequent horizontal strata of hard rock.[5] Fortunately, the rock layers were cracked, meaning that with patient hard work the rocks could be prised loose and removed. Splitting up these rocky layers took weeks of exhausting labour. Neame, an experienced mining engineer from the Western Front in the First World War, said that normally such a task would have required 'a miner's pick-axe, a miner's drill and hammer';[6] the prisoners had to make do with a kitchen knife, a couple of iron bars and some woefully unsuitable carpentry tools.

Some of the rocks were large enough to require two men to roll them back down the tunnel to the shaft for extraction. John Combe became a noted expert in patiently extracting rocks, with Boyd and Miles also very good at this tedious and backbreaking task.[7]

Noise remained a constant concern. De Wiart laid on some 'noises off' – these diversions included loud discussions between officers, the splitting of logs for firewood, and boisterous games of deck-tennis or football, all designed to distract the sentries on the outer wall and cover up any noises from the chapel.[8] Almost all of the prisoners, regardless of rank, were involved in diversions as the digging continued for month after month. Whenever a sentry strayed close to the tunnel, De Wiart would buzz the diggers to stay quiet. It was a nerve-wracking business, and even the usually bluff 'Long John Silver' started to feel the strain.

Buzzing usually started because De Wiart or one of the other watchers had noticed a particular sentry on the wall stop and give the impression of listening to something close by. Sure that the sentry had heard the excavation, De Wiart would curse and press the buzzer, his heart racing, his eye never leaving the Italian. Then, the sentry would lose interest and wander back to his sentry box and De Wiart's panic would subside.[9] This cat-and-mouse game would drag on for almost seven months.

*

Five inches a day was considered good progress through the hard clay and rock. Sometimes it took a week to proceed that tiny distance. That it was done entirely by hand, by middle-aged amateurs using homemade tools, made it an achievement almost beyond imagining.

The tunnel slowly passed beneath the keep's great foundations, which were discovered to be much shallower than Neame or any of the others had imagined for such a massive building. The tunnel was initially four feet two inches high, but as the digging progressed and the miners developed their skills, it was found that they could safely reduce the height to only three feet four inches. The two downsides to a smaller tunnel were reduced airflow and increased heat.[10]

As per Neame's design, the tunnel was dug downhill at an incline of one in eight, meaning that the tunnel dropped four feet by the time it reached the castle's outer curtain wall. But two thick layers of solid rock were encountered in November, requiring intense and exhausting excavations, slowing progress to mere inches on some days. Fortunately, all of the rocks were fissured and cracked, but the diggers had to patiently widen the cracks with their basic tools or undermine the rocks by excavating above and below them. Water was sloshed over the rocks to try to reveal cracks, the men straining their eyes by the light of Sergeant Bain's single-bulb jerry-rigged lamp run down the tunnel attached to stolen Italian wiring. Using water meant that the men had to work in a permanent mud bath, increasing their discomfort greatly, and threatening their health. This practice was soon abandoned.[11]

Every Sunday General Neame would carefully survey the tunnel using his homemade instruments, and any recommendations were noted.[12]

*

Outside it was mostly raining during November. 'Winter is closing in on us here,' wrote Brigadier Todhunter. The rain kept them 'tied to the house which is a bore, but the longer the cold and snow hold off the better'.[13] The plunging temperatures would make working on the tunnel increasingly uncomfortable and heavy rain still managed to penetrate the entrance shaft through leaks in the chapel.

While the digging continued, preparations were begun for the second Christmas at the castle. 'We had a visit from the Swiss Embassy this morning, which makes a change,' recorded Todhunter on 19 December. 'They are very painstaking in looking after us. Both they and the Red Cross say that our parcels may be delayed but luckily we have got a very fair stock here so we shall be all right for a bit.'[14]

When the last team knocked off on the afternoon of Christmas Eve 1942 the prisoners had been labouring on the tunnel for almost four months. Under the most secret and trying conditions, this band of generals and brigadiers had done the impossible. They had sunk a shaft ten feet down from the chapel porch and excavated a tunnel twenty feet in length towards freedom.

'I estimate that we need to dig a further fifteen feet and we've made it,'[15] said Neame that night. It didn't sound like much, but every man knew that they still had months of hard labour ahead of them if they were to be ready for the spring 'escape season'. The distance from the chapel porch to the inside of the outer wall was estimated at about 35 feet.[16]

'Taking into consideration the problems with rock strata and the hard clay, I'm estimating that we should break the surface sometime in mid-March.' Several officers clinked their wine glasses together at this news.

'Here's to a very merry Christmas, gentlemen,' said Neame, raising his glass, 'and to a well-earned holiday in Switzerland come Easter 1943!'

That night Brigadiers Combe and Stirling threw a party for the orderlies, 'but everyone came and enjoyed themselves. We provided some pretty washy beer and Father Christmas in the form of old Armstrong the South African who looks just like him anyhow.'[17]

On Christmas Day, as a sort of treat, the tunnel was opened for inspection to all of the rest of the prisoners at the castle, including the orderlies. With De Wiart's lookouts in place, the visitors were brought down in small groups and given a guided tour. The generals and brigadiers were enormously proud of what they had achieved. James Hargest recorded the reactions of the younger prisoners: 'They were all suitably staggered at the scale of undertaking. Most of them thought we were a few elderly gentlemen full of enthusiasm but rather harmless as miners; but after this inspection they realised we were in earnest.'[18]

'On Xmas Day,' Todhunter wrote, 'we devoured our turkeys which John [Combe] had been nursing so lovingly for so long and very good they were too with plum pudding *a la* Red Cross. G.P. did some quite excellent menu cards, hand painted in watercolour, of various hunts and we had a small Xmas tree with some real candles, so we did our best to be festive.'[19]

*

While the tunnel took shape, careful planning and preparations for the eventual escape were undertaken. Firstly, and most importantly, was to decide how many would escape and who they were to be. There would be three two-man groups: De Wiart and O'Connor, Miles and Hargest, and Boyd and Combe.

'How are the escape outfits coming along?' asked Neame, who, as 'Father of the Camp', chose not to escape; his duty was to lead and represent all of the prisoners at Vincigliata.

'We've got everyone making their own outfits, sir,' said Jim Hargest. 'The idea is that we should pass for Italian workmen. To this end, we're also going to carry the appropriate "props". For example, I'm going out as a bricklayer, so I've got a trowel and plumb-line to carry in the top of my suitcase.'

At night, in the secrecy of their rooms, and after digging during the two day shifts, the escapers worked on manufacturing working men's jackets and caps, modifying bits of uniform. There were some items of clothing left over from earlier escape attempts that had been successfully hidden from the Italians. The idea for most of the escapers was to look workmanlike without appearing shabby or suspicious.

'Rations are being stockpiled, sir,' said Reg Miles, referring to the illicit hoarding of food for the trip, mostly tins of chocolate, malted milk tablets and Red Cross biscuits.

'How about identity documents, G-P?' asked Neame, turning to an exhausted-looking Gambier-Parry.

'It's all in hand, old chap,' replied G-P without emotion, black bags beneath his tired eyes. G-P had managed to obtain a real Italian identity card and was in the process of faithfully reproducing this precious document six times. Because sketching and painting were G-P's hobbies, the Italians had foolishly permitted him inks, paints, brushes, pens and various types of paper, a great deal of which were used for more covert purposes, principally creating splendid maps and identity documents.[20] But making six IDs required many months of exhausting concentration. One mistake on the lettering, a stamp or signature could mean weeks of work down the drain. G-P had no help, as no one else in the small camp possessed his unique skill set. The strain on his eyesight was immense, given that he was often working in the evenings by inadequate light. He also had to be ready to hide his 'artwork' at a moment's notice in the event of a search. He managed to obtain a special ocular device that helped with the fine work, but G-P's nerves were beginning to fray towards the end of the project.[21]

The one seemingly insurmountable problem faced by G-P in the production of Italian identity cards was a lack of passport photos. The Italian authorities did not permit cameras, but each ID had to have a standard-sized black-and-white passport photo glued to it. The other prisoners could not conceive of how G-P could get around this problem. But they underestimated G-P's incredible abilities. As well as art, G-P was passionate about music. He organised and ran the castle choir, with Company Quartermaster Sergeant Tom Morgan as lead tenor. After a great deal of complaining and bargaining, the prisoners eventually secured from Major Bacci a wind-up gramophone for their sitting room.[22] G-P sent off for records, mostly classical music – opera in particular. He would organise weekly recitals. One evening he was extracting a record from its sleeve when he noticed that on the back of the packaging were black-and-white photographs of the featured artists. Even more incredibly, the photos were the exact size and shape as passport images, and printed on virtually the same paper. G-P's idea was simple: find photographs of performers who looked similar to the tunnel escapers and use them on the fake IDs. G-P wrote off for more German and Italian operas until he had a good stock of photographs to choose from. A small committee was formed by the prisoners, who scoured the record covers trying to find faces that matched the six men due to escape. Eventually, close likenesses were found for most of the men, although it proved tricky to find a match for Carton de Wiart. He remained a problem until G-P came upon a photo in an Italian news magazine called *Illustrazione*. The face that most matched Long John Silver's (minus the eye patch) turned out, ironically, to be that of Prime Minister Ion Antonescu, the hardline Axis leader of Romania.[23]

It was important that the escapers learned their new cover identities. Going by the maxim that keeping it simple was probably best, the escapers were encouraged to create their own Italian alter egos. Jim Hargest chose the name 'Angelo Pasco'.[24] He would remember the name with ease, as it was that of a fish merchant friend from Invercargill, New Zealand. Hargest's Pasco would be from Bologna and was, as Hargest had told Neame, a bricklayer by trade.

*

'Tirano,' said Dick O'Connor, pointing with his finger at one of G-P's carefully made maps. 'It's a small town on the Swiss border in the Italian province of Sondrio.'

O'Connor was briefly outlining his plan to walk, accompanied by

Carton de Wiart, to Switzerland. Boyd, Combe, Hargest and Miles had all decided to try to reach Switzerland by rail.[25] General Dick and Carton had, however, decided upon the more strenuous task of trekking – what POWs called 'Boy Scouting' – approximately 270 miles north. De Wiart, owing to his eye patch and missing hand, felt that he was too conspicuous to risk travelling by train, and O'Connor had decided to accompany his friend.[26] They believed that their best chance 'lay in evaporating into the mountains'.[27] But regardless of their planning and physical conditioning constantly running up and down the keep staircases, it would be a major undertaking for a disabled 63-year-old and his 54-year-old companion.

'Our route is very simple,' outlined Air Vice-Marshal Boyd during the meeting. 'We plan to walk to Florence station and, travelling incognito as tradesmen or travelling salesmen, board a train to Milan.' As he spoke he traced the route on the map with his index finger. 'We change trains at Milan for Como, our final destination being the small border town of Chiasso, here. It's about six miles from Como, so we'll walk.'

Chiasso straddles the Swiss–Italian border, with the Swiss part inside Canton Ticino. It's the most southern municipality in Switzerland and lies 88 miles west of Tirano.

'How do you plan to enter Switzerland?' asked General Neame.

'Well, all the frontier crossings are heavily guarded by the Italians *and* the Swiss,' said Boyd. 'Obviously we need to avoid all roads, bridges and railway lines crossing the frontier. But from what we can gather, the Swiss haven't the manpower to completely guard every stretch of the frontier, and neither does the enemy, and the geography is against such a measure. We will hook up into the mountains and cross somewhere quiet.'

'We also have the same idea,' said O'Connor. 'We will cross further north from Tirano at a quiet stretch.'

For the four who were taking the train, their journey to the Swiss frontier should only be a matter of a couple of days, taking into consideration wartime travel on the railways. They would travel light, with just valises or small suitcases. The challenge for them was buying tickets at stations and mingling in with the population. For O'Connor and De Wiart, their journey would take weeks, necessitating them carrying most of what they would need on their backs. O'Connor and De Wiart calculated that their rucksacks, once filled with their food, spare clothing, and maps, would weigh at least 25lbs.[28] Food consisted of Red Cross chocolate, a few tins of bully beef, a few tins of soup, and so on, carefully collected and hoarded over months.

Escape equipment for all three teams was transferred to the chapel for safekeeping,[29] though a reserve was kept elsewhere just in case the Italians blew the tunnel.

*

Just after New Year 1943 Jim Hargest was forced to take a break from digging because of his gammy hip. He was in considerable discomfort, and on Dr Vaughan's recommendation he was sent to hospital in Florence for an x-ray and treatment. As this would require two trips into the city by car, Hargest decided to treat them as reconnaissance missions for the forthcoming tunnel escape. On each trip Hargest persuaded the corporal driving him to go to the hospital by a different route, spinning him a story about wanting to see the sights of Florence. The driver fell for the ruse, allowing Hargest to carefully observe the road junctions and piazzas. The intelligence gathered would prove invaluable in planning a route on foot from the castle to Florence's railway station.[30]

*

One day in late January 1943 Air Vice-Marshal Boyd was working at the tunnel face. The dimensions of the tunnel had narrowed somewhat near the end, and Boyd, a short but powerfully built man, struggled in the constricted space, his burly shoulders pushing against the sides. The labour had become increasingly hellish the longer the tunnel was dug. Though it was winter, sweat poured from Boyd's brow and arms as he worked away at the face with the big kitchen knife, loosening rocks set hard in the clay soil. Behind him squatted his digging buddy Reg Miles, who waited with a half-filled canvas bucket, ready to take back to the entrance shaft to be hauled to the surface and emptied.

'Wait a minute,' muttered Boyd, almost to himself. He stopped digging and took up a handful of dirt.

'What's the matter?' asked Miles, peering over Boyd's filthy shoulder. The bulb that lit the tunnel had been advanced towards the face the day before by Sergeant Bain, but its position and the size of the tunnel created shadows and dark patches.

'Damp,' said Boyd, looking at Miles, his face as grimy as a coalminer's.

'Damp?' repeated Miles, raising one eyebrow.

'Definitely damp. Better get Phil down here,' said Boyd.

When Neame struggled up to the tunnel's face and sampled the soil he agreed with Boyd – it was most definitely damp.

'Well, what does it mean?' asked Boyd impatiently.

'Must be seepage from a water table,' replied Neame, touching the tunnel face. When Boyd's and Miles's faces showed no signs of comprehension, he continued.

'It means, gentlemen, that we are probably close to the castle's outer wall.'[31]

'By Jove,' said Boyd, 'but that's bloody marvellous news!' He clapped Neame roughly on the shoulder with one mud-encrusted hand. 'How much further?'

'I'll fetch my instruments,' replied Neame seriously, backing down the tunnel, his mind already spinning with possibilities.

*

Because space was at a premium inside the tunnel, Brigadiers Stirling and Hargest, the latter now recovered from his hip trouble, widened the shaft at one point to create a bypass for up and down traffic.[32] Boyd and Miles and the other digging teams continued to work at the face until, on Neame's advice, the tunnel was judged to be 35 feet long and should be directly beneath the massive outer wall of the castle. Some wooden propping was necessary only for this damp section.[33] The plan was then to dig upwards, uncovering the foundation of the wall, and then dig along its length for six feet before turning out and creating an exit hole two feet beyond the wall.

On the second day beneath the wall the diggers hit the structure's hard base. It consisted of very large flat stone blocks fitted together with equally resilient mortar.[34] It was decided to use the bottom of the wall as the roof for this section of the tunnel.

Throughout February and March 1943 the tunnel progressed beneath the wall until Neame ordered a course change and the tunnel branched out at a right angle to the wall for two feet.[35] The tunnel now lay an unknown distance below the surface. The next problem was finding out exactly how much earth and rock remained between the tunnellers and freedom.

*

'Not again!' exclaimed Brigadier Stirling, as the tunnel buzzer gave a long blast. This signalled 'stop temporarily' and Stirling, though annoyed at the frequent halts, obeyed instantly. Stirling didn't move. He held one of the improvised iron bars in both hands. He had been working loose a large rock above him when the buzzer had sounded. He knew this meant that a sentry was stood on the wall just twenty feet above Stirling's position. General Neame feared that certain tools made enough noise for the sound to travel through the wall, and that it could potentially be felt or heard by an alert sentry, so every time a sentry came close to the tunnel, the buzzer sounded. Though the constant stops were frustrating for the diggers, it was felt to be a sensible precaution after so much time and effort had been expended on the tunnel.

Time ticked by slowly for Stirling, who was frozen in an uncomfortable position. He had been taking his turn digging upwards just two feet outside the perimeter wall. It was exhausting work at such an awkward angle. Stirling waited, his ears straining for permission to continue. The silence in the tunnel was abruptly shattered by two buzzes, indicating 'carry on again'.

''Bout bally time,' muttered Stirling grumpily, before he resumed levering the large rock from the damp earth. But then the buzzer sounded again. 'For the love of God!' cursed Stirling, freezing once again. Near the end the tunnellers might have been, but the going was getting harder and the impatience of being able to almost see the finishing line wearing even thinner each man's sorely tested patience.

*

In order to minimise the chance of the shaft up to the surface falling in on the diggers, a system of wooden supports was put in by Boyd and Lord Ranfurly. The carpenters 'designed sliding frames to slide up inside a fixed revetment framework at the bottom of the shaft,' explained General Neame, 'and with a roof of removable slats, so that a part of the earth above could be cut away with a trowel while the remainder was safely supported.'[36] The wooden lining for the shaft was increased as the men dug towards the surface.

When the roof had been raised two feet Neame decided to find out exactly how much earth remained above their heads. It was not simply a case of digging to the surface and creating an exit hole. That would only be done when the conditions for the actual escape were ready. Neame decided to probe the surface with a hollow stair rod. Nothing – they were still too deep.

After the diggers reached three-and-a-half feet upwards, Neame returned to try again. At this point the probe broke through. Neame turned to some of the others who had gathered in the tunnel behind him, expectant expressions on their muddy faces.

'Four-and-a-half feet to the surface,' announced Neame in a

harsh whisper. The others grinned or silently shook hands. Working upwards had been incredibly difficult, with large and difficult rocks blocking the shaft on several occasions, their removal requiring all of the diggers' ingenuity.[37] It had seemed that the castle was determined not to let them go just yet.

The buzzer's shrill single warning suddenly broke Neame's and the others' reverie. They all looked towards the ceiling. They knew that up there were armed men with explicit orders to shoot anyone seen on the wrong side of the walls. They all remembered the sneering Captain Pederneschi pointing at the strand of wire erected five feet inside the outer wall and his chilling warning: 'This is the line of death ... No prisoner is allowed to cross it ... If you do you *will* be shot!'

CHAPTER 13

Through the Night of Doubt and Sorrow

'The work [on the tunnel] was crushingly hard, and only iron determination prevented the workers from giving up the struggle.'

Flight Lieutenant John Leeming

A few days after General Neame had successfully probed the surface through the remaining four-and-a-half feet of soil covering the tunnel exit, it began to rain. A strong wind blew up and the rain increased in ferocity, great sheets lashing the castle like a ship at sea. The generals looked out of their accommodation with alarm. Water was running off the roof in a torrent and forming great pools in the courtyard and gardens as the drains to the moat were overwhelmed.

A team was sent to check on the tunnel. As they climbed down into the entrance shaft the rain drummed loudly on the chapel roof high above them. Brigadier Hargest spotted water running down the shaft in a steady trickle. As he reached the base of the shaft his foot sank into a couple of inches of muddy water. Clambering along the tunnel, water was pooling at its lowest point. Hargest quickly reported to Neame, who came to inspect.

After a thorough inspection of the tunnel, Neame told the others that there was a crack in the castle's wall that was allowing water to percolate into the tunnel shaft. He asked Hargest and Miles to make a sump in the tunnel to draw off the worst of the water.[1] It was a disgusting job, the two brigadiers working in cold, mud and rainwater, but they managed and the tunnel dried out after a couple of days (though work recommenced the day after the rain had stopped).[2]

*

'My God!' exclaimed Air Vice-Marshal Boyd. 'How on earth are we supposed to get through this lot?' The tunnel was now only four feet from the surface, according to Neame's probings, but Boyd and Brigadier Miles had run into a problem. They were slowly excavating what appeared to be another layer of rock that ran right across the roof of the shaft. Neame was called upon to inspect it. Neame's probe must have somehow passed through a crack or hidden gap. Boyd pointed out, quite rightly, that excavating such a solid mass of rock right above the diggers' heads was incredibly dangerous. Boyd suggested changing the direction of the exit shaft to avoid the rock, but Neame refused to countenance such an idea. Time was of the essence. They were well into March 1943, and any serious delay might scupper their chances of getting away. And there were other factors to consider, as Neame explained: 'I saw no chance of concealment in driving horizontally out of the hill-slope, and we had not enough timber to make changes of direction in gallery and shaft, and would, in all probability, have struck the same layer of rock.'[3]

There was nothing for it but for the diggers to find some way of breaking the rock layer up and removing the material. Boyd and Miles volunteered for this onerous task, having already mastered rock removal during the construction of the main tunnel. A long discussion followed about how to prop up the rocks that they would be working on to prevent a terrible accident. Boyd and Miles eventually overcame the layer of rocks by widening the shaft until they discovered seams. Immense labour and considerable risk were necessary to lever out these huge rock pieces, which weighed 40–50lbs each. In fact, the rocks were so heavy that they were not removed from the tunnel – instead, the diggers rolled them down to the base of the entrance shaft and stored them there.

Slowly, but surely, the roof of the exit shaft was raised inch by painful inch towards the surface. Neame continued to carefully probe the overhead soil until there was only six inches remaining. Then a halt to the work was called.[4]

'That's it,' said Neame, turning to the small handful of diggers who had crowded into the shaft and tunnel to hear the results of the latest probe. 'Gentlemen, the tunnel is finished.' It was 20 March 1943. It had taken the middle-aged excavators nearly seven months of punishingly hard labour to drive 52 feet of shafts and tunnel deep beneath the great castle's foundations. Only six inches remained to be cut away, and that would happen on the night of the escape. If the tunnellers needed evidence of their incredible feat of engineering they had only to glance at the massive pile of spoil that stood ten feet high inside the chapel.

The shaft was timbered up and Lord Ranfurly put a strong roof in place, so that anyone who walked over the exit shaft would not collapse the six inches of soil and reveal the tunnel beneath.

In the meantime, Ranfurly had also been busy making a cover for the exit hole. The wooden lid was painted and covered with earth and pine needles, creating a very convincing camouflage. It was intended that the tunnel would be used several times, so concealment remained paramount.

*

'I say, that's a really remarkable likeness,' said Dick O'Connor. The others all grunted their agreement.

'Right down to my bare patch,' said Hargest, touching his balding crown with one hand. 'Howes has done a first-class job.'

Hargest, O'Connor, Neame and the other escapers were standing in the doorway to Hargest's bedroom and staring intently at his bed. The bed was occupied, a human shape lying bundled up beneath the blankets, a head resting on its side on the pillow complete with ear, dark hair and bald spot. The view was slightly obscured by a mosquito net that hung down over the bed, suspended from a bamboo frame.

'It's really uncanny,' said Neame, folding his arms as he stared at the figure in Hargest's bed. Neame turned to the young private who stood just inside the door.

'Fine work, young man. Very fine work indeed,' said Neame seriously. Private J.E. Howes, Brigadier Hargest's batman, stiffened to attention.

'Thank you, sir,' he replied slightly embarrassedly.

The manufactured figure in the bed was an ingenious answer to a difficult question that General Neame had posed a month before. It was planned that the six escapers would exit the tunnel around 9.00pm on the day chosen for the breakout. But there was a very serious problem. The Italians ensured that the duty officer, accompanied by a sergeant, checked that all of the prisoners were in their beds at around 1.30am, giving the escapers barely four-and-a-half hours to get clear of the castle and out of Florence before they would be missed. They couldn't leave much earlier than 9.00pm because they needed full dark, and anyway the Italians checked them during the early evening. They needed to find a way of fooling the duty officer into thinking that the six escaped generals were still in their rooms in order to buy more time. The morning roll call was not taken until 11.00am, and a fourteen-hour head start could very well be the difference between success and failure.

The moment the Italians realised that some of the prisoners were missing an alert would be transmitted to all police stations, barracks, train stations, ports and frontier posts. Descriptions of the men, along with their photographs, would be circulated and every official would be looking for them. Patrols would be dispatched to likely points, such as railways stations, where escapers might try to transit, and spot checks on identity papers would be rigorously instituted. For the two teams that planned to catch a train from Florence to Milan, and then change trains to Como, any delay was vitally important. Travel during wartime was fraught with overcrowding and delays, and they knew that their journey north could be slow.

The brilliant idea of making dummies was proposed and accepted a few weeks before the tunnel was finished. It was important that each dummy should have as strong a likeness as possible to the escaper that it was based upon. Fortunately, one group of prisoners in the castle had long been observing the escapers – their batmen or army servants. So the task of making the dummies fell to the very young soldiers who looked after the senior officers.

The dummy representing Hargest was typical of those manufactured by the batmen. Private Howes had asked Hargest to grow his hair out and had then saved the clippings retrieved from Able Seaman Cunningham, the castle's barber. Constructing the head was relatively simple. Howes had taken a large handkerchief and soaked it in glue. Hargest's hair clippings were then stuck to it, remembering to leave a bald spot on the crown. The handkerchief was then stuck on to a stuffed balaclava and a cloth ear sewn on to one side.[5] The 'body' under the blankets was simply a roll of Hargest's clothing.

Each of the six dummies was different. General O'Connor and Brigadier Combe were fair-haired, while Miles and De Wiart were bald.[6] From a distance, at night, the dummies might just fool the Italians. Neame ensured that the illusion was stronger by diffusing the light. He applied for mosquito nets for the prisoners and they started using them at night immediately, even though not a single insect had yet been seen. The Italians soon grew used to seeing the officers sleeping soundly beneath these nets, which made it harder to clearly see the bodies in the beds. But it had been obvious to Neame and the others that the dummies would only pass inspection if they were viewed from some distance away. To this end, Neame made several complaints, both to Commandant Tranquille and to the Red Cross, explaining that the duty officer's habit of entering an officer's room during the 1.30am inspection was severely disrupting the prisoners' sleep.[7] After much arguing and negotiation, Tranquille agreed that in the interests of allowing his elderly prisoners a good night's sleep, the duty officer would instead merely open the door to a prisoner's room and use a handheld torch to conduct a quick inspection. On no account was the officer to enter the prisoners' rooms during the inspection. Neame and the others knew that viewed through a mosquito net by the light of a torch, the dummies should pass for real people.[8]

*

For several days after the tunnel had been completed, the escapers checked their disguises, papers and maps. Flight Lieutenant Leeming had manufactured some more of the little compasses that were housed in Italian Bakelite shoe polish boxes, so all of the teams were properly equipped. All now looked to General Neame for a final decision about when to launch the escape. He, and he alone, held responsibility for ordering 'Zero Day'.

It all came down now to the right weather conditions. Wind was essential to cover any noise that the escapers made as they excavated the last six inches of dirt from the exit shaft before charging off into the night. Rain was the second prerequisite, in order to hopefully hold the wall sentries inside their guard boxes instead of prowling the battlements just two dozen feet above the tunnel exit. It was a matter of waiting until those two weather conditions occurred on the same night.[9]

It didn't look promising. Each day and night was 'fair': dry, with little or no wind. All of the escapers had taken to constantly reporting on the weather on an hourly basis in the days that followed the completion of the tunnel. In the meantime, the final details of the escape plan were settled.

'So it's agreed that Ranfurly will remove the final six inches of soil in the shaft,' said General Neame. 'I will assist as required. We'll begin excavations at 8.00pm, leaving us an hour before the final kick-off.'

Ranfurly nodded. He had been selected for the final dig largely because of his height – six foot three inches.

'I'll then camouflage the hole with the special cover I've made,' stated Ranfurly.

'All of the escape kit, which is currently stored in the chapel, will be brought up to the rooms ready for the teams to change into,' continued Neame.

'What about the dummies?' asked Brigadier Miles.

'Those too – have your servants bring them up ready to be placed in the beds.'

Neame explained that a system of watchers would be placed to give warning of any Italians approaching, though this was deemed unlikely.

'Right, let's go through the plan one more time regarding the tunnel,' said Neame.

'I enter first, sir,' said John Combe. 'I'm to reconnoitre the ground immediately after getting out of the shaft.'[10]

'I'm next,' said Miles. 'I'm to work with John and guide the rest of the party to some spot concealed from the castle road.'

'Then it's my turn,' said Air Vice-Marshal Boyd. 'Behind me will be Jim and Dick,' he said, referring to Brigadier Hargest and General O'Connor.'

'Yes, and Hargest and I will help Carton out of the exit,' said O'Connor.

'And then I close the exit using Dan's special cover, sprinkle some more soil over it, obliterate footmarks and then make my way to the hidden RV where the others will be waiting,' said Hargest.[11]

It all sounded so simple – but doing it for real: that would be the greatest test of nerve they had faced since they were last in action.

*

'It's raining!' declared an excited Dick O'Connor on the morning of 28 March. The rest of the escapers and their helpers went to the windows of the sitting room or the door to the courtyard. O'Connor was right. The sky was overcast and a steady rain had begun to fall.

As it was a Sunday, Neame would hold religious services for the prisoners in the dining room at midday as usual. G-P, in charge of music, added a hymn to the service in direct reference to the day's possible significance: 'Through the night of doubt and sorrow goes the pilgrim band'.[12]

*

Two hours later it was still raining.

'What do you say, Phil?' asked O'Connor expectantly. General Neame stood at the window, arms folded, staring at the rain that tapped gently against the glass. He didn't move for some time. Behind him the escapers waited for an answer, sitting or standing around the comfortable room, the only sound the logs that fizzed and crackled as they burned in the great stone fireplace. Presently, Neame turned from the window, his face set.

'Right chaps: it's on,' nodded Neame. The frozen tableau of generals and brigadiers exploded into life, a burble of excited conversation erupting as they headed for their rooms to begin final preparations for the off.

*

General Neame continued to monitor the weather for the next several hours, as did many of the officers and men. With departure set for 9.00pm, the escape teams checked and rechecked their kit and clothes, their stomachs oily with pre-performance nerves. The desire to 'get cracking' suffused their muted conversations like a mantra. Lord Ranfurly prepared to enter the tunnel and complete the final excavation, opening the shaft to the outside. But then word came at 7.30pm that everyone was to assemble in the sitting room.

'I'm sorry chaps,' began Neame, one hand resting on the fireplace's marble mantelpiece, 'show's off.'

'But why?' exclaimed General De Wiart rather sharply. There was a fair amount of grumbling among the rest and much shaking of heads in disbelief.

'You placed me in command of this operation,' said Neame, 'and you gave me the authority to determine when Zero Day would be.' Everyone quieted down out of respect. 'Well, I'll tell you why. It's the weather … it's not quite right.'

'But Phil,' said Dick O'Connor in a reasonable voice, 'I was *just* at the courtyard door and it's still raining.'

'I know it is,' replied Neame, '*but* it's slackening off and the wind's dropped. Look, I know what you chaps are going through, but I can't let you go ahead until the weather conditions are absolutely perfect. At the moment they are not quite right. We've all worked too damned hard to risk falling at the last fence.'

Neame was talking sense, but the let-down was hard to take for men who were raring to go. For nearly seven long and arduous months they had laboured on the tunnel with one thought in mind – the night when they would crawl through it to freedom. Now, at that victorious moment, they had been told to wait. Several tried to persuade Neame otherwise, but he firmly told them that they *would* wait.[13] 'A feeling of depression followed this verdict,' wrote O'Connor, 'as some thought that we were missing a real chance. But General Neame very properly stuck to his guns, and our disappointment proved short lived.'[14]

*

Monday 29 March 1943 dawned bright and clear. The 'weather watchers' were soon at their allotted windows and doorways, smoking cigarettes and pipes and glancing heavenward. The day looked like a bust, but in the afternoon the sky started to cloud over and grow overcast. The clouds took on the dark, pregnant look of rain. Then it began, a few dark spots appearing on the courtyard's flagstones until the heavens fully opened and the rain came in steady sheets, driving the sentries into their boxes for cover. By 6.00pm the rain was still continuing to fall steadily, with no sign of letting up. The escapers had retired to their rooms after dinner, hardly daring to believe that tonight could be *the* night, especially since the previous evening's disappointing cancellation. The men sat on their beds and stared into space, feeling like pent-up racehorses champing at the bit but confined to enforced idleness. They reread letters from loved ones without really taking in their import, glanced at photographs or tried to busy their minds by going over the plan and their part in it for the thousandth time. More than one paced the stone floor of his room, puffing nervously on a cigarette and often pausing by his window to stare out into the wet darkness.

'Jim,' said a voice behind Hargest as he leaned ruminatively on his windowsill, the smell of rain freshening him as a light wind blew droplets against his face through the open pane. The voice made Hargest jump and he turned quickly. General Neame was leaning around the door frame. 'I think you had better dress,' said Neame. Hargest took a pace towards him, his face blank.

'It looks as though tonight will be a good one,'[15] added Neame, throwing him a big grin before his head and shoulders disappeared from the doorway and Hargest heard his footsteps moving down the corridor to another escaper's room with the joyous news.

Hargest moved quickly, pulling on the escape outfit that he had concealed in his room. Watchers had already been posted in case of a sudden Italian appearance, though no officers or guards were expected in the prisoners' quarters until the 1.30am check.

*

'Blast!' exclaimed Dick O'Connor when he pulled out his rucksack from its hiding place. Rats had eaten two large holes in it.

'Don't worry, sir, I'll fix that in a jiffy,' said his batman, Trooper Stones. In 30 minutes Stones had the holes patched and the rucksack fit for service again.[16] It needed to be, for O'Connor would be carry-ing upwards of 25lbs of rations and kit inside of it.

While the six escapers dressed in their civilian outfits, assisted by their loyal batmen, and the suitcases and rucksacks were checked and rechecked, General Neame and Lieutenant Ranfurly, the latter wearing only a pair of underpants, clambered down into the tunnel. The escapers went down to the dining room for a last meal before the off, though most had little appetite. Ranfurly had also had sandwiches made and hard-boiled eggs readied, and these were distributed to the escapers as extra rations to tide them through the first 24 hours of their journeys.

Jim Hargest brought a bottle of rum down to the dining room and filled six small medicine bottles, one for each of the escapers. He also took with him, in his suitcase, a small bottle of red wine.[17]

It was a time for goodbyes. The escapers all shook hands with the other officers, who would not be going yet, though it was planned that another six men would make the attempt in a day or two. The generals and brigadiers then shook hands with their batmen, the young soldiers who had become like sons to many of these old warriors. They had in some cases fought side-by-side for years and had shared the trials and tribulations of imprisonment together. Though separated not only by age and rank but also by the social class conventions of the era, the batmen and orderlies had nonetheless become their friends.

Deep beneath the castle Dan Ranfurly and Neame laboured on the final half-foot of imprisoning earth and stones.

'Right sir, I'm in position,' murmured Ranfurly, his long frame reaching up the exit shaft. Below him crouched General Neame. He glanced at his watch. It was a few minutes after 8.00pm.

'Okay, Dan,' whispered Neame, 'proceed.'

Ranfurly needed no further urging. Balancing himself against the wooden sides of the exit shaft he reached up and pulled aside the boards at the top, exposing the dark, damp earth above. Then he began to dig with the trusty old kitchen knife, soil and stones cascading down over his outstretched arms and his face as he excavated. For ten minutes Ranfurly worked like a man possessed, hacking and gouging at the earth while Neame backed into the tunnel away from the torrent of mud that fell from above. Then all was quiet.

'Sir,' whispered Ranfurly, almost silently. Neame gingerly moved into the bottom of the shaft and looked up. Ranfurly's mud-blackened face was almost invisible in the darkness, except for his white teeth. He was grinning. Ranfurly pointed upwards with the tip of his knife. Neame allowed his eyes to adjust. Clouds scudded past the fresh hole that Ranfurly had cut at the top of the shaft.[18] Cold rain fell on to Neame's upturned face, cleansing and refreshing after the filth and heat of the gloomy tunnel. Grinning widely himself now, he gave Ranfurly a thumbs-up before disappearing back down the tunnel towards the chapel with the good news.

*

'Officer coming!' hissed one of the watchers into the crowded dining room. Everyone froze for a second. Then they began to scatter. The alert had come from Brigadier 'Rudolph' Vaughan's room, one of the main lookout points. The six escapers snatched up their cases and rucksacks and dashed for their rooms. They had to conceal their luggage and escape outfits before the officer arrived. To add to the confusion, General Neame had sent word from the chapel for the escapers to assemble in the tunnel.[19]

But a few minutes later everyone was called back to the dining room, hearts still in mouths. It had been a false alarm. A watcher had seen an Italian NCO making his rounds on the battlements and mistook the situation. The order arrived telling the escapers to make their way to the chapel.[20] The strain was beginning to tell. Fortunately, 'Rudolph's' namesake Captain Ernest Vaughan, the castle's doughty new medical officer, took charge and gathered the escapers together and started directing them into the chapel.[21]

*

When the escapers entered the darkened chapel they discovered Lord Ranfurly sitting at the top of the shaft. He refused to shake hands with any of them owing to his filthy state. The escapers had taken extra precautions with their outfits to protect them from the rigours of crawling through a muddy tunnel and the rainy night that they could expect at the other end. Each man wore an outsized pair of pyjamas over his clothes and a large handkerchief tied over his home-made flat cap. The men's shoes were covered with old socks, with the legs of their pyjamas tucked firmly in.[22]

The escapers clambered down into the tunnel, Ranfurly helping each with his bag. Moving quickly down the tunnel to the exit shaft they were met by General Neame at the bottom, his face lit by a very low light.

'Right, you know the drill,' whispered Neame. 'The watchers report that all of the sentries are in their boxes. It's raining quite steadily.'

Brigadier Combe would be the first to go. He carried his leather suitcase, a length of rope and a blanket. His job was to spread the blanket outside the exit to prevent the escapers' shoes chewing up the wet grass and leaving an obvious mark that would attract the attention of any sentry who peered over the battlements during daylight. He was then to 'secure the rope round a post on the top of a stone wall just down the hillside from the battlements'. This, wrote Hargest, 'was our last obstacle, five feet high on the uphill side and about ten feet on the downhill or road side. The rope was to steady us; we could hang on to it while descending.'[23]

Neame glanced at his watch, then along the tunnel where seven darkened and tense-looking faces, including that of Ranfurly at the far end, stared back at him. He looked at his watch again. It was time. 'Right John,' he said to Combe, 'Good luck and see you after the war.' Combe, awkwardly encumbered by the suitcase, coiled rope and blanket, muttered his response, briefly shook Neame's hand and then began to climb up the exit shaft. Behind him, the remaining six shuffled forward, Neame raising one hand to steady them while staring up the shaft as Combe struggled to the top.

At 9.00pm Brigadier John Combe's head appeared beneath the

castle's massive curtain wall. Rain lashed at his face – a clean, crisp and beautifully cold rain. The air that accompanied the rain was fresh and invigorating after the stale tunnel. A wave of fierce exhilaration swept over Combe as he struggled out of the hole and set to work. He was alive … and he was free.

CHAPTER 14

The Pilgrim Band

*'We were free … and freedom is a precious thing and worth the
highest price a man can pay, and that moment I tasted it in full.'*

Major-General Adrian Carton de Wiart

The next man out of the tunnel was Brigadier Miles, who in
addition to carrying his personal kit was also hauling out Lord
Ranfurly's carefully camouflaged three-ply exit hole cover. Once
he'd deposited the cover by the exit Miles was to help Brigadier
Combe down at the five-foot-high castle road wall. As soon as he
emerged, Miles quickly dropped the heavy board and scurried down
the slope towards where Combe crouched in the lee of the wall. Air
Vice-Marshal Boyd was next out – he only carried his suitcase. His
task once clear of the exit was to go to the road and keep watch.
There was always the fear that the Italians might have a ground sentry
outside the curtain wall during the hours of darkness. Brigadier Jim
Hargest was number four. He carried his suitcase, a long rope with
an iron hook on one end, and a sandbag full of pine needles and soil.
When General Neame gave him the signal to start climbing up the
exit shaft Hargest pushed his case ahead of him, while grasping the
heavy sandbag in his other hand. The tunnel was wet and slippery,
and it was difficult work making the top.[1]

Hargest was shocked by how light it was when he clambered
awkwardly out of the exit shaft. Unbeknown to the prisoners, the
Italians had placed some lights under the wall and they were reasonably bright.[2] Hargest glanced up nervously at the top of the high castle

wall. He couldn't see anyone, but if a guard did glance over the edge the escapers would be easily seen. However, it was still raining hard and the sentries had decided to remain dry inside their little wooden guard boxes atop the battlements. Hargest placed his suitcase and the sandbag on the blanket. Then he took off the coil of rope that he was wearing across his torso and passed it back down the hole, hook first. After a few seconds the rope went taut, and a single strong tug was the signal for Hargest to haul. Up came General De Wiart's heavy pack, which Hargest unhooked and placed with the other equipment on the blanket. Then he fed the rope back down into the hole. This time he hauled up General O'Connor's rucksack. Hargest paused, expecting De Wiart to appear, and preparing to give him a helping hand if needed, but instead he heard a voice whisper fiercely, 'The rope!'

Inside the shaft General De Wiart had begun his ascent when he stopped and leaned back down, whispering something to Neame at the bottom. Neame didn't hear what he said and, assuming that the tall one-armed man was stuck, started pushing on his legs.[3] But De Wiart resisted and leaned back down again. 'I've forgotten Connor's bloody gamp!'[4] hissed De Wiart roughly. Neame turned to look at O'Connor, who quickly thrust a rolled black umbrella into his hands. 'Well, it *is* raining,' said O'Connor defensively. Neame raised one eyebrow before quickly passing the umbrella up to the impatient De Wiart.

Up top Hargest complied with the third request for the rope and dangled it back down the hole. Another tug and he hauled to the surface a walking stick and O'Connor's black umbrella. Next came De Wiart, muttering something under his breath about a 'bloody gamp' as he was helped from the tunnel. The tall figure picked up his pack and stick and was soon away. Lastly emerged O'Connor, who was horribly surprised by the lights. 'It's like Piccadilly in peacetime,'[5] he whispered to Hargest before he was also away towards the darkness of the road wall. Hargest scooped up the sodden blanket and tossed it into the hole. Then he fitted Ranfurly's heavy cover over the exit and emptied the contents of his sandbag over it, pausing for a few seconds to carefully spread the material and camouflage the hole as best he could. Satisfied with his work, Hargest snatched up his suitcase, the empty sandbag and the rope and headed off after the others.[6]

*

Inside the tunnel everything went dead quiet once Hargest had fastened the cover over the hole. General Neame sat for a few seconds at the bottom of the exit shaft.

'And that's that,' he said reflectively, before making his way back towards the chapel. He still had plenty of work to do.

'Everything okay, sir?' asked Ranfurly, caked in mud and still dressed only in his underwear.

'Yes, the chicks have flown the nest,' replied Neame. 'Come on, you'd better get cleaned up and help the others with the dummies.'

It was essential to protect the secret of the tunnel at all costs. Plans were afoot to send a further six officers through it over the coming days, so the Italians had to be fooled into thinking that the first six had escaped over the castle's outer wall. To this end Neame had planned a diversion. The long rope that Hargest had used to haul rucksacks and equipment to the surface would be dropped somewhere where it would be easily found in the morning. Hopefully, the Italians would fall for this ruse and not suspect a tunnel.[7] In the meantime, the dummies had to be moved up to the bedrooms and made ready for the night-time inspection.

*

At the low wall outside the castle that led to the road the escapers had a huge stroke of luck. Set into the wall was a great iron gate that stood twelve feet tall. Everyone had assumed that this portal would be securely locked, necessitating clambering over the wall itself to reach the road. But when Boyd tried the gate, it opened. Quickly everyone filed through and then Boyd tried to close it. But the gate was stiff and, perhaps at that moment forgetting where he was, Boyd slammed the gate with some force. Everyone ducked when the iron gate closed behind them with a loud boom.[8] Boyd looked at them sheepishly in the rainy darkness and mouthed a silent 'sorry'. Then all eyes turned to the battlements. It seemed inconceivable that a sentry hadn't heard the almighty crash. No movement was discerned, the distance, wind and rain snatching away the hard noise before it reached the lofty sentry posts.

'Come on, let's get moving,' said O'Connor, and the six fugitives headed off downhill into the dripping woods below the castle where they were grateful to be swallowed up by shadows. Before they departed, the rope was poorly hidden. After a while they stepped over a wire fence into an olive grove and then clambered awkwardly over bramble-covered terraces as they headed deeper into the valley. O'Connor called another halt, and the escapers quickly divested themselves of their soaked and filthy overclothes used to protect their civilian outfits, stashing them in the undergrowth along with Hargest's empty sandbag.[9] After another 600 yards the path branched into two routes; this was where O'Connor and De Wiart were to part company with the other two teams.

By now, the rain had eased off. The six men stood in their groups for a few minutes, O'Connor and De Wiart conspicuous by their very different outfits and large rucksacks. They were dressed for the countryside rather than as smarter workmen or travelling salesmen as favoured by the other four. De Wiart wore an old pair of corduroy trousers given to him by General Gambier-Parry, a civilian collarless shirt and an old pullover, with his raincoat over the top and a rag loosely knotted around his neck as a rudimentary scarf. On his feet he wore brown leather mountain boots that he had purchased at Sulmona before the move to Vincigliata.[10] O'Connor was similarly disguised, both men also wearing homemade workmen's caps. They were posing as Austrian tourists on a hiking holiday, which would account for their strange accents when speaking Italian and

O'Connor's fair hair. But their identity documents carried Italian names and listed Bologna as their place of domicile, to enable them to pass themselves off as local peasants should the need arise. They would swap between the two identities as the situation required.

'We shook hands silently,' recalled De Wiart of the parting, 'and let the darkness swallow us up.'[11] With O'Connor beside him, De Wiart set off in a northeasterly direction towards the Apennines. Their target was to cross the grand Bologna–Milan trunk road between Modena and Reggio.[12]

For the other two teams, the target was Florence station. When they parted from O'Connor and De Wiart, the remaining four fugitives were six miles from their target. Moving fast through the night, they crossed a bridge above a mill and hit the tarred road to the city. Stopping briefly, they determined to make themselves more presentable. They stripped off the old socks that had protected their shoes and shins during the escape and threw them into the fast-flowing, rain-swollen mill stream, then crouched on the bank and washed their suitcases clean of mud from the tunnel.[13] It was now about 10.00pm.

*

Back at the castle, at 10.00pm General Neame ordered the dummies placed in the escaped officers' beds.[14] The orderlies fussed over their placement, and the hanging of the mosquito nets, until Neame conducted an inspection and declared everything to be ready. The real test would come at 1.30am when the Italians made their customary inspection.

*

Miles and Boyd set a cracking pace down the road towards Florence. In fact, it was too fast. Hargest caught up with them.

'Look here, we should slow down a bit,' said Hargest to Miles and Boyd. Everyone was wearing a lot of thick clothing and overcoats, brought along in case they encountered snow in the Alps during their crossing into Switzerland, and their faces were running with sweat. 'Our train doesn't leave until 0035 hours and we've only half-a-dozen miles to cover.'[15]

Boyd protested, worried that they might need extra time if they lost their way on the route into Florence. But Hargest was adamant and they slowed down accordingly. He didn't think that it was wise to arrive too early and in an exhausted state – they might attract unwanted attention.

On they marched. As they entered Florence's blacked-out suburbs they started seeing people, some finding their way in the dark with torches while others rode bicycles with shielded lamps. The escapers were pleased to note that no one took the slightest interest in them. Soon they were deep into Florence, passing through mostly quiet streets towards the railway station. Before very long they arrived at their destination. Hargest glanced at his wristwatch.

'Twenty-three thirty-five hours,' he murmured to the others as they stood in the shadows of an apartment building across from the huge station hall. The Milan train would depart in one hour's time, at 12.35am.

'Well, we can't hang around here,' said Boyd. 'We'd look less conspicuous waiting inside the station itself.' The others agreed, and they picked up their suitcases and strode nonchalantly across the piazza and through the great iron and glass doors into the station.

Florence railway station was a hive of activity, with civilians, soldiers and police milling around its huge ticket hall. Occasional announcements blared out over tinny speakers and all around them were passengers' conversations and the sounds of trains shunting, whistles blowing and steam escaping from engines. The hall was brightly lit and even in the middle of the night it was crowded with people. The fugitives glanced towards the far end of the vast, echoing hall where the ticket office was located. Several railway officials and *Carabinieri* stood around chatting or watching the crowds.

'Let's split up for a while,' suggested Miles, and the four escapers moved away from each other to wait singly. Hargest decided to test his disguise. He sauntered over to a group of Italian soldiers who were waiting next to a pile of kitbags. Hargest was pleased to note that they didn't look at him twice. Using discreet signals, the four fugitives drifted back outside to compare notes.[16]

'Right, who's going to buy the tickets?' murmured Boyd. No one replied.

'Very well, *I'll* do it,' said Boyd irritably, breaking the embarrassed silence.

'Only three third class, remember,' piped up John Combe as Boyd prepared to go back into the station. 'I'm going second class.' Combe was posing as a travelling salesman and was dressed well in comparison to his companions. He would travel in a different carriage to Milan, but he'd have to purchase his own ticket.

*

Back inside the noisy and overcrowded station Boyd made his way towards the ticket office. There was a queue, which he joined. In his mind he went over his line several times, confident that his Italian would suffice. Then came his turn. Boyd presented himself before one of the little grill windows.

'*Tre biglietti di terza classe ritorno a Milano*,' said Boyd confidently. The clerk understood, but then launched into a loud and long diatribe in staccato Italian, Boyd only managing to pick out the word 'Bologna' with any clarity. The clerk stopped speaking and stared at Boyd as if waiting for a reply, but Boyd's mind had gone blank. He hadn't understood what the clerk had said, or even whether he had asked him a question. He might simply have been giving him some important instruction. Boyd glanced to his right. A *Carabiniere* had turned and was staring at him, both thumbs hooked into his gun belt. Boyd could hear the queue of people behind him muttering impatiently. His stomach turned over with nerves. He licked his lips and uttered a low '*scusami*', before he walked away from the window without any tickets. He could feel the *Carabiniere*'s eyes boring into his back as he walked towards the exit.

Once outside, he confessed what had happened to the others.[17]

'The clerk chappie was probably giving you instructions about changing trains at Bologna,' said Miles. 'Never mind, I'll get the tickets.' Miles strode off into the hall, accompanied by Brigadier Combe, who would have to go to a different window to purchase his second-class return ticket.

Miles and Combe bought their tickets without any problems.[18] With plenty of time to kill until their train, the four escapers decided to walk around the streets of Florence for a while.

*

Dick O'Connor and Carton de Wiart were, in the meantime, making excellent progress on foot. They covered five or six miles before De Wiart took a wrong turn in the dark and they became momentarily lost. Map reading had never been De Wiart's strong suit, so O'Connor took over and they managed to find the way again.[19]

Neither man intended to stop for a rest throughout the hours of darkness and the two generals pushed on with the pace of men half their age. They successfully crossed the River Sieve before threading their way through the sleeping Borgo San Lorenzo, a town of over 16,000 people twelve miles northeast of Florence. At one point a searchlight beam suddenly stabbed out in the darkness, pinning them in the bright light. Both men froze, fearing they were about to be challenged, but after a few seconds the searchlight swung away over surrounding countryside and the two Britons hurried on.[20]

Soon they found the main Bologna road, following it northeast. A quick glance at his watch showed O'Connor that they were making excellent time.[21]

*

Jim Hargest, standing outside Florence station, glanced nervously at his watch again.

'Five minutes till the train departs,' he murmured to Boyd, Miles and Combe. It was 12.30am.

'Right, let's get on with it,' replied Boyd grimly. They strode into the station and made their way towards the platforms, tickets in their hands. The crowd was being funnelled through several gates that were manned by ticket inspectors and guarded by bored-looking *Carabinieri*. The four escapers shuffled forward with the crowd and presented their tickets. The inspectors barely looked at them, simply checked their tickets and waved them through. So far so good. In about an hour the duty officer at the castle would make his rounds. Hopefully the dummies would do their jobs and no alarm would be raised. By the time the inspection was finished, the four escapers would be well on their ways north.

The platform was cold and damp, and there was no train waiting for the two teams. They waited and waited, scared to sit down in case they were drawn into conversation with other travellers, but increasingly exhausted by the ordeal. Hargest and the others constantly glanced at their watches, but still no train appeared. At 1.30am Hargest turned to Boyd, placing his hand over his mouth as he spoke.

'Night-time check,' he murmured. Boyd looked at his watch and nodded. If those dummies failed to pass muster, the station would soon be crawling with troops looking for them. It was one of the obvious places to begin casting the net for escaped prisoners of war. Stamping his feet to try to keep warm, Hargest looked along the lit tracks beside the platform. Still no damned train.

*

Captain Pederneschi, accompanied by a sergeant, tramped up the stone steps to the next level of bedrooms, his way lit by a handheld torch. It was 1.30am and the castle was deathly quiet. The sergeant opened the first door on the left and Pederneschi shone his torch inside. A figure lay asleep beneath a mosquito net. The security officer moved on. It was the same in each room. Everything was in order. He yawned and rubbed his eyes. It had been a long day and he was due to come off duty once he had completed his check of the orderlies' accommodation. Pederneschi turned and, followed by the sergeant, tramped off towards another part of the castle.

General Neame lay on his back in his darkened room, his ears straining as he listened to Pederneschi's jackboots clumping away down the corridor. He smiled – the Italian had bought it; the dummies had passed muster. Neame thought of his friends who had escaped and wondered how they were getting along. He also thought of the new day to come and the challenges he and the remaining prisoners would face. Neame stared at the ceiling. It was a long time before sleep came.

*

Shortly after Captain Pederneschi began his inspection the Milan train finally puffed into Florence Station. Hargest glanced at his watch – 1.45am. '*So much for Fascist efficiency,*' he thought. Every compartment was crammed to capacity and the corridors were full as well. As soon as the train squealed to a shaky halt the several hundred people who were waiting on the platform surged forward in a dense mass of clamouring, arguing and shoving humanity, each determined to board. The people trying to get off the train stood little chance, and Hargest and the three other escapers were swept along in this confusion towards a carriage. Such was the level of overcrowding that some passengers even boarded through the carriage windows. The escaped officers tucked their bags securely under their arms and, using their shoulders, bulled their ways on to the train. Boyd found himself miraculously inside the crowded corridor of a carriage and quickly spotted Jim Hargest at the other end. The train did not linger; shortly after arriving it puffed out of

Florence, the previously raucous and fractious passengers settling down, and soon the corridor was filled with laughter and the melodic flow of Italian affability.

The problem was the very friendliness of the average Italian. Jim Hargest found himself pushed up against a *Carabiniere*, who suddenly decided to engage him in conversation. Hargest ignored his first attempt, but the *Carabiniere* was insistent and, tugging at Hargest's sleeve, asked him another question. Realising that his poor Italian was a complete giveaway, but also recognising that to ignore his questioner would only make him suspicious, Hargest fell back on a carefully worked-out ruse. He leaned closer to the *Carabiniere* and whispered in hoarse Italian: 'I'm sorry, but I am very deaf.' The *Carabiniere* nodded, shrugged his shoulders, then turned away and began chatting to another man.[22]

The distance from Florence to Bologna, where the escapers would have to change trains for Milan, was 45 miles. The train was fast, but not fast enough, arriving at 3.00am. The Bologna to Milan train was supposed to depart at 3.00am, and the escapers were terrified that they would miss their connection. But they had reckoned without wartime railways in Italy. On arrival at Bologna station another interminable wait began on the cold platform for the delayed train. The delays were a cause for serious concern. Come 11.00am, the escapers fully expected to be noted as missing from the castle. It seemed inconceivable that the Italian officer who inspected them at morning roll call in the dining room could miss six officers. Then the alert would be issued and the train stations would suddenly be blockaded by soldiers and *Carabinieri* carrying the escaped officers' descriptions and tasked with inspecting the papers of travellers. The infernal delays meant that Boyd, Hargest, Miles and Combe were practically half a day behind schedule. They were supposed to have been arriving at Milan at 6.00am and Lake Como, near the Swiss frontier, at 8.00am. In their original plan, worked out from purloined intelligence at the castle, they would have crossed the frontier around the time the Italians realised that they were missing, and before an alert could be fully put into effect.

The wait on the platform at Bologna station was very uncomfortable for the four middle-aged escapers. They had missed a night's sleep and had not even managed to sit down since they entered the escape tunnel at the castle over eight hours before. It was imperative that they find some hot food and a drink to perk them up, so Hargest was left guarding the bags while the others scoured the station for refreshments. Before long someone tapped him on the shoulder.

'Are these your bags?'[23] asked a nosy Italian railway policeman. Hargest replied in the affirmative and the policeman just nodded and strolled off. It wasn't the last question that he had to field in his schoolboy Italian, as several passengers asked him about trains and timetables. He was relieved when his friends reappeared, but they had failed to find any hot food or drinks.

The Milan train finally departed from Bologna at 5.20am. Getting aboard was the same dreadful scrimmage as at Florence, and it almost brought dire consequences for Brigadier Hargest. Just as he was hauling himself aboard a carriage, someone in the crowd pulled at his suitcase. Seconds later and Hargest was left holding only the broken handle – his case with his clothes, wine, food and tools had disappeared beneath the riotous crowd. He made a snap decision to retrieve it and launched himself like an enraged bull into the mass of humanity and by sheer force managed to find his case and climb back aboard the carriage. By the time he made it inside a corridor he was exhausted and starting to feel unwell. He reattached the handle to his case using a bootlace, pressed his back against a wall and tried to catch his breath. Looking around he saw Brigadier Miles at the other end of the corridor, also looking exhausted and ashen-faced, while Owen Boyd was wedged in about six feet behind Hargest.[24]

*

With the coming of dawn, Generals O'Connor and Carton de Wiart were still shadowing the Bologna road. One of De Wiart's feet was hurting, and he cursed his stupidity in not joining the others for more escorted walks around the vicinity of the castle.

''Bout time for a feed, don't you think, Connor?'[25] said De Wiart, grimacing slightly from the pain in his foot.

The two men branched off from the road and climbed up a little tree- and scrub-covered hillock where they gratefully stripped off their heavy rucksacks and sat down on the grass. De Wiart removed his boots. One of his big toes was badly blistered.

'We'll take a breather for a few hours,' said O'Connor. 'We're pretty well concealed from the road, I think.'

The two men broke out some of their rations. They had covered over fifteen miles on foot since breaking out of the castle, and intended to push on once rested.

*

Aboard the Bologna to Milan train the journey seemed interminable, and unlike O'Connor and De Wiart, Brigadiers Hargest, Miles and Combe and Air Vice-Marshal Boyd were powerless to increase their speed or deviate from the route. They were trapped aboard the slow-moving and horrendously overcrowded train and becoming increasingly conscious of the time issue. Jim Hargest found himself buttonholed by a little old Italian man who was determined to chat. Hargest again deployed his deaf act, whereupon the old man started making jokes at Hargest's expense to the carriage in general. The very last thing Hargest wanted to be was the centre of attention, but he couldn't move away. 'He was a mean little man,' recalled Hargest, 'and I would have loved to wring his neck.'[26]

The train regularly jerked to a halt at stations along the way to pick up or deposit passengers. In preparation for the journey Hargest had committed to memory the names of the major towns along the route, so at each halt he took care to mentally note the station names. First was Modena, followed by Parma, Piacenza, and then Lodi.[27] Finally the train steamed lazily over a bridge spanning the fast-flowing and wide Po River and on to the Plain of Lombardy. The sky grew dark and overcast and soon heavy rain battered the carriage windows like flung sand.

The atmosphere inside the carriage, in spite of the weather, was jolly and the Italians chattered away telling stories and jokes. At one point a young couple tried to draw Hargest into a joke they were telling to the carriage in general, when the little old man suddenly interjected. 'It's no use talking to him,' said the old man, pointing to Hargest who had a sickly smile plastered across his face. 'He's deaf. Anyway, I think he's a German.'[28]

*

'Right, Carton, let's get cracking,' announced Dick O'Connor after they had rested for three or four hours. They packed up their kit, stood, and shouldered their heavy rucksacks. 'I'm afraid we'll be bush-whacking from now on,' said O'Connor. They couldn't afford to follow the main Bologna road any longer as the chances of running into police or *Carabinieri* were simply too great. Instead, the two generals would go cross-country, 'up hill and down dale',[29] as De Wiart would recall, through pretty rolling countryside and the occasional village. The months of intensive fitness training that the two men had put in on the keep staircases paid off, notwithstanding Carton de Wiart's blister. For some of that period O'Connor in particular had been up and down those stone steps 75 times a day, 'which in height added up to between 3,000 and 4,000 ft – a *very* boring performance!'.[30] Now the two men with a combined age of 115 were back eating up the miles towards their target frontier crossing at Tirano.[31] O'Connor had his rolled umbrella tied to the top of his pack, while De Wiart made full use of his stout walking stick, which he had relied on to help him keep his balance since losing an eye.

*

Jim Hargest glanced at his wristwatch and silently cursed. From Milan, the four escapers had planned to catch the 8.00am train to Como near the Swiss frontier. From Como it was a six-mile hike to the border town of Chiasso and freedom. But as the train finally pulled into Milan's vast main station Hargest knew that they had in all probability missed their connection, leaving them 40 miles short of Switzerland. Hargest glanced at Miles, who was standing close by. When their eyes met, Hargest briefly glanced back at his watch and then shook his head. Miles looked miserable. It was 8.20am on 30 March 1943 when a gloomy Hargest, Boyd, Miles and Combe finally disembarked from the train in Milan.[32]

CHAPTER 15

Elevenses

*'I watched Boyd and Miles wilt and go grey, and
my hip was troubling me a good deal.'*

Brigadier James Hargest

'So, what now?' asked Brigadier Reg Miles in a low voice. He was standing inside Milan's huge main station with Jim Hargest, Owen Boyd and John Combe. It was dangerous to stand around too long in discussion, but they were in a quandary. It was 8.30am on 30 March 1943 and the clock was ticking. The escapers knew that they only had until 11.00am before the alarm would be raised at Vincigliata Castle when the Italians finally noticed that six officers were missing from roll call. In two-and-a-half hours the Italian authorities would be informed, and within three-and-a-half at most their descriptions and photographs would begin to be circulated to all police, *Carabinieri*, army posts and border crossings.

'The Como train has definitely departed,' said Hargest, rubbing his tired eyes. 'Let's find out when the next one is due.'

The little group split up and mingled with the hundreds of passengers and staff that were milling around the huge, echoing station. Miles quickly examined a train timetable before drifting back once more into a loose huddle with the others.

'Next train to Como isn't until twelve hundred hours,' he said. They all knew that by noon the Italian operation to find them would be in full swing.

'We can't hang around here for another *three-and-a-half hours*,' murmured Boyd.

'Look,' said Hargest, 'we're about 40 miles from the frontier. Lets take a taxi as far along the Como road as we can.'[1]

'And then what?' asked Boyd, his brow creased.

'We walk,' said Hargest flatly.

This idea was vetoed as too risky. They had neither the energy nor the kit for such an undertaking. And they would stick out like sore thumbs on the main roads once the Italians started hunting for them.

'Well then, it will have to be the train. I'll buy us four tickets. We can wait on the platform,' said Miles. The others agreed and Miles went off to the ticket office, returning a few minutes later. But when they tried to enter the platform gate, hoping to rest and disappear from view until the train came, the guard told them to come back at noon.[2] The four escapers split up and wandered around for a while trying to think of a solution before coalescing again.

'I have an idea,' said Combe quietly. 'I remember hearing that there is a private railway line that goes up to Como from the Gardo di Nord.' This was quite far away across Milan. The others looked unconvinced.

'Well, it's worth a try,' said Combe sharply. 'It's certainly better than standing around here all morning and waiting to get caught.'

'How do we get to the North Station?' asked Miles.

'We'll take a tram,' replied Combe. 'They run right past the front of this station. I suggest we break into our respective teams and make our own ways there.'

Combe glanced around and immediately noticed a youngish man in civilian clothes and a fedora hat staring at the group. He looked away when he caught Combe's eyes, but when Combe looked back the man was staring again as he leaned against a wall. Combe decided to get moving.[3] He and Boyd walked outside and headed for a tram that was just starting to pull away. Hargest and Miles followed them to the piazza and watched as their friends ran across, each of them boarding the tram from a different end of a carriage as it began to move.[4] They didn't notice the Italian man jog quickly over and also board at the back of the carriage.

'We'll give them a few minutes, then follow,' said Hargest to Miles, who nodded solemnly.

After a suitable period of waiting, Hargest and Miles walked down to the tram stop and boarded the next vehicle that came along. They felt good – they were moving again *and* they had a plan. Hargest held on to an overhead rail and looked out of the window. He was tired but captivated by Milan. He stared intently as the tram bumped and ground down the street past La Scala and the famous cathedral.

*

Boyd and Combe arrived outside the North Station at about 9.50am. Like everywhere else it was busy with people coming and going. They went inside and waited, hoping that Hargest and Miles would shortly join them. They tried to act normal, waiting with their suitcases on the floor in front of them, just two middle-aged travellers going about their lawful business. Combe discreetly glanced around. People were queuing for tickets or standing chatting, while the usual uniformed railway officials and police stood around and a janitor cleaned part of the floor with a mop. But then Combe saw the young man from the main station again. And he had definitely seen Combe and Boyd.

'Stay here,' muttered Combe under his breath. 'I'll check the timetable.' Before Boyd could reply, Combe picked up his case and marched off in the direction of the information boards. He hoped to lure the watcher away from Boyd and their friends who would surely be arriving in a few minutes.[5] Hardly daring to look around, Combe stood before the busy boards and pretended to read the train lists, his heart pumping wildly. He had almost calmed himself down when a hand gripped his right shoulder and an Italian voice said: 'Excuse me, sir, but can you come with me?'[6]

*

Owen Boyd stood in the busy station hall for several minutes, wondering where on earth Combe had got to. There was no sign of Hargest or Miles either. He turned around slowly and scanned the hall, searching for Combe. As he looked over towards the information boards he suddenly saw Combe's tall figure. He was talking to a shorter man in a fedora hat who was showing him something in his hand. Then Combe began to walk away with the man, his new companion holding Combe's upper arm as if to guide him.

'Good Lord!' exclaimed Boyd, forgetting for a moment his composure. Then it dawned on him. Quickly picking up his suitcase, he walked in the opposite direction and disappeared into the densest part of the crowd of milling passengers.

*

When John Combe had turned around and seen the same man that had been following him since the main station, his stomach had performed a nervous flip. His questioner had not smiled, but had produced an identity card from an inside pocket of his cheap dark suit. The word 'Polizia' was emblazoned prominently on its front. As the man reached inside his jacket it bulged slightly and Combe caught sight of a shoulder holster and automatic pistol.

'Please accompany me, sir,' said the policeman in Italian. Combe was led away to an office in the station.[7] As he went he looked but he couldn't see Boyd or the others. For that he was thankful. Hopefully Boyd would manage to make himself scarce and warn the others.

*

A few minutes after Combe had been arrested, Jim Hargest and Reg Miles stepped off a tram outside the North Station and walked inside. After looking around for a short time, they couldn't see Combe or Boyd and assumed that they had already gone through to the platform. Owen Boyd, after seeing Combe taken, had decided to do just that and had hastily bought a ticket to Como and passed through the gate.

Miles went off to purchase tickets for himself and Hargest, noting that the next train to Como would depart at 10.30am. This was 90 minutes earlier than the next train from Milan's main station, meaning that the escapers should be nearing the Swiss frontier when the alarm was sounded back at Vincigliata Castle. They might still make it across before the Italians managed to activate enough troops and police to start hunting for them.

Jim Hargest went into the station buffet and ordered two coffees and newspapers. Then he sat down at a window table to look out for Miles's return and watch the platform, hoping still to see Combe and Boyd.[8]

Miles soon returned with the tickets but no news of the others. The two New Zealanders sipped their coffees and read their Italian newspapers, peeking occasionally at a large clock on the wall of the buffet. No one seemed to take any notice of them; the café was noisy with customers and filled with cigarette smoke.

Just before 10.30am Hargest stood up, carefully folding his paper and tucking it under his arm before picking up his suitcase. Miles followed suit and the two men calmly walked over to the platform gate, presenting their tickets for inspection.

For once, the train was on time: a small engine and half-a-dozen shopworn carriages. The train was only half-full, which was a distinct relief after the overcrowded Florence service, and the two brigadiers found a compartment and settled in, getting out their sandwiches from the castle. Then, precisely on time, the little train gave a lurch and slowly began to pull out of the station. Hargest glanced at his watch once again and grimaced. They were cutting it fine, *very* fine indeed. And what on earth had become of Boyd and Combe?

*

At that precise moment, the plain-clothes policeman in an office at Milan's North Station was expertly searching Brigadier John Combe. Combe stood with his arms raised while the policeman went through his pockets, emptying their contents on to a scuffed wooden desk: some coins and a small roll of banknotes, some of Gambier-Parry's maps and the painstakingly forged identity card. The policeman examined the identity card with great interest, comparing the photograph carefully with the tall man standing before him, and asking Combe various questions about his identity, which Combe managed to answer. The policeman picked up the homemade maps, turning them over in his hands.[9] It was clear from the policeman's line of questioning that he suspected Combe was not who he purported to be. Combe's Italian stretched only so far. Shortly after arriving in the office, the policemen picked up the receiver of a black telephone on the desk and began an animated conversation. A few minutes later two uniformed police officers arrived. Combe was told that he was to be taken to a police station for further questioning, and one of the policemen produced a pair of steel handcuffs and locked Combe's wrists tightly together in front of him. The other policeman picked up the material on the desk and Combe's suitcase while the plainclothesman led the way outside. As Combe was frogmarched across the station hall people turned and stared. Outside, he was bundled into the back of a black Fiat and driven off at speed.

*

Unbeknown to Hargest and Miles, Owen Boyd was still at liberty. Somehow he had missed seeing his friends on the long and busy platform, but he had slipped aboard the last carriage and settled himself into a quiet compartment. As far as he knew, he was the only one of the quartet to still be at liberty, but he remained absolutely determined to reach the frontier, come what may. He still had his maps, his compass and some money; he was moving and thus far had not attracted any untoward interest from the authorities. He felt that he had an excellent chance of making it, though, like Hargest and Miles, he too glanced periodically at his wristwatch and noted how little time remained until the morning roll call at the castle. The little train was annoyingly slow and the horrible feeling of being late for the party stalked Boyd's mind like a wraith.

*

John Combe's only thought was to buy time for Boyd, Hargest and Miles. He thought that he could do so by giving evasive answers to questions and trying to confuse and confound the police. Every minute that Combe's real identity failed to be discovered meant that the others edged that little bit closer to freedom.[10] But the Italians were not giving Combe an easy ride.

At the police station Combe was taken to an interview room where he was searched again, this time much more thoroughly. But it was not thorough enough, for the Italians never found Combe's Bakelite compass, which was sewn into a secret pocket in the back of his coat, nor did they find his equally well-hidden best maps.[11]

'So, you will tell us why you have a forged identity card,' said an interrogator in Italian, holding Gambier-Parry's artwork up in front of Combe's face. Combe shrugged his shoulders like a local and spread his palms. He claimed to be the man in the photograph, just a travelling salesman from the Italian Tyrol.

'You are lying!' yelled the interrogator, a surly-looking police captain of early middle age. He slammed his palm down on his desk, making Combe jump. On the wall above the policeman's head a portrait of Mussolini stared down with undisguised belligerence. The interrogator's brown eyes narrowed. 'Why were you at the North Station?' he demanded in a more reasonable tone. Combe, who understood most of what he was being asked after months of Italian study at the castle, mumbled an evasive answer about 'work'. The interrogator slammed his fist down again on the table. 'Lies!' he shouted. 'You will tell me the truth! Why do you have maps of northern Italy? You are a spy, no?'

'I am a travelling salesman,' replied Combe.

'Your accent is very strange,' said the interrogator. 'I think that you are a foreign spy.' Combe glanced to the left, where a clock was fastened to the wall. It read 10.55am. 'I told you, I'm from the Tyrol,' replied Combe calmly. He knew that if he could keep up this act for even a few more hours, Boyd and the others might yet make it. Even if they were discovered missing from the castle in a few minutes' time, it would take time for the wheels of Italian bureaucracy to start to turn.

The interrogator sighed deeply and folded his arms.

'We shoot spies in Italy,' he said casually.[12]

*

At Vincigliata Castle, General Neame and the remaining officers waited nervously in their dining room for the 11.00am check. The dummies had all been removed from the beds and hidden in the chapel. They had five minutes until the duty officer would appear through one of the gates in the white wall. Neame was racking his brains trying to think of some way that he could keep up the pretence of a full house with six warm bodies missing. Word from one of the watchers arrived that the Italian officer had been spotted.

'It's the new boy,' said Brigadier Todhunter, glancing out of the window at the approaching officer. The very young Second Lieutenant Solera, really still a teenager and new to the castle and the ways of its prisoners, was strutting across the courtyard.

'I say, Ted,' said Neame to Todhunter. 'Let's make him welcome. We'll invite him in to elevenses. Have the other chaps walk in and out of the dining room to give the impression of a full house.' Neame dashed towards the door to head off Solera with an invitation to join him for a cup of Bovril while Todhunter quickly outlined the plan to the others. They all prayed that Neame could keep Solera busy in conversation so that he didn't pay as much attention to the business of actually counting the prisoners.[13]

The mantle clock began to strike. Todhunter glanced in its direction. 'Eleven hundred hours,' he muttered under his breath.

'Right chaps,' he said, looking at Brigadier Stirling and General Gambier-Parry, 'better pray to God that this works.'

*

Young Second Lieutenant Solera didn't stand a chance. Within seconds of entering the prisoners' dining room he was buttonholed by General Neame and Brigadier Todhunter and had a steaming cup of Bovril thrust into his hands. An affable young man who was surprised and flattered by the attention of a gaggle of aged military heroes, Solera failed to spot that he was being deceived. While he chatted away with Neame and Todhunter, discussing the many problems with the castle, the other senior officers milled around the dining room, constantly popping out, changing their clothing slightly, then reappearing again. The effect was of a full house, and Solera fell for the ruse hook, line and sinker.[14] He failed to do his job correctly, something he would later be taken to task over by Captain Pederneschi, but he was really no more than a callow youth. Departing fifteen minutes later, he reported that all British officers were present and correct.

Neame couldn't believe his luck. Unless some misfortune befell them, the missing officers should remain undetected by the Italians until evening.

*

Aboard the Milan to Como train Brigadiers Hargest and Miles sat in a compartment staring at the passing countryside. The sun was shining, which after the wet and stormy conditions of the past two days seemed to be a sign of good times to come. Hargest and Miles were both exhausted and eternally grateful to be finally sitting down and able to rest. Hargest's hip had been causing him some discomfort for hours. Both men slowly started to regain their strength. But a worry remained hanging over them like the Sword of Damocles – ready to end their pleasant sojourn and cast them back into prison. They had no idea if a reception committee awaited them at Como station.[15] It was past 11.00am, so they had to assume that their absence had been reported by now at the castle. How long it took the Italians to alert railway stations was anyone's guess, but Hargest and Miles knew that it wouldn't take long for orders and descriptions to be sent by telephone and teleprinter from *Carabinieri* headquarters in Florence. The train was due to arrive at Como in about half an hour. There was no possibility of jumping from the train before it reached its destination – Hargest certainly couldn't contemplate such a drastic measure with his hip. There was also the nagging worry of what had become of Air Vice-Marshal Boyd and Brigadier Combe. If they had fallen into Italian hands, perhaps they had already been identified and an alert sounded? Hargest watched as Reg Miles slowly peeled a hard-boiled egg brought with him from the castle. Hargest found that his appetite had left him.

Five carriages back Owen Boyd felt much the same as Hargest and Miles. As far as he was concerned, he was the only one of the four who had successfully escaped from Milan. He'd definitely seen John Combe get picked up, and Hargest and Miles had never arrived. And like the two New Zealanders he kept glancing nervously at his wristwatch – the talismanic time of 11.00am had been surpassed, meaning he was now a hunted man. He had to be. He couldn't conceive of how six officers could remain unaccounted for following the morning check at the castle. Boyd stared out of the window, noting how the little train was ascending into the mountains. The scenery was stunning, but it was hard to concentrate. He closed his eyes and tried to doze, but even though utterly exhausted he found that he was too pent-up to switch off. A nagging knot of tension deep in the pit of his stomach refused to leave him, and Boyd knew that he was still in immense danger. Like the others, he kept glancing at his watch. It was all a question of time and Boyd was starting to think that he didn't have quite enough.

CHAPTER 16

Boy Scouting

'I was threatened several times with shooting.'

Brigadier John Combe

Back in Milan, Brigadier John Combe's interrogation continued at police headquarters. He was roughly searched again, with many of his clothes taken off him, but by a miracle the police still failed to locate both his compass and his best maps.[1]

The tone of the questioning was becoming more hostile and violent, with some pushing and shoving interspersed with the threats. On several occasions Combe was actually threatened with execution if he failed to reveal all. Though rattled by the experience, Combe had resolved to hold out as long as he could to give his friends a chance before revealing his rank and prisoner of war status. He felt that the Italians were bluffing – though there was a small part of him that was beginning to doubt this assessment. The police knew something was wrong, but they had yet to establish he was an escaped POW, probably owing to his age. Of course, Combe expected the hammer to fall any time after the 11.00am check at the castle. But miraculously, so far his connection with Vincigliata had not been established. For now, Combe remained evasive, his basic Italian and taciturn demeanour confounding his inquisitors.[2]

*

'Heads up, Reg,' murmured Jim Hargest, tapping Miles's boot with his own. Miles had nodded off, but came to with a start. 'Como,' said

Hargest, nodding towards the window. The train had slowed to a crawl and was trundling the last few hundred yards along the line into the pretty town that bordered the stunning Alpine lake of the same name. Both men leaned forward in the bright sunshine that streamed through the window and tried to see the approaching platform. It was a make-or-break moment.

'We'll soon know,' whispered Miles. Then the train pulled alongside the platform, coming slowly to a halt. The New Zealanders studied the platform intently – it was almost empty. Hargest had been expecting police officers and soldiers waiting to arrest them, but there was no one. Either the alert order had been slow to leave the castle, or by some miraculous means the six officers had not yet been missed. The two brigadiers looked at each other in amazement, a feeling of relief washing over them.

Hargest and Miles stood, taking down their luggage from the overhead racks, and shuffled out into the corridor. Miles headed for an exit towards the front, while Hargest opened a carriage door at the rear. It was an elementary precaution to avoid both men being immediately picked up, should their worst fears be realised and the authorities be lying in wait for them. Gingerly, both men opened their carriage doors and stepped down on to the platform, mingling with the other disembarking passengers. Miles and Hargest stared down the length of the platform. No police or soldiers could be seen. Hargest glanced at his watch – it read 11.55am. 'Almost an hour since the morning roll call at the castle,' he thought. He strolled over to Miles, who was lighting a cigarette.

'I'll walk up to the gate and watch for the others leaving,' he said under his breath. 'You walk the length of the train and see if they get off.' Miles nodded, picked up his case and started to walk back down the platform beside the stopped train, glancing into compartments and watching people alighting. Hargest moved over to the exit gate and stood waiting, in case Boyd and Combe showed up.[3]

*

As the train had coasted into Como station, Owen Boyd had stood up, pulled on his flat cap and picked up his suitcase. He too was worried about a nasty reception committee waiting for him so he decided to take the precaution of getting off the carriage from the side opposite to the main platform. The train had actually run into a siding with platforms on either side.[4] He didn't realise that on the other side of the train Reg Miles was at that moment looking for him.

*

Hargest and Miles could only linger for a few minutes – any longer and they might begin to look suspicious. There was also the genuine fear that the alarm might yet go out from the castle, and the last place they needed to be when the searches began was a public train station. Miles walked over to Hargest and together they surrendered their tickets and passed out of the station without incident. What had happened to Boyd and Combe was anyone's guess, though they evidently had not caught the Milan to Como train. Perhaps they would come up on the next one; perhaps they had been caught … Such concerns had to be pushed out of the minds of the two New Zealand brigadiers. The important thing now was their self-preservation and successful escape.

'It's about five miles to Chiasso on the frontier,' said Hargest to Miles as they walked out of Como's red-brick Victorian Lago station towards the famous lake. As they strolled down towards the waterfront in bright sunshine, it was hard to believe that there was a war on. The massive lake stretched away before them, framed by green-covered hills and the Alps behind. The dome of the 14th-century Como Cathedral dominated the town, surrounded on the waterfront by terracotta- and light yellow-coloured buildings giving an impression of prosperous peace. People bustled about, and the cafés and restaurants were full. The war had yet to touch this corner of Europe. Still wearing their greatcoats, Hargest and Miles were soon sweating in the mountain air but keen to crack on to Chiasso.

*

After walking along part of the waterfront, Hargest and Miles branched off through Como town, heading towards the road to Chiasso. They passed several soldiers and policemen without anyone showing any signs of recognition or challenging them. Hargest unfortunately lost his wine when the handle of his suitcase snapped once again and the bottle broke. Soon the two brigadiers were out in the countryside, following the road as it grew steeper and steeper. The country was dotted with pretty villas and gardens. Their plan was to follow the road most of the way to Chiasso then go south up on to the San Fermo Pass, before striking due west.[5] Once the villas ended and the highway only passed through wooded countryside, the two escapers decided to get off the road as soon as possible so that they wouldn't look suspicious. They were incongruously dressed for the season and carrying hand luggage rather than mountain rucksacks. And they knew that the border area would be crawling with soldiers and police – they had passed several groups already.

*

Owen Boyd was also taking the road to Chiasso, though he was way behind Hargest and Miles having hung around at Como station for a while. His intention was to skirt the country close to the Swiss frontier until he found a railway line that crossed it, and then, hobo-style, jump a train and ride to freedom.[6]

*

'Stand up!' said the interrogator in a harsh manner. Brigadier Combe stood as ordered. Another policeman replaced the handcuffs, before Combe was led from the interrogation room down a long corridor and outside into the bright sunshine. He had already been interrogated several times, but he had not divulged his real name even though threatened with execution.[7] Outside the back door of Milan Police Station was a black police truck. The driver unlocked the door and forced Combe into the hot and stuffy interior, connecting

234

the handcuffs that he wore to a stout chain on the hard bench seat in order to prevent escape. A couple of young Italian men were already shackled inside. Once they were moving Combe asked one of the other prisoners where they were going.

'San Vittore Prison,' replied the man sullenly, before the guard who was riding in the back with the prisoners told them to be quiet. San Vittore was the main civilian prison in Milan.[8] The fact Combe was being sent there rather than to a military establishment indicated that the authorities clearly had no idea of his true identity. They seemed to think that he was some sort of common criminal or perhaps a black marketeer or smuggler, judging by his false papers and maps. Or, perhaps, a spy.[9] Combe determined to keep up his vague act until he was sure enough time had elapsed that his travelling companions should have crossed the frontier. Combe reckoned on at least two more days of discomfort in the hands of the Italian police.[10]

*

The road to Chiasso was steep and grew steeper the closer Hargest and Miles got to the town. Finally, after a hot and exhausting trek, Miles spotted a small white stone set beside the road that read '*Chiasso 1km*'. At this point the two New Zealanders left the road and headed into the countryside. They crossed the railway line that ran back to Como and then started up the hill again. After a while they came to a deep gully that ran under the road. It was shaded with much foliage and Hargest and Miles dived gratefully into it, climbing on for a further half a mile under excellent cover.[11]

'Let's have a break,' suggested Hargest, wiping sweat from his brow with his handkerchief. He and Miles sat down in the shade to rest and eat some of their meagre rations. They shared a tin of Red Cross bully beef and washed it down with their little remaining water.[12] They examined their maps. The hike was proceeding according to plan. Hargest glanced up at the wooded hill that loomed above them.

'Right, Reg, let's crack on,' he said, picking up his suitcase. Together, the two escapers started to climb once again. After much effort, they made it to the summit and were rewarded with a stunning view. They could see Lake Como far below, the sun glinting off its glassy surface. They could see the funicular railway running from the lake up to the small mountain village of Brunate. Turning around, they could see down on to the flat Lombardy Plain across which the train from Milan had brought them. The men turned back again and stared in the direction of freedom once more. To reach Switzerland they would have to traverse a deep valley.

'Looks like home,' said Miles as he stared at the snow-covered Alps that loomed like a great granite wall in the distance. Hargest agreed that the view was strongly reminiscent of New Zealand, and it reassured both men.[13] The steep climb up to the top of the hill had exhausted them, so they lingered at the summit to rest and drink in the views. They looked into the valley that they would have to cross and could discern a road and a railway line running towards the Swiss town of Lugano. They could also see what appeared to be a fence running through the snow, bisected by the railway. It was a strange moment to be able to see the path to freedom laid out so starkly – it looked deceptively simple to just cross the valley and climb the steep mountain on the other side and pass through that fence, which from their current position, was a tiny black line again the white snow. But a closer inspection revealed that there was more to the frontier than just a fence – little buildings could be seen, buildings that Hargest and Miles took to be barracks for Italian frontier troops. As they progressed with their hike, they would encounter more evidence of defensive measures and troop activity in the valley and mountainsides along the frontier, making movement increasingly risky.

*

Air Vice-Marshal Boyd worked his way up the road towards Chiasso before deciding to follow the railway line that, according to his maps, ran over the frontier into Switzerland. Eventually, and after some difficulty, he closed up on a stretch of line that was less than a mile from the frontier and ducked down into deep undergrowth to wait for dark and observe train movements while plotting how to jump a locomotive. He would spend the rest of the day dozing fitfully, nibbling on his remaining rations and watching.[14] He was tantalisingly close to the frontier, but he knew that any precipitate action might lead to his immediate recapture, so he would wait until dark to make his move. Hargest and Miles had opted for the less direct route, swinging on a long and arduous detour into the high mountains near Chiasso. While the New Zealanders trekked, Boyd lay in silence behind some bushes, trainspotting and conserving his energy for the final push to freedom.

*

Hargest and Miles stumbled and crouched as they worked their way cautiously along the high ridgeline above the valley. There was little cover and they were concerned about running into an Italian patrol. The evidence of a military presence was all around them, with small collections of buildings, fences and trenches on both sides of the valley. Two shabbily dressed men wearing ordinary shoes and carrying old suitcases would have a hard time explaining their business in the high Alpine country should they be challenged.

By 3.00pm both men were exhausted by the terrain and the stress and decided to rest once again. Hargest took out his bricklayer's trowel from his case and helped Miles scrape out a couple of holes in the ground into which they lay, covering themselves with dead leaves. It was the best that they could do on the largely open ridgeline. They tried to sleep, but regardless of their physical exhaustion, neither man could.[15]

*

About 4.00pm, Hargest and Miles rose from their shallow trenches, dead leaves festooning their clothes and hair. Though still very tired, they decided to push on. They crossed a deserted road and headed for a higher wooded mountain beyond. As they were walking up they had a sudden start when they heard the sounds of men's voices up ahead. Hargest and Miles dived behind some bushes and crouched low. Fearing a patrol, they listened carefully. There was a sound of hammering mingled in with the voices. Hargest crept forward cautiously for a better look. A group of men were making repairs to an electricity pole.[16] Hargest crept back to Miles and reported what he had found. Though the men were civilians, the New Zealanders decided that it was probably unwise to be seen in case some loyal Italian should report their presence to the authorities. Creeping off, the brigadiers gave the working party a wide berth, conscious of every snapping twig and rustle of dead leaves as they trod.

*

At Vincigliata Castle, everything was progressing as normal. The Italians still had no inkling that a major escape had occurred the night before. The routine of the castle remained unchanged. Already General Neame had had some discussions with the remaining senior officers about the possibility of trying to fool the Italians for a second night running by placing the dummies back into the six empty beds. Neame was all for it, though some of the others thought that the British were pushing their luck.

The next problem to arise concerned Air Vice-Marshal Boyd. He was scheduled to have an Italian lesson with the castle's interpreter at 6.00pm. Before escaping, Boyd had had the good sense to write a note to the interpreter cancelling his lesson due to ill health, and had given this to Neame to pass on in his absence. Hopefully, the interpreter or one of the Italian officers would not follow up the note by visiting Boyd to check on his health. At 4.30pm, Neame had the note sent in and hoped for the best.[17]

*

At the moment Boyd's note was being sent to the Italian interpreter at the castle, the Air Vice-Marshal was still crouched behind some bushes on an elevated position above the railway line that ran into Switzerland. After some desultory attempts at sleeping, and a feed, Boyd had started carefully observing the trains that rumbled up the line towards the north.[18] The locomotives were hauling goods wagons into Switzerland, presenting Boyd with the beginnings of a daring plan. He noticed after a while that each train stopped about half a mile from the frontier. When the third train under observation had done this, Boyd had exclaimed his surprise. But he couldn't work out why it was happening. The trains would loiter in a stationary position for exactly five minutes (Boyd timed them carefully with his watch) before piling on steam once more and chuffing off to the frontier. During those five minutes no one appeared to be checking the trains; they just stopped. Perhaps the track was defective, thought Boyd, mystified.

Continued observation of further trains over the next couple of hours confirmed the pattern. Boyd realised that he could use the five-minute stop to break cover and make his way down to the track and hitch an unauthorised lift in one of the goods wagons at the rear of the train. He had noted with delight that once a train was moving again it didn't appear to stop at the frontier, but rather steamed straight through in the direction of Lugano.[19] It all looked too easy. Boyd glanced at the sky and then at his watch. He would wait until it was dark and then make his move.

*

Soon after avoiding the party of workmen in the woods, Hargest and Miles almost blundered into a man who was chopping wood outside a small farmhouse. As the two escapers hurried past, the man stopped what he was doing and leaned on his axe, staring at them. Moving quickly on, Hargest and Miles started to climb the steep, wooded mountain. 'Whenever I looked back, I could see the axeman watching us intently,'[20] wrote Hargest. It was not a good feeling.

Once deeper into the woods that covered the mountain slopes, they were no longer under observation, but again the two New Zealanders were exhausted. They flopped down on a patch of shady grass to catch their breath. After so many months of captivity, hiking in the mountains was proving very challenging, and Hargest's hip was aching almost constantly. Suddenly, a gunshot blasted out.[21] Hargest and Miles involuntarily ducked, then scrambled behind some trees. It had come from the direction of Como. Had they been reported and were soldiers now coming for them? The brigadiers dared not break cover lest they be fired at, so they waited, panting in the heat, their hearts fit to burst out of their chests. Silence. Nothing. No shouted commands or the sounds of men coming up the trail. But then the mountain stillness was broken by more gunfire. It seemed to be a little way off, and both brigadiers had seen enough action to know when they were being directly fired at. This was *not* one of those occasions. Perhaps troops were exercising nearby or hunters were out in the woods. Hargest let out a long breath and looked at Miles, who shook his head ruefully. Slowly, the men stood up, brushed the leaf litter from their coats and, picking up their suitcases, resumed their weary ascent.

Hargest checked his compass. They were now southeast of Chiasso station. From their lofty position hundreds of feet above they could see the station clearly. Little did they know that not far from the station lurked Owen Boyd, who continued with his lonely trainspotting. Hargest and Miles's plan was to continue round to the southwest. They moved on to another long ridge. Going slowly, Hargest calculated that they needed to continue for about two miles to bring them south of the border town of Chiasso.

At 5.00pm Hargest and Miles halted south of Chiasso for another rest and a meal break. There was some man-made cover available – some old abandoned slit trenches half-full of leaves were as inviting to the exhausted brigadiers as feather beds, and they slid down grate-fully inside them. They ate some more rations, but they were by now dehydrated after the long climb, and had run out of water. Hargest had a single orange from the castle, which he shared with Miles, but it did little to slake their thirst.[22]

*

At Vincigliata castle an old peasant, one of several who tended the grounds outside the walls, led a horse and cart through the outer garden gate, the same gate that the prisoners had found miraculously and mysteriously unlocked the night before. The peasant left the gate wide open, and a guard was sent down to close and lock it. The *Carabiniere*, a rifle slung over his shoulder, sauntered down from the castle drive with a set of large iron keys held in one hand. As he started to pull the tall iron gates shut he suddenly noticed something out of the corner of one eye. Walking over to investigate, the sentry was mystified to see that someone had left a coil of rope tucked up against the wall beside the gate. He pulled some out and inspected it in the failing light. It was not regular rope, but appeared to be made out of linen bedsheets sewn together. Then he realised what he was looking at. Quickly scooping up the coil of rope, the sentry trotted back towards the castle.[23]

A few minutes later the sentry presented himself before Captain Pederneschi's desk and saluted.

'Well, what is it?' asked Pederneschi in a bored tone.

'I found this, sir,' said the sentry, placing the coil of rope on the desktop.

Pederneschi quickly sat forward in his chair and examined the rope.

'Where did you find this, private?' demanded Pederneschi, his eyes flashing with excitement. After the sentry explained, Pederneschi jumped to his feet, putting on his cap and starting for the door. He gave orders to fetch a sergeant and more men, and Mickey, the dog left behind by Lieutenant Ricciardi. Pederneschi's face was set in a determined grimace. Something was going on and he was going to

241

get to the bottom of it. He paused, opened his leather holster and took out his Beretta pistol. He extracted the magazine, checked it, and then slammed it back into place before replacing the pistol in its holster. 'Come on!' he barked at the sentry before marching off towards the gate, his jackboots drumming ominously on the flag-stoned driveway.

CHAPTER 17

Mickey Blows the Gaff

'The next moment the world was full of the sound of bells. We fled.'

Brigadier James Hargest

Within minutes of leaving his office, the castle's stern security officer, Captain Pederneschi, accompanied by a small section of guards, had descended on where the sentry had discovered the coil of rope. Pederneschi stood contemplating the scene. The sun was going down, casting evening shadows across the castle and its grounds. It looked as though the British prisoners had made another attempt to climb over the outer wall of the fortress. But Pederneschi was confused – none had been reported absent at the 11.00am check. It seemed inconceivable that any prisoner could have emulated General O'Connor's daring escalade – Pederneschi had put paid to any further such attempts by increasing the number of wall sentries, wiring them in on their wooden catwalk, and by installing the carefully watched 'line of death' on the inner side of the wall. Pederneschi ordered the section of guards to fan out around the outside walls of the castle and search the ground for any further clues. In the meantime, the great white dog Mickey had wandered off and was sniffing around. Suddenly, Mickey began pawing at the ground and barking, his tail flapping wildly.

Pederneschi stamped over to the dog. With his front paws Mickey was trying to dig, whimpering and barking as he did so.[1] Pederneschi grabbed the dog by its collar and wrenched him aside. As he pulled the dog, Pederneschi stepped sideways, and suddenly there was a hollow sound beneath one of his jackboots. Pederneschi tapped the ground again with his boot, and the hollow sound was there again. He immediately crouched down and ran his hand roughly over the surface. Something wasn't right. The vegetation came away revealing a painted wooden board. Jamming his fingers around the join Pederneschi pulled up the board revealing a dark hole. There was a sound as well – the faint sound of an electric buzzer.[2]

'Sergeant, a torch, quick!' shouted Pederneschi. The sergeant ran over and handed over a small handheld flashlight. Pederneschi switched on the light to reveal a deep, wood-lined shaft and ladder. 'A tunnel!' blurted out Pederneschi in genuine amazement. By now the other sentries had rushed over and were all peering into the hole with slack-jawed amazement.

'Get down that hole,' Pederneschi ordered the sergeant, 'and find out where it comes out.'[3] He handed the torch to the sergeant, who gingerly climbed down and disappeared.

'You two, stand guard here until I relieve you,' said Pederneschi to two of the sentries. 'The rest of you follow me. I have to see the commandant.'

*

'They've found the tunnel!' yelled Lord Ranfurly as he ran into the dining room. There was a considerable commotion out in the courtyard as Italian soldiers, bayonets fixed to their rifles, gathered outside the chapel.

To the assembled officers it was naturally a grievous blow, but they had some housekeeping to take care of before the Italians descended mob-handed to search the POW accommodation. The buzzer that Captain Pederneschi had heard inside the tunnel was not supposed to be active, Neame having ordered Sergeant Bain to disconnect it after the escape. But somehow it had accidentally been reconnected and had since gone haywire, ringing continuously.[4]

'Have the boys burn the dummies,' ordered General Neame.

Over the next few minutes the dummies were taken back out of the six empty beds and the heads thrust into fires in the kitchen and other rooms by the orderlies.[5]

Neame glanced at the clock above the mantelpiece.

'Twenty-two hours, gentlemen. We've given them a 22-hour head start.' It was 6.00pm. It was an amazing achievement under the circumstances and far better than they could have hoped for. But the loss of the tunnel was a terrible blow. Plans had been afoot for another six officers to escape through it.

*

On receipt of the news of a tunnel from Captain Pederneschi, Commandant Tranquille ordered that a roll call of the prisoners be taken immediately, preparatory to a thorough search of the castle for contraband and escape equipment. Pederneschi was pleased – he knew that all prisoners had been accounted for at 11.00 that morning, and the sentries had reported no incidents on the walls or gates. It looked as though Pederneschi had foiled a major escape attempt. As he strode over towards the keep beside Tranquille, he had a slightly cruel smile fixed to his face.

Second Lieutenant Solera was detailed to assemble the prisoners. He approached Neame wearing a triumphant smile, believing, like Pederneschi, that a major plot had just been foiled. 'Do you know what Mussolini said, General?' opined Solera proudly. 'He said that the best general was the one who had his troops on the field fifteen minutes before his opponent.'[6]

The sergeant sent down the tunnel had emerged in the lift lobby. When the officers inspected, they discovered the hole into the chapel, and the chapel piled ten feet high with spoil. It was almost inconceivable that such an excavation could have been carried out right under their noses. Guards were posted on the tunnel exit.

At 6.30pm a head count was taken. Second Lieutenant Solera, who earlier in the day had reported all prisoners present and correct now stood to attention before the commandant. His face was flushed with embarrassment.

'Well?' asked Tranquille, his hawk face casting a balefully triumphant glance around the dining room, where Neame and the other senior officers had assembled.

'Six missing, sir,' said Solera quietly, hardly daring to look the commandant in the eye.

'What!' exploded Captain Pederneschi angrily. He then proceeded to count all of the prisoners, including the orderlies. But he soon realised that some distinctive faces were missing. When he returned to Tranquille, Pederneschi's face was ashen.

'Six *are* gone, Commandant.'

'Who?' spat Tranquille.

'O'Connor, Carton de Wiart, Boyd, Hargest, Miles and Combe.'

'Search the castle from top to bottom!' shouted Tranquille. 'Captain, see me in my office immediately.'

As Pederneschi turned to follow Tranquille out of the room he caught a glimpse of General Neame's face. It had split into a huge grin.

*

Owen Boyd looked at his watch in the fast disappearing light: 6.30pm. Another goods train was puffing slowly past his concealed position, a long column of black smoke billowing into the air, contrasting starkly with the brilliant white snow that gleamed in the last of the sunlight on the upper mountains. Boyd watched closely as the squeal of brakes met his ears once again, and the train ground to a halt at exactly the same position as all the others. It would be dark soon, and once the sun had set Boyd would make his move and catch the next train to make the mysterious five-minute stop. He glanced around the countryside but could see no one. It was a good sign.

*

After hiking all night and all of the next day, by 7.00pm Generals O'Connor and Carton de Wiart were exhausted and looking for somewhere to shelter. If anyone asked, they were simply elderly Austrian tourists enjoying a walking holiday in Northern Italy. O'Connor spotted a farmhouse in the evening twilight and decided to try his luck. He rapped on the door. It was opened by an elderly Italian peasant, who was surprised by the strange foreign visitors, but clearly also honoured by their visit. O'Connor, who spoke good conversational Italian after his many hours of dutiful study at the castle (conducted with the express purpose of aiding his escape), asked the farmer whether he could put them up for the night. The farmer showed them to his cowshed, where a few milking cows were corralled, and O'Connor and De Wiart settled themselves upon straw beside the animal stalls. They were about to break out their meagre rations when the farmer reappeared and invited them into the main house for a meal.

The farmhouse was filled with three generations of the family, and the two escapers were treated as honoured guests. The farmer's wife produced fresh bread and heaps of pasta, all washed down with the local red wine. The conversation was lively, with the Italians warm and boisterous.

Suddenly, the farmhouse door was wrenched open and in stepped an Italian soldier. O'Connor immediately ceased chattering and De Wiart's heart sank. But then the soldier smiled and was soon embracing and kissing family members. He was one of the farmer's sons, home on leave. O'Connor 'rose magnificently to the occasion', remembered De Wiart, 'broke into voluble Italian and jabbered away to the whole family as to the manner born, whilst I confined myself to eating and inwardly blessing the more studious Dick.'[7]

*

'Someone's coming!' whispered Brigadier Miles. 'Hide!' Moving quickly, he and Hargest burrowed down under the leaves inside the trenches where they had been resting.[8] They could hear men's voices close by. Then footsteps. The two New Zealanders barely dared to breath, screwing their eyes shut and almost gagging on the smell of musty, rotting vegetation. After a few minutes, silence returned, with just the noise of birds in the trees looking for roosts before the twilight. Hargest gingerly put up his head over the lip of his trench.

'All clear, Reg,' he whispered to Miles.

Crawling out of their temporary hides, the two brigadiers began walking along the ridge. They had not gone far when a siren sounded, its shrill klaxon call loud enough to freeze blood. It gave Hargest and Miles a bad start, until they realised that it was probably a factory whistle down in the valley indicating the end of the working day rather than anything to do with frontier defence.[9] By now, their nerves were beginning to get more than a little frayed by the cat-and-mouse game that they were playing.

Eventually they reached the end of the woods and were confronted by a deep valley. Hargest glanced compulsively at his watch. 'Nineteen thirty hours,' he said to Miles, who nodded. The valley had virtually no cover whatsoever. On the other side the ground reared up into an almost vertical wooded hillside. Ominously, both men could discern rifle pits on the far side, the top of the range of hills having been cleared of vegetation.[10]

'I'm terribly thirsty,' said Miles. 'I can see a water hole down the bottom.' He pointed to where the last rays of the sun glinted off a patch of water. Neither man had any water left and they were suffering badly.[11]

'Look over there,' said Hargest, pointing into the distance where the occasional wooden hut could be made out. 'Looks like a frontier patrol.' As Hargest and Miles watched, a column of tiny figures could be discerned marching across the Alpine landscape and meeting another orderly party.

'Which mountain do you think that one is?' asked Miles, pointing in the direction of the massive wooded hill across the valley. Hargest took out a map and examined it carefully.

'I'd say it's Olimpino. The frontier fence should run behind it.'[12]

'Well,' sighed Miles, 'we'll have to wait for dark before we try and get through those patrol areas.'[13] Hargest agreed and the two men settled down to wait. Time passed slowly.

*

Owen Boyd glanced at the new train as it arrived. It was almost completely dark now and the train was just a darker shape moving against the valley floor. The only light came from the footplate, where the boiler fire glowed warmly. As predicted, the train slowed and then came to a halt exactly as before. Boyd didn't hesitate. He jumped up and started down the short hillside as fast as he dared and charged up the railway tracks to the back of the train, where a single red caboose lantern glowed like a malevolent eye.

He moved along the train to the second-to-last truck, conscious of the noise of his footsteps on the gravel beside the rails. He turned and looked behind him several times as he moved forward. Moving fast, he climbed up on to a foot rail and started fiddling with the door release. It was stuck. Boyd cursed. He knew that he had only a couple of minutes before the train started shunting forward. Up ahead towards the engine he heard someone laughing, the noise carrying on the still night air. Holding himself steady with one arm, his legs aching as he balanced on the foot rail, Boyd pulled at the door release with all his might. It gave with a harsh metallic clunk that seemed loud enough to warrant investigation from the footplate. Gingerly, he ran the door back a few inches on its rail and quickly swung inside. He pulled the door shut just as the train gave a lurch, the wheels and bogeys spinning on the shiny rails before taking the weight of the trucks. Then the train was moving, the engine settling into a steady rhythm. Boyd crouched by the door, hardly believing his luck. He'd made it.[14]

*

The first stage in the process of apprehending the escapers began soon after the discovery of the tunnel at Vincigliata Castle. All *Carabinieri*, army and police commands were notified of the escape by teleprinter messages, and the alert was further disseminated down to individual posts by telephone or face-to-face meetings. Steps were immediately taken to strengthen the frontier defences with Switzerland and France, and search parties mobilised to begin scouring the countryside.

For the first time since North Africa, the Germans were involved with the senior officer prisoners. Though German forces would not move into Northern Italy in force until September, Italy was an important supply base for German forces in North Africa, meaning that there were many units in the country. The most important was *Generalfeldmarschall* Albert Kesselring's *Luftflotte* 2, which controlled several air bases and air force ground units throughout the region. Soon teleprinters at Kesselring's headquarters and subsidiary units were chattering like machine guns as a strongly worded alert was quickly spread:

> On the evening of 29 March 1943, six captured British generals escaped from a prisoner of war camp near Florence. They speak German well. It is possible that they will try acts of sabotage during their escape and will appear in German or Italian uniforms or in civilian clothing for this purpose.[15]

*

A sea of twinkling lights across the valley transfixed Hargest and Miles. While Italy was under blackout regulations, neutral Switzerland suffered no such rules and Chiasso and its surrounding villages were brightly lit. It had been a very long time since the two New Zealanders had seen such a sight.

By now, their desperate thirst had driven the brigadiers from their lofty perch and down into the darkened valley in search of water.

When they arrived at the water hole, Miles took out his enamel mug and dipped it in. 'When he raised it,' Hargest recalled, 'something scrambled out – a frog! The hole was stagnant.'[16] They were now in an exposed position, making a lot of noise stumbling through the rocky valley floor and well lit by the lights of Chiasso.

'We won't avoid detection for long in this light and quiet,' whispered Miles fearfully. 'Let us go back to the trenches and hope for better luck tomorrow.'

'But we agreed to go on,' replied Hargest. 'Besides, we can't hang on for another day without water.' They agreed to continue. The only water that was to be had was small puddles formed in animal footprints – the two brigadiers pressed their faces into the mud and sucked up this stagnant water gratefully.[17]

*

O'Connor and De Wiart wandered back to the farmer's cowshed tired, stomachs full of good home-cooked food and pleasantly mellow after several glasses of wine. They crashed out on the soft straw. De Wiart's badly blistered toe was hurting, but he tried to push it out of his mind.

'You know, Carton, I haven't worked out exactly how far we've walked,' said O'Connor, tugging a map out of his rucksack. After contemplating it for some time he looked up.

'I reckon we've covered 33 miles, or thereabouts,' announced O'Connor.[18]

'Damned good show! And more so as we are lugging these blessed things about,' said De Wiart, pointing with one boot at his 25lb rucksack.

If they could keep up this kind of pace they should make the Swiss frontier in about seven days.

*

Aboard the goods train, everything was going to plan. Boyd crouched in the dark, the train steaming along slowly as it headed for the frontier. But suddenly Boyd felt the train begin to slow down once more. With much squealing and juddering the train came to a stop. Boyd's mind was a riot of emotions: perhaps they would now check the wagons at the frontier – if that was the case he was sunk. Then, with another jolt, the train started to shunt backwards! He could feel it change direction on the track before it came to another halt. It felt as though the train had backed into a siding.[19]

Boyd's ears strained to hear what was going on outside. There were some metallic clanking sounds and bumps, followed by silence. Then the train started up again, moving off noisily in the direction of Switzerland – the problem was Boyd's wagon didn't move. He realised with growing horror that his part of the train had been uncoupled and left in a siding.[20] He cursed his bad luck. The frontier was only a few hundred yards away.

Boyd remained crouched beside the door trying to decide what to do. Perhaps the next train along would pick up the uncoupled wagons; or perhaps they would be left on the siding all night. He was trapped like a rat in a barrel if any checks were carried out on the wagons. For the time being, he decided to wait. He would see what happened before attempting anything drastic.

*

'Christ!' hissed Hargest, flattening himself against the snowy hillside. Reg Miles dived down beside him. Hargest pointed ahead in the darkness. There was a sentry box. The two brigadiers had almost blundered into it in their exhaustion.

'Wait here, I'll have a look,' whispered Hargest, before setting off, bent double. He skirted around the box, but couldn't see a sentry. It was deserted. Hargest walked over and peeked inside. Empty.[21]

The two brigadiers sat on their haunches for a few minutes, trying to get their bearings in the darkness. According to their understanding, the frontier was on the other side of the hill upon which they sat. Hargest looked up the steep incline. There was something ahead, some distance behind the sentry box. They moved forward to examine it. A large pole was cemented into the ground. 'I lay and looked upward to get a view against the light of the sky,' wrote Hargest. 'At once it dawned on me – *this* was the frontier.'[22] It was a stout fence, twelve feet high, angled on the steep hillside. The top was hung with bells, which any vibration would set off.[23] Hargest reached out and gently shook the fence. The bells jangled loudly.

Hargest turned to Miles, who was staring transfixed at the obstacle, as if in a daze. 'Quick,' whispered Hargest, 'give me the wire cutters.'[24]

*

Air Vice-Marshal Boyd had made up his mind. Simply sitting inside a freight wagon in the hope that something positive may eventually happen was not his style. A man of action, Boyd had decided that if he was going to cross the frontier, he would have to do it himself. The train gambit had failed, so it was up to him to find an alternative way, whether that be jumping another train or emulating Hargest and Miles and walking out of Italy. The longer he spent inside the goods wagon, the greater the chance of discovery and capture.

Gingerly, Boyd slid the wagon door back a couple of inches and peered outside. Everything appeared quiet. Pushing the door back further on its rails, Boyd slid gently out and placed a foot on the step. Once fully out, he carefully slid the door back into place and locked it. Then he jumped down to the ground and crouched. He could detect no movement. Boyd stood up, and carrying his suitcase in one hand, he started to walk away. Suddenly, a torch was switched on, illuminating him. For a second he considered running, but the sentry's challenge in Italian made it clear that the man was armed.[25]

Boyd stood still, raising his arms above his head. The sentry approached, his boots crunching along the side of the railway track until he was only a few feet from Boyd. He pointed his rifle at Boyd, then asked him in Italian: 'Are you a British general?'[26]

Boyd was astonished. Clearly, the Italians had discovered the escapers' absence from the castle and had flashed an alert to all their police and military forces. Boyd sighed deeply and slowly nodded. He was only a quarter of a mile from the Swiss frontier.

*

Reg Miles fumbled in his bag for a pair of wire cutters that he had fortuitously liberated from a workman at the castle some weeks before. Jim Hargest waited impatiently by the fence until Miles had retrieved the cutters. Grasping the fence, Hargest pulled it as tight as he could to prevent it vibrating and setting off the row of bells mounted along its top. Miles came forward and dropped to his knees before the fence. Each man looked both ways along the length of the barrier. Hargest nodded and Miles positioned the jaws of the cutters over the first piece of wire. Then he squeezed. The stout wire suddenly parted with a loud click.[27] At that moment, it was the finest sound in the world.

CHAPTER 18

Night Crossing

'For the first time in many months a warm peace entered my soul.'

Brigadier James Hargest

'Get through!' gasped Brigadier Reg Miles slightly breathlessly as he pried back the cut pieces of the tall frontier fence. Jim Hargest crouched down and crawled through the opening, his clothes collecting a thick coating of snow as he went. Once he was through, Hargest turned back and extended his arms.

'The coats and bags, Reg,' he said, beckoning with his fingertips. Moving fast, Miles snatched up their greatcoats, rolling them into balls before passing them through, followed by their suitcases. Miles glanced behind him, then turned back to the fence and 'shot through like a rabbit.'[1] The two brigadiers jumped to their feet, scooped up their things, and dashed like mad up the steep slope into the thick fir trees above.

Once in among the trees Hargest and Miles sat down in the snow. All was quiet. Miles turned to Hargest, his face beaming in the moonlight.

'Jim, we're in Switzerland!'

Hargest stared back at him, his face also creased by a victorious smile. He uttered a little prayer of thankfulness. 'My heart was tight-packed with gratitude,' he later wrote.[2] Hargest opened his little suitcase and rummaged around for a few seconds before pulling out the 3oz bottle of rum that he'd brought with him from the castle. Miles did the same.

'To freedom, Reg,' said Hargest, clinking his bottle against Miles's.

'To freedom, Jim,'[3] repeated Miles, and then they both took a deep slug of rum, savouring the moment.

*

Brigadier John Combe was settling down to his first night behind bars as a common criminal at the San Vittore prison in Milan. The corridors echoed with shouts and the slamming of iron doors. His cell was a spartan affair, with just a simple bed and a bucket toilet. Most of his clothes and all of his equipment and supplies had been taken away from him. At his last interrogation, Combe had stuck resolutely to his cover story, and it was clear that the Italians had yet to join up the dots and link him with the escape from Vincigliata Castle. But worryingly, his police interrogators had warned him that he could expect a two- or three-year prison sentence for being in possession of false identity documents. Combe rolled over on his hard mattress and tried to sleep. He thought of his companions and wondered what had become of them.[4]

*

Air Vice-Marshal Owen Boyd had been taken to a *Carabinieri* post near the frontier after his apprehension in the rail yard. He was bitter at the nature of his recapture, literally within a stone's throw of freedom. His kit had been taken away from him, along with his maps and fake identity card, but Boyd had admitted who he was, showing his captors his identity tag as proof. He was told that on the following day he would be sent back to the castle for punishment.[5]

*

Generals O'Connor and Carton de Wiart remained in play, though they were stretched out on the straw of a farmer's cowshed just over 30 miles from the castle, snoring fitfully after their exhausting march.[6]

So far, they had encountered no problems and felt optimistic that they could reach their target, the border town of Tirano, in about seven days, *if* they could keep up the pace. Before O'Connor had fallen asleep he had reflected that all the hard endurance training that he and De Wiart had undertaken at the castle during the months of careful preparation was now paying off.[7] They were as fit as any men could expect to be in late middle age and psychologically conditioned to succeed.

*

Although Brigadiers Hargest and Miles had made it to Switzerland, they now had to ensure that they would remain. It was of paramount importance that they contact the British authorities. But the first stage was to give themselves up to the Swiss authorities and let the wheels of bureaucracy take over. This proved easier said than done. They were high up in the mountains in the night-time, with little idea of what lay ahead and absolutely no contacts in the country. Their first task would be to descend to a less challenging altitude and find some form of civilisation.

It was very dark as the two New Zealanders started to descend through the snow and trees. Branches constantly struck them as they fumbled and flailed through the forest in the poor light. Hargest slipped, sliding and rolling downhill, still clutching his suitcase, until his sudden descent was arrested painfully by a tree. Then Miles took a nasty tumble, in the process losing his cap in the snow.[8]

By now, the pair had been without water for too many hours, and both were dehydrated and exhausted. After a long climb they came to a path that led to a beautiful mountain stream. Hargest and Miles dropped to their knees beside the stream and using their hands as cups they greedily drank the freezing cold Alpine water before washing their faces and hands. They rested beside the stream, eating the last of the bully beef and bread from the castle and washing it down with their rum.

Instead of avoiding people, as they had been attempting to do since their escape from the castle, Hargest and Miles now had to actively seek out company, which felt strange to them. Ironically, it proved difficult to find anyone to surrender to at such a late hour. The first village they came to, Novazanno, was eerily quiet. The New Zealanders slaked their thirst once again, this time at the village fountain, before moving on. The occasional car drove past them, but there was little sign of life. To add to their woes, it began to rain.[9]

The temperature dropped with the rain and soon both men were shivering violently, wet and determined to find cover. After sheltering in a shed open to the weather on three sides, they were so cold that they couldn't stand it any longer and at 3.00am Swiss time (one hour behind Italy) they went into the nearest village and banged on the door of a restaurant, behind which the two escapers could hear singing.[10] There was no response. Hargest tried again, standing in the rain outside wearing every item of clothing that he possessed in a vain attempt to stay warm.

'Hello!' bellowed Hargest, in between hammering on the door. 'Can you hear me. We are Englishmen.' No response. He turned to Miles, who shrugged his shoulders.

'Hello, hello!' shouted Hargest again. 'We are English officers, can you open the door?'

The singing had stopped and Hargest could hear some low conversation from inside the restaurant. He sighed, and banged on the door again.

'We are two British generals who have escaped from Italy. We need shelter.'[11]

Hargest was on the point of giving up and trying elsewhere when someone drew back the bolts on the door and it was cautiously opened, light and warmth spilling out. Three Swiss men stood inside the doorway staring out at the bedraggled visitors before one of them broke the spell and gestured for them to come inside. Hargest and Miles went immediately over to the fire and crouched down, rubbing their frozen hands together over the dancing flames.

The proprietor and his companions were a little drunk, but sobered up when presented with the problem of the strange visitors. Hargest asked if he and Miles could remain by the fire till the morning. The proprietor, Antonio Soldini, gave them a large bottle of beer and questioned them thoroughly. Then he slipped out to make a telephone call. On his return Soldini brightened up and plied the frozen brigadiers with more alcohol followed by coffee.[12] Evidently, he had spoken to the local police, for a short time later two uniformed officers arrived and joined in with the merriment.

Hargest and Miles bade a fond farewell to Soldini and his family and went with the policemen in their car to Mendrisio. At the station they were booked in, handed over all of their possessions, made brief statements and then were escorted into a two-man cell where they slid into a grateful sleep beneath warm woollen blankets.[13]

*

Shortly after dawn Generals O'Connor and Carton de Wiart, their rucksacks fastened securely to their backs, their legs stiff after so much exercise the day before, left the farm where they had sheltered for the night and began their day's trek.

The weather was with them, for it was bright and sunny. Their objective was to cross the grand Bologna–Milan trunk road between Modena and Reggio, so they quickly turned off the main Florence–Bologna road and headed cross-country in a northeasterly direction.[14] The countryside, cut by numerous valleys, was alive with a carpet of wild violets. The combination of freedom, flowers, fresh air and sun lifted their spirits: 'We gloried in our escape from prison bars,'[15] wrote De Wiart, and the two generals marched off with a spring in their step. O'Connor navigated for them using one of Flight Lieutenant Leeming's compasses and General Gambier-Parry's maps and they never got lost.[16]

*

Later on the morning of 31 March, the Swiss police roused Brigadiers Hargest and Miles in their cell. After rudimentary ablutions and some breakfast and coffee the two New Zealanders were put in another car and driven through the town of Lugano to the Swiss Army headquarters in Bellinzona. Once there, the commandant and a colonel carefully questioned the brigadiers. 'We made statements about ourselves – name, rank, where we had been imprisoned, and other minor details,'[17] recalled Hargest. The colonel rose and spoke.

'Gentlemen,' he said, in excellent English, 'we believe what you have told us. But you *did* enter Switzerland uninvited, and without papers, so with regret we must continue to hold you in arrest.'[18] This news came as something of a shock to Hargest and Miles, who had fully been expecting to be able to contact the British authorities and go free.

'If you give us your word that you will not try to contact the British Consulate or the British Legation in Berne, or speak to anyone else or try to escape, we will send you to a hotel until tomorrow.' Hargest and Miles both gave their word.

'What happens tomorrow, Colonel?' asked Hargest.

'Tomorrow we will send you to Berne under escort,'[19] replied the Swiss officer. Hargest and Miles were satisfied – at least that was one step closer to the British Legation.

'Now, gentlemen, Private Knuzler here will be your escort during your stay in Bellinzona.' Ernst Knuzler, a young reservist army clerk who spoke perfect English, stiffened to attention. Knuzler changed into civvies and then escorted the brigadiers to their hotel. There they luxuriated in steaming hot baths and took a meal in the dining room. It was all rather surreal to be free to mingle with ordinary people. In the afternoon Knuzler took them up to the old fortresses above the town for a stroll. The views were stunning, plunging down to Lake Maggiore. For Hargest it marked a special moment. 'Sitting there with my legs over the parapet I was able to view dispassionately all that had passed in the last three years. For the first time in many months a warm peace entered my soul.'[20]

*

Later that evening, as Brigadiers Hargest and Miles sat down to another pleasant meal in their hotel dining room, Generals O'Connor and Carton de Wiart came to the end of a long day of hiking across difficult terrain. As the day had worn on they had started to see more and more villages, which was not a good thing. They had intended to keep contact with the locals to a minimum, so as not to attract undue attention. After days on the road they were looking bedraggled, their clothes soiled and beards starting to take.[21] Coupled with their non-Italian looks and De Wiart's eye patch and missing hand, they stuck out like the proverbial sore thumb. O'Connor was concerned how long the 'Austrian tourists' wheeze might last, especially if questioned thoroughly.[22]

Finding shelter became a priority as evening came on, but, probably due their scruffy appearance and foreign bearing, they were turned away from at least three of the farms that they tried.[23] On their fourth attempt they spoke to a very kindly lady, who seemed concerned that two elderly tourists needed shelter. She suggested, to O'Connor and De Wiart's growing disbelief and alarm, that they go to a local barracks where the soldiers would happily give them shelter. 'It took all Dick's flattery to persuade her that the charms of her shed were infinite,'[24] recalled De Wiart. So, for the second time, the two generals bedded down gratefully with Italian cows and slept the sleep of utter exhaustion. They were now almost 70 miles beyond the castle.

*

Brigadiers Hargest and Miles were not free yet. This was demonstrated on the morning of 1 April during a train ride through the spectacular 6,909-foot-high St Gotthard Pass on the way to Berne.

When locals tried to speak to the escapers, the police sternly forbade any communication. There was the ever-present worry that because they had entered Switzerland illegally, the Swiss *might* send them back to Italy.

Rain began to fall as the train passed the Zugersee and steamed into pretty Lucerne. At Lucerne Hargest and Miles and their escort changed trains for Berne. On arrival in Berne the police handed the brigadiers over to another party of military police commanded by the tall and imposing Colonel Schaffroth. Taken to a house on the outskirts of the town, Schaffroth interrogated the New Zealanders for many hours until he was fully satisfied of their identities and stories. But the escapers were disappointed when at the end of the interrogation Schaffroth refused permission for them to telephone the British Legation. Instead, he told them that they would be taken to the Hotel Baren and held under the same conditions as before.[25] It was extremely frustrating for the escapers to know that less than a mile away was the British diplomatic mission and sanctuary.

*

O'Connor and Carton de Wiart were up early, and after a simple breakfast from their limited rations they began hiking. They walked on a compass bearing, constantly checking their maps. The first thing that they noticed was the alarming preponderance of soldiers everywhere. They didn't appear much interested in the generals, but it was unnerving to see so many Italian troops in villages and out in the countryside. Around lunchtime O'Connor brought them to a halt.

'There's a deep ravine up ahead,' he said, pointing out the river on his map. 'There's a bridge here,' he continued, moving his finger. 'That's where we'll cross.' Quickly covering the distance to the ravine, O'Connor and De Wiart were in for a shock. They hid in some bushes a few hundred yards from the ravine and observed silently.

The ravine was very deep, plunging down to a relatively small stream below. The bridge was suspended above the chasm, and under normal circumstances it would have taken them just minutes to get across and on their way. But Italian sentries, the sun glinting off their steel helmets, stood at each end of the long bridge, leaning on their rifles. O'Connor and De Wiart watched as they flagged down cars and trucks that wanted to cross and checked the drivers' documents.[26] The hunt was evidently on for the escaped British officers. It was obvious that trying to bluff their way across, even with Gambier-Parry's excellent forged passes, would mean running a huge risk. They had walked so far that it seemed stupid to risk their gains by attempting to fool the sentries on the bridge.

'We'll cross the ravine further down, out of sight of the sentries,' said O'Connor. But it was obvious that such an undertaking was going to put them behind schedule. They crept away from their cover and took a wide detour around the bridge until they found a spot that was quiet. De Wiart peered down into the ravine from the bank, his face set in a grimace.

'Damned deep, old boy,' he murmured.

'We'll go slow,' replied O'Connor, his face also showing the strain. 'Come on, let's get on with it.' Speed was of the essence. If anyone saw them crossing the ravine in such a fashion, climbing down and then up its steep, rocky sides, it would be obvious that they had something to hide. Any regular civilian would have used the bridge rather than risk a broken leg scrambling on the rock face.

*

'I'm a British officer,' stated John Combe matter-of-factly to the prison governor. He had demanded to be taken to see the official in charge of San Vittore prison. After two days locked in a cell, and facing an uncertain future, Brigadier Combe felt that he had given his comrades an excellent head start. Now it was time to end the charade and reveal his identity.

The prison governor was not convinced by Combe's admission, and soon police were summoned to interrogate him.

'My name is Combe, John, Brigadier, British Army,' repeated Combe to the new inquisitors. 'I escaped from *Campo* 12 at Vincigliata on 29 March.' It took a while for him to be believed. The police seemed more interested in the fact that he had been caught in possession of false Italian identity papers, and the two- to three-year prison sentence was brought up again.[27] But Combe knew his rights under the Geneva Convention. After some bureaucratic wrangling, confirmation of his identity and status was received at the prison from the *Carabinieri* authorities in Florence. Combe was told that he was to be sent back to Vincigliata the following day for punishment. After the horrible conditions inside the civilian prison Combe was actually looking forward to once more being in the hands of the Italian military. He also burned with a desire for some news of his escape partners. He felt a personal victory – he had withstood some pretty strident questioning and harsh imprisonment, including several times being threatened with execution, but had managed to fool his captors for over two days.[28] Though he was bitter at his own capture so early on, he felt justifiable pride in his performance in captivity.

*

Air Vice-Marshal Boyd arrived back at Vincigliata Castle in handcuffs. As he was driven up to the massive entrance gates he felt very mixed emotions. Climbing out of the military car, his handcuffs were taken off and he was handed over. There was no sign of Major Bacci or Captains Tranquille or Pederneschi. It became apparent that they had been relieved of their positions in the fall-out from the escape of six senior Allied officers from right under their noses.[29] The new commandant was Major Vivarelli, an officer whom General Neame described as 'a most objectionable and spiteful person'.[30]

On arrival, Vivarelli, a hardened Fascist officer, had immediately ordered that all remaining British officers at the castle be confined to their rooms for 48 hours. All exercise had been cancelled and two nightly checks instituted, the *Carabinieri* making as much noise as they liked, disturbing the generals on purpose.[31] General Neame had immediately demanded an interview with Vivarelli. 'I had a first-class row with him,' recalled Neame, 'for which I was awarded seven days' solitary confinement by the Italian Chief of the General Staff, for the offence of "using language unsuited to a prisoner-of-war and insulting the Italian General Staff"!'[32] In Neame's opinion Vivarelli 'was deliberately out to annoy and provoke us'.[33] Neame later recorded the result of these constant night checks in an official complaint to Rome: 'I am certain as a result of these continuous disturbances at irregular times, I now suffer from insomnia and my nerves are suffering severely.'[34]

Shortly after his arrival back at the castle, Owen Boyd was brought before Vivarelli who with a sneer sentenced him to 30 days' solitary confinement.[35] It was very clear that a new regime was in command at the castle, and that all those connected to the escape were to be severely punished, as much to restore Italian face as anything else. News of the escape had gone all the way to Mussolini himself, who was apparently furious. Boyd, stewing in solitary 'after having been so nearly successful … found this punishment the hardest to bear; he craved for someone with whom to talk it over,' Hargest would later write.[36]

*

Generals O'Connor and De Wiart stumbled, slid and awkwardly climbed their way down into the deep ravine, their heavy rucksacks threatening to pitch them headfirst into the abyss. It was the most unpleasant terrain that they had yet encountered,[37] De Wiart with his missing eye and impaired balance finding it particularly precarious.

Reaching the bottom of the ravine safely, the two escapers rested before crossing the small stream and ascending to the surface. The climb up was a little easier than clambering down, but they were completely exhausted by the time they struggled out on to flat land again. The whole enterprise had eaten into their timetable and stocks of energy.

They marched on again until the early evening when they once more sought shelter from strangers. O'Connor was forced to virtually beg a woman to be allowed to spend the night in her cowshed; 'judging from the expression on her face and her undisguised reluctance,' wrote De Wiart, 'she deemed it very hard luck on the cows.'[38]

*

Brigadiers Hargest and Miles were roused early in their Berne hotel room on 2 April by two Swiss Army clerks, come to take yet more statements. This took up several hours. By now, the two New Zealanders had grown used to retelling the story of their escape into Switzerland. While one of the clerks packed up his typewriter, and Hargest and Miles wondered what was going to happen next, the door opened and in stepped a young military police captain. He saluted formally and faced the two prisoners.

'Brigadier Hargest, Brigadier Miles,' said the officer stiffly, 'I am to tell you that you are free.'

For a second or two the Swiss officer's words did not sink in. Before Hargest and Miles could respond, the officer continued.

'You have a visitor. Shall I show him in?'

'Yes, of course,' said Hargest, rather shell-shocked by the sudden good news.

In stepped Colonel Henry Cartwright, British Military Attaché. He shook both of their hands warmly, congratulating them on their incredible achievement. Hargest and Miles recognised Cartwright from his book *Within Four Walls* that they had both read. It was virtually the textbook on how to escape from a prison camp and was written from experience. During the First World War, Cartwright had attempted to escape dozens of times, eventually succeeding on his 23rd attempt. It was rumoured that the Germans even used Cartwright's book to plan the security in their prisoner of war camps.[39]

'There's someone who is dying to meet you,' said Cartwright brightly. Within five minutes Hargest and Miles had dumped their kit and tatty old coats in Cartwright's office. Then they walked over to a rather grand house in the better area of town.

They entered its large hallway, framed by a grand staircase. A butler showed them into the drawing room where a small crowd of well-dressed men and women turned and stared at them. Hargest and Miles felt completely out of place, their homemade civilian clothes ragged and soiled from their long journey, their faces pale and strained from their ordeal. A lean middle-aged man in an immaculately tailored pin-striped suit who wore black-framed spectacles stepped from the crowd and advanced towards them, his face beaming with a welcoming smile.

'Brigadier Hargest, Brigadier Miles, so good of you to come. I'm Norton, the Minister here.' Clifford Norton shook their hands. 'You've made it,' he continued, 'for this is sovereign British soil. You are *free* men.'

Hargest and Miles were overwhelmed. The other people in the room broke into spontaneous applause at Norton's remarks. Hargest could scarcely contain the wave of emotion that broke over him, and Miles wiped his damp eyes.[40] They really had made it. Nothing could touch them here. Soon they were shaking hands and being clapped on the back as the laughing and happy crowd surged around them: 'English faces,' recalled Hargest, 'English voices.'[41]

Epilogue

The 3rd of April 1943 passed in much the same way as the previous days out on the road for Generals O'Connor and Carton de Wiart. They plodded along, rucksacks on, across countryside that was increasingly dotted with villages and small towns, which of course meant people. They also passed the local *Carabinieri* without any problems.

After another night sleeping alongside Italian livestock, O'Connor and De Wiart started early on the 4th, but in the afternoon they were pulled over by a local Fascist official who demanded their papers. This was the great test of General Gambier-Parry's forging skills. His handiwork passed with flying colours, helped along by O'Connor's facility with the language. 'O'Connor rose to further heights of Italian fancy and poured out answers to the volley of questions put by this unattractive man,' wrote De Wiart. 'I turned on my deaf-mute act, and soon the creature was satisfied, and allowed us to pass on.'[1] Praise for G-P's forging skills was running high as the two generals continued on the road north.

By evening they were near the town of Vignola, separated from it by a heavily guarded bridge over a river. There was no possibility of trying to cross further down – the river was too substantial. For once, O'Connor failed to secure them any lodgings for the night. In the end they had to make do beneath a cart in a quiet farmyard.[2]

They rose very early on 5 April and managed to cross the bridge before the guards were posted. Once a couple of miles beyond

Vignola they paused by a little stream and washed and shaved as best they could, as their ragged appearance was starting to attract undue attention from the locals.

The following day, 6 April, found them in the Po Valley, due south of Verona.[3] They became lost in the myriad of little villages and stopped to consult a map. Two passing *Carabinieri* on bicycles spotted the generals, stopped and dismounted. They demanded their papers. 'They scrutinised them and could find no fault with them,' De Wiart recalled, 'but, in fact, they proved to be that rare thing, men with an instinct.'[4] De Wiart suspected that it was his and O'Connor's tatty appearances that piqued the interest of the policemen, as G-P's documents had again passed scrutiny without comment. Either way, the *Carabinieri* would not let the generals go, and seemed particularly fascinated by De Wiart's injuries. They forced him to show them his stump. The *Carabinieri* sergeant had noticed that O'Connor's identity card listed him as from Bologna, a city that he knew well. Conversely, it was soon obvious that O'Connor did not know Bologna at all. The sergeant told them that they must come to the local police station.[5] 'We knew the game was up,' wrote De Wiart, 'but when we informed our two captors of our identity, they nearly embraced us and were so overcome with joy that they insisted we should finish the journey to the *Carabinieri* post in a cart, making a triumphant entry.'[6]

And thus were captured the last escapers from Vincigliata Castle. They had marched 150 miles in an incredible show of courage and tenacity, doubly impressive given their ages. They felt pride in their achievement, which though tinged with regret at capture was an amazing accomplishment in itself. 'We were twice the men we had been when we started,'[7] wrote De Wiart honestly. 'We were a bit weary at times,' wrote General Dick, 'but we could have got on easily to the frontier as far as walking was concerned.'[8] They now faced interrogation and the obligatory 30 days of solitary confinement back at Vincigliata Castle.

What happened afterwards ...

Bertram Armstrong

'O Bass' Armstrong received the Distinguished Service Order while a prisoner in 1942 for his performance in command of the 5th South African Infantry Brigade in the desert campaign. He escaped from Vincigliata Castle in company with all of the other prisoners when Italy changed sides in September 1943, walking over the Apennine Mountains to Romagna, which was very taxing for a man with a game leg. Promoted to Major-General, Armstrong was appointed Chief of the General Staff of the South African Union Defence Forces, retiring in 1953. Armstrong died in South Africa in 1972 aged 79.

Owen Tudor Boyd

Boyd eventually made it back to England after escaping from Italy with Generals Neame and O'Connor in late 1943. He had just been appointed to a new RAF command when he died of a massive heart attack in 1944 at the age of 54. For his successful escape from the castle in March 1943 Boyd was Mentioned in Despatches.

Adrian Carton de Wiart

De Wiart served 30 days' solitary confinement for his success-ful escape from Vincigliata Castle in March 1943. In August of the same year he was asked by the Italians to accompany General Zanussi to Lisbon in neutral Portugal to meet with Allied repre-sentatives to discuss the Italian surrender. Released in Lisbon, De Wiart was flown home to England. Shortly afterwards Winston Churchill appointed him as his personal representative to the Chinese Nationalist leader Generalissimo Chiang Kai-shek, promoting him to Lieutenant-General. On his way to the Far East De Wiart attended the Cairo Conference with Churchill, Chiang Kai-shek and US President Franklin D. Roosevelt before arriving in Chungking in December 1943. He often flew to India, and was there able to meet General O'Connor, who was commanding British troops in the east of the country. In 1945 De Wiart was appointed a Knight of the Order of the British Empire (KBE). During the last months of the war he toured the Burma Front and also was aboard the battleship HMS *Queen Elizabeth* during the bombardment of Sabang in the Dutch East Indies.

His final wartime duty was attending the Japanese surrender in Singapore in September 1945. During his journey home he stopped over in Rangoon where, coming down some stairs, he slipped on a coconut mat and fell badly, breaking several vertebrae and knocking himself unconscious. Hospitalised in the UK, he eventually recovered, but not before surgeons took the opportunity to remove large amounts of First World War shrapnel from his body.

Carton de Wiart finally retired from the army in 1947. His wife died in 1949 and in 1951 De Wiart married again (his second wife would live until 2006, reaching 102) and they settled in the Republic of Ireland, buying Aghinagh House in County Cork. There De Wiart lived the life of a country gentleman, shooting and fishing until his death in June 1963 at the age of 83. He is buried in the grounds of Aghinagh House.

John Combe

Brigadier Combe served his 30 days of solitary confinement at Vincigliata Castle. Upon escaping again in September 1943, Combe joined the Italian Partisans in Romagna until finally reaching Allied lines in May 1944. In October 1944 he was given command, with the reduced rank of Colonel, of the 2nd Armoured Brigade. In 1945, temporarily a Major-General, Combe briefly commanded the 78th and 46th Infantry Divisions in Austria after the German surrender. He was awarded a Mention in Despatches for his escape in 1943. In October 1946, his rank was made permanent and he was appointed Deputy General Officer Commanding British Troops Austria. Combe retired in 1947 and married the same year. Appointed a Companion of the Order of the Bath (CB) in 1947, he was also honoured by the United States, being appointed an Officer of the Legion of Merit in 1948. From 1945 to 1957 he served as Honorary Colonel of the regiment he had led in the desert against Rommel, the 11th Hussars, including taking part in the funeral procession of King George VI.

John Combe died in 1967 aged 71.

Michael Gambier-Parry

'G-P' escaped along with the other prisoners in September 1943 and managed to find sanctuary in a Rome convent until the Allies liberated the city. He retired from the army in 1944 and lived in Castle Combe near Chippenham. Gambier-Parry served as Deputy Lieutenant of Wiltshire and died in 1976 aged 85.

James Hargest

Hargest and Miles were stuck in Switzerland for many months with little to do following their successful escape from the castle. Both men desired to get back to Allied lines, but the only way was by travelling secretly through German-occupied France to neutral Spain and thence to England via Gibraltar. Hargest left Switzerland and with the help of a French evasion line he made it to the British Consulate in Barcelona, eventually arriving safely in England in December 1943. For his escape from Vincigliata Castle and his evasion through France Jim Hargest was awarded a second Bar to his Distinguished Service Order and made a Commander of the Order of the British Empire (CBE). Sadly, his son Geoffrey died of wounds received in Italy at the Battle of Monte Cassino in March 1944. On 6 June 1944 Hargest landed in Normandy as New Zealand's military representative attached to the British 50th (Northumbrian) Infantry Division. Tragically, as he was leaving the front on 12 August 1944 Hargest was killed by a German shell and was buried in France. He was 52 years old. The James Hargest High School in Invercargill, New Zealand is named after him.

John Leeming

Leeming escaped from Italian captivity by the novel method of feigning mental illness. He began this act at Vincigliata Castle and was so convincing that both the Italian Army and the Red Cross recommended his repatriation to England in April 1943, a couple of weeks after the successful tunnel escape. Leeming immediately returned to RAF duty. After the war he became a successful novelist, often touching upon his wartime imprisonment at the Villa Orsini and Vincigliata Castle. John Leeming died near Manchester in 1965 aged 69.

Reginald Miles

Jim Hargest's partner in the tunnel escape languished in Switzerland after arriving safely in 1943. He decided to attempt the dangerous evasion across France to Spain before Hargest. He too received a Bar to his DSO for his escape. But on arrival in Spain, in a depressed and exhausted state the 50-year-old committed suicide, shooting himself in Figueras on 20 October 1943. He was buried with full military honours in Spain. Miles was posthumously appointed a CBE.

Sir Philip Neame

With Boyd, O'Connor and some other prisoners from the castle, Neame trekked hundreds of miles south following the Italian Armistice until he met Allied troops at Termoli on 20 December 1943. Arriving in Britain on Christmas Day, he found that there was no job for him. In August 1945 Neame was appointed Lieutenant-Governor of Guernsey with the rank of Lieutenant-General, a post he held until 1953. He was Colonel Commandant of the Royal Engineers from 1945 to 1955, and Honorary Colonel of 131 (Airborne) Engineer Regiment, Royal Engineers from 1948. Made a Knight of the Order of the British Empire in June 1946, in the same month he was also appointed a Knight of the Order of St John. In 1955 Neame was appointed a Deputy Lord Lieutenant of Kent, where he died in April 1978, aged 89.

Sir Richard O'Connor

With the help of Italian Partisans O'Connor reached Allied lines at Termoli on 21 December 1943. In the New Year he was Mentioned in Despatches for his escape attempts. O'Connor assumed command of VIII Corps during the Normandy campaign. Under his leadership, the formation took part in several famous operations around Caen and during the US breakout, including Epsom, Goodwood and Bluecoat. VIII Corps next supported Brian Horrocks' XXX Corps during Operation Market Garden in Holland. On 27 November 1944 O'Connor was removed from command, allegedly for not being tough enough on American subordinate commanders, and ordered to take over as General Officer Commanding-in-Chief, Eastern Command, India. This new job involved controlling the lines of communication to Bill Slim's 14th Army in Burma. In April 1945 O'Connor was promoted to General and in October appointed GOC-in-C North West Army India. Between 1946 and 1947 he was Adjutant General to the Forces and an ADC to King George VI. O'Connor resigned in September 1947 from his military post following a disagreement, but shortly afterwards was appointed a Knight Grand Cross of the Order of the Bath.

After retirement O'Connor remained very active, being Commandant of the Army Cadet Force Scotland from 1948 to 1959, Colonel of the Cameronians (Scottish Rifles) 1951–54, Lord Lieutenant of Ross and Cromarty 1955–64 and Lord High Commissioner to the General Assembly of the Church of Scotland in 1964. In 1971 his service to Scotland was recognised when O'Connor was made a Knight of the Order of the Thistle. General Dick died in London in June 1981 at the age of 91.

The Earl of Ranfurly

Dan Ranfurly reached Allied lines with Brigadiers Vaughan, Combe and Todhunter on 30 May 1944 after many adventures with the Italian Partisans. He worked for Lloyd's of London before Churchill appointed him Governor of the Bahamas, a post he held until 1957. His wife's famous wartime diaries were published to great critical acclaim. The Countess of Ranfurly was instrumental in the creation of an organisation known today as Book Aid International. Lord Ranfurly took up farming on his estate in Buckinghamshire. He was appointed a Knight of the Order of Saint Michael and Saint George (KCMG). Dan Ranfurly passed away in 1988 aged 74.

Douglas Stirling

'Pip' Stirling was infamously prosecuted by court martial in 1943 for using insulting language about the Italians in a letter that he sent home, calling them 'bastards'. He was sentenced to several years' imprisonment but, honour satisfied by the verdict, the Italians returned him to the castle where the whole matter was quietly forgotten. Like the others, Stirling escaped in September 1943 and successfully arrived in Allied lines. He later wrote to General O'Connor in the hope of securing command of an armoured brigade in Normandy, but without success. Pip Stirling died in 1958 aged 61.

Edward Todhunter

Escaping Vincigliata Castle in September 1943, Todhunter joined the Italian Garibaldi Partisan Brigade, reaching Allied lines at Ancona in May 1944. He served as High Sheriff of Essex from 1964 to 1965 and was a magistrate. Edward Todhunter died in 1976 at the age of 76.

Edward Vaughan

Brigadier Edward 'Rudolph' Vaughan reached Allied lines in May 1944 and was appointed Commanding Officer, Delhi Area, India later that year, being made a Companion of the Order of the Bath (CB). From 1945 to 1948 Vaughan was an ADC to King George VI. He retired from the army in 1948 and died in Sussex in 1953 aged 59.

The Italians

Major Bacci died of cancer a few months after his removal from command following the tunnel escape.

Baron Ricciardi changed sides in September 1943, finding himself attached to an Indian unit during the fighting in Italy. He survived the war.

Dr Bolaffio, who had risked everything helping the British escape attempts, returned to private practice in Florence after the war. No evidence could be found to indicate that he was rewarded for his service by the British government following General Neame's request in writing.

General Chiappe was shot by the Germans after the Italian Armistice.

The fates of **First Captain Tranquille** and **Captain Pederneschi** remain unknown.

Vincigliata Castle

Temple-Leader's monstrous creation that so perplexed and confounded the British prisoners of war is still there atop its hill just outside Florence, a brooding and somewhat beautiful presence. These days it's a part of a thriving vineyard business and is used to host society weddings from all over the world. Externally, it's little changed from its 1943 appearance. The tunnel was filled in with concrete and the chapel emptied of spoil. The wooden sentry platform around the wall has been torn out and the wire and searchlights long scrapped. But if you narrow your eyes to the Tuscan sun, you can still imagine that rainy and windswept night in March 1943 when a motley collection of perhaps the unlikeliest escapers in military history emerged from beneath its towering outer wall with a dream fixed firmly in their minds – the sweet dream of freedom and home.

Acknowledgements

I should like to extend my enormous thanks to the following people, institutions and organisations for their superb and generous assistance during the researching of this book.

My very great thanks to the following relatives and friends of the men involved in the escape from Vincigliata Castle for taking the time to share with me anecdotes, documents and photographs that have proved so invaluable to the writing of this book: Lady Caroline Simmonds, daughter of the 6th Earl of Ranfurly, for giving me permission to use her late mother's diary as a source; Anne Myers and Anthony Gambier-Parry, the daughter and grandson respectively of Major-General Michael Gambier-Parry, for granting me interviews; Nigel and Philip Neame, the twin sons of Lieutenant-General Sir Philip Neame, for permission to use their late father's autobiography, photographs, unpublished 'Narrative of Events' and many other invaluable documents, and for attempting to put me in contact with John Leeming's family; Lady Anne Tidbury, Iona O'Connor and Mrs J.K.J. Pollok-McCall, for kind permission to use General O'Connor's unpublished 'Escape Narrative'; Major James Nairn, General O'Connor's close friend, for sharing his personal memories of 'General Dick' with me, for advice on sources and for arranging permission to access O'Connor family documents at King's College London; Michael Todhunter, son of Brigadier Edward Todhunter, for granting me a fascinating interview, for his kind provision of access to family documents, letters and photographs, and for his efforts to get me into Vincigliata Castle. Efforts to contact the copyright holders of John Leeming's book *Always*

To-Morrow and James Hargest's *Farewell Camp 12* were unfortunately unsuccessful.

A great many thanks to Briege Hunter and Brett Irwin, Public Record Office of Northern Ireland; Jodie Double, University of Leeds Library; Adam Sutch, Researcher, RAF Museum; Lianne Smith, Liddell Hart Centre, King's College London; Alan Sinclair, Ditsong National Museum of Military History, South Africa; Rebecca Pike, Senior Reporter, *The Canterbury Times*; Kathryn Tye, Communications Executive, Shepherd Neame Ltd; South African National Defence Force Archives; The National Archives (Public Record Office), Kew; Cambridge University Library; The British Library.

Many thanks to my splendid agent Andrew Lownie, whose advice and enthusiasm are much appreciated. The team at Icon Books have been brilliant, and I'd like to thank my editors Duncan Heath and Robert Sharman for all of their hard work.

Lastly, I'd like to thank my beautiful and accomplished wife Fang Fang for her encouragement of and enthusiasm for this project. Her insightful observations and critical eye are much valued, and I appreciate her also acting as (unpaid) research assistant and travelling companion during the researching of this book in Italy, Switzerland and the UK.

Photo acknowledgements

Photograph of Brigadiers Hargest and Miles: 'Senior NZ officers await Greek Minister of War, Maadi. New Zealand.' Department of Internal Affairs. War History Branch: Photographs relating to World War 1914–1918, World War 1939–1945, occupation of Japan, Korean War, and Malayan Emergency. Ref: DA-01430-F. Alexander Turnbull Library, Wellington, New Zealand. http://natlib.govt.nz/records/22779228.

All other images courtesy of Michael Todhunter, all rights reserved.

Bibliography

Private papers
Private papers of Lieutenant-General Sir Philip Neame, VC, KBE, CB, DSO, KStJ
Private papers of Brigadier E.J. Todhunter, TD, DL

Archives
Liddell Hart Centre for Military Archives, University College London
Escape Narrative of Lieutenant-General Sir Richard O'Connor: OCONNOR 4/5/1 1941 Apr.–1943 Apr.

National Archives (Public Record Office), Kew
AIR 19/229 – Proposed Exchange of Air Marshal O.T. Boyd for an Italian General
HS 9/1228/7 – Thomas Daniel Knox, Earl of Ranfurly, Special Operations Executive: Personnel Files
WO 208/3319/1921 – Lieutenant-Colonel (Acting Brigadier) J.F.B. Combe, DSO & Bar
WO 208/3319/1922 – Lieutenant-Colonel (Local Brigadier) E.J. Todhunter
WO 208/3319/1923 – Brigadier E.W.D. Vaughan, MC
WO 208/3320/48 – Gambier-Parry, M.D. Prisoner of War Section. Escape/Evasion Reports: MI9/SPG: 1961
WO 208/3444 – Report on escape of British Generals from prison camp in Italy by Major General P. Neame
WO 208/5582/5583 – MI9/S/PG Interrogation Report Lieutenant-Colonel (Acting Brigadier) J.F.B. Combe, DSO & Bar
WO 32/10706 – Prisoner of War: General (Code 91[A]): Vincigliata (Prison Camp No. 12): Reports:
- Camp for British Generals at Vincigliata, Red Cross Report, 29 November 1941

- Lieutenant-General P. Neame to the Protecting Power, 14 May 1942
- Camp for British Generals at Vincigliata, Red Cross Report, 30 May 1942
- Report of Captain Leonardo Trippi, Assistant Military Attaché, Swiss Legation, Rome, 3 June 1942
- Inspection of Prisoner of War Camp No. 12, Red Cross Report, 23 June 1942
- Memorandum from the Italian Ministry of Foreign Affairs to the Swiss Legation Rome, 25 July 1942
- Report No. 2 On Inspection of Prisoner of War Camp No. 12, Red Cross Report, 1 July 1942
- War Office (Directorate of Prisoners of War) to the Foreign Office (Prisoners of War Department): Treatment of British Generals in Italian Hands, November 1942
- Report No. 4 on Inspection of Prisoners of War Camp No. 12, Red Cross Report, 15 October 1942
- Lieutenant-General Sir Philip Neame to The Italian War Ministry, Rome, 13 April 1943

Published sources

Books

Baynes, John, *The Forgotten Victor: General Sir Richard O'Connor, KT, GCB, DSO, MC* (London: Brassey's, 1989)

Butler, Daniel, *Field Marshal: The Life and Death of Erwin Rommel* (London: Casemate, 2015)

Carton de Wiart, Sir Adrian, *Happy Odyssey* (London: Jonathan Cape Ltd, 1950)

Cumming, Michael, *Pathfinder Cranswick* (London: William Kinder, 1962)

Evans, Bryn, *The Decisive Campaigns of the Desert Air Force, 1942–1945* (Barnsley: Pen & Sword Aviation, 2014)

Evans, David, *Understand Mussolini's Italy* (London: Hodder Education, 2012)

Foot, M.R.D. & J.M. Langley, *MI9: Escape & Evasion, 1939–45* (London, Book Club Associates, 1979)

Hargest, James, *Farewell Campo 12* (London: Michael Joseph, 1954)

James, Henry, *Transatlantic Sketches* (Boston: James R. Osgood, 1875)

Krige, Uys, *The Way Out: Italian Intermezzo* (London: Collins, 1946)

Leeming, John, *Always To-Morrow* (London: George G. Harrap & Co. Ltd, 1951)

Leeming, John, *The Natives are Friendly* (New York: E.P. Dutton & Company, 1951)

McGibbon, Ian (ed.), *The Oxford Companion to New Zealand Military History* (Auckland: Oxford University Press, 2000)

Mead, Richard, *Churchill's Lions: A Biographical Guide to the Key British Generals of World War II* (Stroud: Spellmount Books, 2007)

Mollo, Andrew, *The Armed Forces of World War II: Uniforms, Insignia and Organisation* (London: Black Cat, 1987)

Neame, Sir Philip, *Playing With Strife: The Autobiography of a Soldier* (London: George G. Harrap & Sons Ltd, 1947)

Ranfurly, Countess of, *To War With Whitaker: The Wartime Diaries of the Countess of Ranfurly, 1939–45* (London: Mandarin Paperbacks, 1997)

Richards, Denis, *Royal Air Force 1939–45*, Vol. 1 (London: Her Majesty's Stationery Office, 1975)

Ufficio Storico dell'Aeronautica Militare, *Ordine Militare d'Italia 1911–1964* (Rome: Ufficio Storico dell'Aeronautica Militare, 1969)

Zabecki, David T. (ed), *World War II in Europe: An Encyclopedia* (New York: Routledge, 1999)

Magazines and periodicals
Lawrence Journal-World
News Chronicle
Time

Notes

Prologue

  1. Sir Adrian Carton de Wiart, *Happy Odyssey*, (London, Jonathan Cape Ltd, 1950), p. 197

Chapter 1

  1. 'Prize Catch', *Time*, 2 December 1940

  2. Sir Philip Neame, *Playing With Strife: The Autobiography of a Soldier* (London: George G. Harrap & Sons Ltd, 1947), p. 285

  3. 'British Air Marshal Tudor Boyd Captured by Italians in Sicily', *Lawrence Journal-World*, 21 November 1940

  4. Michael Cumming, *Pathfinder Cranswick* (London: William Kinder, 1962), p. 73

  5. Denis Richards, *Royal Air Force 1939–45*, Vol. 1 (London: Her Majesty's Stationery Office, 1975), p. 270

  6. 'Italy Claims Air Marshal as Prisoner', *Brisbane Courier-Mail*, 23 November 1940

  7. John Leeming, *Always To-Morrow* (London: George G. Harrap & Co. Ltd, 1951), p. 12

  8. John Leeming, *The Natives are Friendly* (New York: E.P. Dutton & Company, 1951), p. 195

  9. Bryn Evans, *The Decisive Campaigns of the Desert Air Force, 1942–1945* (Barnsley: Pen & Sword Aviation, 2014), Kindle edition, unpaginated

10. John Leeming, *Always To-Morrow* (London: George G. Harrap & Co. Ltd, 1951), pp. 13–14

11. Ibid: p. 14

12. 'Prize Catch', *Time*, 2 December 1940

13. John Leeming, *Always To-Morrow* (London: George G. Harrap & Co. Ltd, 1951), p. 15

14. John Leeming, *The Natives are Friendly* (New York: E.P. Dutton & Company, 1951), p. 196

15. John Leeming, *Always To-Morrow* (London: George G. Harrap & Co. Ltd, 1951), p. 17

16. Ibid: p. 18

17. 'Prize Catch', *Time*, 2 December 1940

18. *Ordine Militare d'Italia 1911–1964* (Rome: Ufficio Storico dell'Aeronautica Militare, 1969)

19. John Leeming, *Always To-Morrow* (London: George G. Harrop & Co. Ltd, 1951), p. 21
20. Ibid: p. 22
21. Ibid: p. 23
22. Ibid: p. 28
23. Ibid: pp. 28–9
24. Bryn Evans, *The Decisive Campaigns of the Desert Air Force, 1942–1945* (Barnsley: Pen & Sword Aviation, 2014), Kindle edition, unpaginated
25. Associated Press report, Rome, 2 January 1941

Chapter 2

1. 'Lord Ranfurly's Report on his Capture', in *To War With Whitaker: The Wartime Diaries of the Countess of Ranfurly 1939–45* (London: Mandarin, 1997), p. 232
2. David T. Zabecki (ed.), *World War II in Europe: An Encyclopedia* (New York: Routledge, 1999), p. 437
3. John Leeming, *Always To-Morrow* (London: George G. Harrap & Co. Ltd, 1951), p. 80
4. Daniel Butler, *Field Marshal: The Life and Death of Erwin Rommel* (London: Casemate, 2015), p. 210
5. John Baynes, *The Forgotten Victor: General Sir Richard O'Connor* (London: Brassey's, 1989), p. 136
6. Thomas Daniel Knox, Earl of Ranfurly, HS 9/1228/7 Special Operations Executive: Personnel Files (The National Archives [Public Record Office], Kew)
7. 'Lord Ranfurly's Report on his Capture', in *To War With Whitaker: The Wartime Diaries of the Countess of Ranfurly 1939–45* (London: Mandarin, 1997), p. 232
8. Ibid.
9. John Baynes, *The Forgotten Victor: General Sir Richard O'Connor* (London: Brassey's, 1989), p. 137
10. 'Lord Ranfurly's Report on his Capture', in *To War With Whitaker: The Wartime Diaries of the Countess of Ranfurly 1939–45* (London: Mandarin, 1997), p. 232
11. Ibid: p. 233
12. Brigadier E.J. Todhunter to Colonel Whitmore, Essex Yeomanry, 13 May 1941
13. John Baynes, *The Forgotten Victor: General Sir Richard O'Connor* (London: Brassey's, 1989), p. 136
14. Brigadier E.J. Todhunter to B.E. Todhunter, 28 April 1941
15. John Baynes, *The Forgotten Victor: General Sir Richard O'Connor* (London: Brassey's, 1989), p. 136
16. Brigadier E.J. Todhunter to Colonel Whitmore, Essex Yeomanry, 13 May 1941
17. Brigadier E.J. Todhunter to B.E. Todhunter, 28 April 1941

18. John Baynes, *The Forgotten Victor: General Sir Richard O'Connor* (London: Brassey's, 1989), p. 136

19. Brigadier E.J. Todhunter to B.E. Todhunter, 28 April 1941

20. Brigadier E.J. Todhunter to B.E. Todhunter, 14 April 1941

21. B.E. Todhunter to E. Parker, ICI (Egypt) S.A., Cairo, 14 July 1941

22. Ibid.

23. Ibid.

24. Brigadier E.J. Todhunter to B.E. Todhunter, 28 April 1941

25. 'Revealed: Desert Fox Erwin Rommel was given his legendary goggles by a British PoW in return for retrieving a stolen hat', by Hannah Flint, *The Mail on Sunday*, 12 April 2005

26. Ibid.

27. Rommel's cap, adorned with Gambier-Parry's goggles, is preserved in the Rommel Museum, Herrlingen, Germany

28. Brigadier E.J. Todhunter to B.E. Todhunter, 28 April 1941

29. 'Lord Ranfurly's Report on his Capture', in *To War With Whitaker: The Wartime Diaries of the Countess of Ranfurly 1939–45* (London: Mandarin, 1997), p. 233

30. Ibid.

31. Ibid.

32. Sir Adrian Carton de Wiart, *Happy Odyssey* (London: Jonathan Cape Ltd, 1950), p. 179

33. 'Adrian Carton de Wiart: The unkillable soldier' by Peter Crutchley, *BBC News Magazine*, 6 January 2015

34. Sir Adrian Carton de Wiart, *Happy Odyssey* (London: Jonathan Cape Ltd, 1950), p. 89

35. Ibid: p. 182

36. Ibid: pp. 182–3

37. Ibid: p. 183

38. Ibid: p. 183

39. 'Brief Narrative of Events at the British Generals' Prisoner of War Camps in Italy, Apl. 1941 to Sept. 1943' (unpublished), private papers of Lieutenant-General Sir Philip Neame

Chapter 3

1. James Hargest, *Farewell Campo 12* (London: Michael Joseph, 1954), p. 60

2. John Leeming, *Always To-Morrow* (London: George G. Harrap & Co. Ltd, 1951), pp. 48–9

3. 'Brief Narrative of Events at the British Generals' Prisoner of War Camps in Italy, Apl. 1941 to Sept. 1943' (unpublished), private papers of Lieutenant-General Sir Philip Neame

4. Sir Adrian Carton de Wiart, *Happy Odyssey* (London: Jonathan Cape Ltd, 1950), p. 189

5. John Leeming, *Always To-Morrow* (London: George G. Harrap & Co. Ltd, 1951), p. 48

6. Ibid: p. 48
7. Ibid: p. 49
8. Sir Adrian Carton de Wiart, *Happy Odyssey* (London: Jonathan Cape Ltd, 1950), p. 185
9. James Hargest, *Farewell Campo 12* (London: Michael Joseph, 1954), p. 60
10. John Leeming, *Always To-Morrow* (London: George G. Harrap & Co. Ltd, 1951), p. 51
11. 'Brief Narrative of Events at the British Generals' Prisoner of War Camps in Italy, Apl. 1941 to Sept. 1943' (unpublished), private papers of Lieutenant-General Sir Philip Neame
12. John Leeming, *Always To-Morrow* (London: George G. Harrap & Co. Ltd, 1951), p. 51
13. Ibid: p. 53
14. Ibid: p. 60
15. Ibid: p. 66
16. Ibid: pp. 66–7
17. Ibid: p. 73
18. Ibid: pp. 74–5
19. Ibid: pp. 73–5
20. Ibid: p. 76
21. 'Brief Narrative of Events at the British Generals' Prisoner of War Camps in Italy, Apl. 1941 to Sept. 1943' (unpublished), private papers of Lieutenant-General Sir Philip Neame
22. Sir Adrian Carton de Wiart, *Happy Odyssey* (London: Jonathan Cape Ltd, 1950), pp. 183–4
23. Ibid.
24. Ibid: p. 184
25. 'Brief Narrative of Events at the British Generals' Prisoner of War Camps in Italy, Apl. 1941 to Sept. 1943' (unpublished), private papers of Lieutenant-General Sir Philip Neame
26. Brigadier E.J. Todhunter to B.E. Todhunter, 28 April 1941
27. Ibid.
28. Brigadier E.J. Todhunter to Mrs. Todhunter, 30 April 1941
29. Sir Adrian Carton de Wiart, *Happy Odyssey* (London: Jonathan Cape Ltd, 1950), p. 184
30. Ibid.
31. Brigadier E.J. Todhunter to Mrs. Todhunter, 30 April 1941
32. John Leeming, *Always To-Morrow* (London: George G. Harrap & Co. Ltd, 1951), p. 76
33. Ibid: p. 77

Chapter 4

1. 'Brief Narrative of Events at the British Generals' Prisoner of War Camps in Italy, Apl. 1941 to Sept. 1943' (unpublished), private papers of Lieutenant-General Sir Philip Neame

2. John Leeming, *Always To-Morrow* (London: George G. Harrap & Co. Ltd, 1951), p. 81
3. Ibid.
4. Ibid.
5. Sir Adrian Carton de Wiart, *Happy Odyssey* (London: Jonathan Cape Ltd, 1950), p. 180
6. John Leeming, *Always To-Morrow* (London: George G. Harrap & Co. Ltd, 1951), p. 92
7. Brigadier E.J. Todhunter to Mr B.E. Todhunter, 4 May 1941
8. Sir Adrian Carton de Wiart, *Happy Odyssey* (London: Jonathan Cape Ltd, 1950), p. 186
9. Brigadier E.J. Todhunter to Mr B.E. Todhunter, 11 May 1941
10. John Leeming, *Always To-Morrow* (London: George G. Harrap & Co. Ltd, 1951), p. 89
11. Brigadier E.J. Todhunter to Mrs Todhunter, 4 May 1941
12. 'Brief Narrative of Events at the British Generals' Prisoner of War Camps in Italy, Apl. 1941 to Sept. 1943' (unpublished), private papers of Lieutenant-General Sir Philip Neame
13. Brigadier E.J. Todhunter to Mrs Todhunter, 4 May 1941
14. Brigadier E.J. Todhunter to Mr B.E. Todhunter, 2 June 1941
15. John Leeming, *Always To-Morrow* (London: George G. Harrap & Co. Ltd, 1951), p. 96
16. Ibid: p. 95
17. Ibid: pp. 93–4
18. Brigadier E.J. Todhunter to Mrs Betty Todhunter, 30 April 1941
19. Sir Adrian Carton de Wiart, *Happy Odyssey* (London: Jonathan Cape Ltd, 1950), p. 188
20. Brigadier E.J. Todhunter to Mr B.E. Todhunter, 2 June 1941
21. Brigadier E.J. Todhunter to Mr B.E. Todhunter, 28 June 1941
22. Brigadier E.J. Todhunter to Mr B.E. Todhunter, 14 July 1941
23. Ibid.
24. Brigadier E.J. Todhunter to Mrs B. Todhunter, 16 June 1941
25. Brigadier E.J. Todhunter to Mr B.E. Todhunter, 14 July 1941
26. Brigadier E.J. Todhunter to Mrs Todhunter, 16 June 1941
27. Ibid.
28. Brigadier E.J. Todhunter to Mr B.E. Todhunter, 10 August 1941
29. John Baynes, *The Forgotten Victor: General Sir Richard O'Connor* (London: Brassey's, 1989), p. 141
30. M.R.D. Foot & J.M. Langley, *MI9: Escape and Evasion 1939–1945* (London: Book Club Associates, 1979), p. 148
31. Ibid: p. 54
32. 'Escape Narrative' by General Sir Richard O'Connor (OCONNOR 4/5/1 1941 Apr–1943 Apr), Liddell Hart Centre for Military History, King's College London
33. Brigadier E.J. Todhunter to Mrs Todhunter, 27 July 1941

34. John Leeming, *Always To-Morrow* (London: George G. Harrap & Co. Ltd, 1951), p. 96
35. Brigadier E.J. Todhunter to Mr B.E. Todhunter, 16 August 1941
36. Ibid.
37. Brigadier E.J. Todhunter to Mr B.E. Todhunter, 22 August 1941

Chapter 5
1. 'Brief Narrative of Events at the British Generals' Prisoner of War Camps in Italy, Apl. 1941 to Sept. 1943' (unpublished), private papers of Lieutenant-General Sir Philip Neame
2. Ibid.
3. Brigadier E.J. Todhunter to Mr B.E. Todhunter, 2 September 1941
4. John Leeming, *Always To-Morrow* (London: George G. Harrap & Co. Ltd, 1951), p. 102
5. Ibid: p. 103
6. Ibid: p. 103
7. James Hargest, *Farewell Campo 12* (London: Michael Joseph, 1954), p. 69

Chapter 6
1. Brigadier E.J. Todhunter to Mr B.E. Todhunter, 2 September 1941
2. James Hargest, *Farewell Campo 12* (London: Michael Joseph, 1954), p. 70
3. 'Escape Narrative' by General Sir Richard O'Connor (OCONNOR 4/5/1 1941 Apr–1943 Apr), Liddell Hart Centre for Military History, King's College London
4. Andrew Mollo, *The Armed Forces of World War II: Uniforms, Insignia and Organisation* (London: Black Cat, 1987), p. 88
5. Sir Philip Neame, *Playing With Strife: The Autobiography of a Soldier* (London: George G. Harrap & Sons Ltd, 1947), p. 286
6. Ibid.
7. 'Brief Narrative of Events at the British Generals' Prisoner of War Camps in Italy, Apl. 1941 to Sept. 1943' (unpublished), private papers of Lieutenant-General Sir Philip Neame
8. John Leeming, *Always To-Morrow* (London: George G. Harrap & Co. Ltd, 1951), p. 106
9. 'Camp for British Generals at Vincigliata', Red Cross Report, 30 May 1942, WO 32/10706, (The National Archives [Public Record Office], Kew)
10. Report of Captain Leonardo Trippi, Assistant Military Attaché, Swiss Legation, Rome, 3 June 1942, WO 32/10706, (The National Archives [Public Record Office], Kew)
11. 'Camp for British Generals at Vincigliata', Red Cross Report, 30 May 1942, WO 32/10706, (The National Archives [Public Record Office], Kew)
12. Report of Captain Leonardo Trippi, Assistant Military Attaché, Swiss Legation, Rome, 3 June 1942, WO 32/10706, (The National Archives [Public Record Office], Kew)

13. 'Camp for British Generals at Vincigliata', Red Cross Report, 30 May 1942, WO 32/10706, (The National Archives [Public Record Office], Kew)

14. John Leeming, *Always To-Morrow* (London: George G. Harrap & Co. Ltd, 1951), p. 108

15. Ibid.

16. Ibid: 108–9

17. Sir Adrian Carton de Wiart, *Happy Odyssey* (London: Jonathan Cape Ltd, 1950), p. 191

18. 'Lord Ranfurly's Report on his Capture', in *To War With Whitaker: The Wartime Diaries of the Countess of Ranfurly 1939–45* (London: Mandarin, 1997), p. 233

19. Ibid.

20. Ibid.

21. Ibid.

22. Ibid: p. 234

23. Ibid: p. 234

24. John Leeming, *Always To-Morrow* (London: George G. Harrap & Co. Ltd, 1951), p. 109

25. Ibid.

26. Ibid: pp. 109–10

27. Ibid: p. 109

28. Ibid: p. 110

29. Sir Adrian Carton de Wiart, *Happy Odyssey* (London: Jonathan Cape Ltd, 1950), p. 191

30. Ibid.

Chapter 7

1. Sir Adrian Carton de Wiart, *Happy Odyssey* (London: Jonathan Cape Ltd, 1950), p. 192

2. John Leeming, *Always To-Morrow* (London: George G. Harrap & Co. Ltd, 1951), p. 108

3. Sir Adrian Carton de Wiart, *Happy Odyssey* (London: Jonathan Cape Ltd, 1950), p. 192

4. John Leeming, *Always To-Morrow* (London: George G. Harrap & Co. Ltd, 1951), p. 107

5. Ibid: p. 107

6. Ibid: p. 108

7. Sir Adrian Carton de Wiart, *Happy Odyssey* (London: Jonathan Cape Ltd, 1950), p. 192

8. 'Inspection of Prisoner of War Camp No. 12, 23 June 1942', WO 32/10706 (The National Archives [Public Record Office], Kew)

9. Henry James, *Transatlantic Sketches* (Boston: James R. Osgood, 1875), pp. 287–8

10. The Earl of Ranfurly to The Countess of Ranfurly, 3 October 1941, in *To War With Whitaker: The Wartime Diaries of the Countess of Ranfurly 1939–45* (London: Mandarin, 1997), p. 123

11. Sir Philip Neame, *Playing With Strife: The Autobiography of a Soldier* (London: George G. Harrap & Sons Ltd, 1947), p. 289

12. John Baynes, *The Forgotten Victor: General Sir Richard O'Connor, KT, GCB, DSO, MC* (London: Brassey's, 1989), p. 144

13. The Earl of Ranfurly to The Countess of Ranfurly, 3 October 1941, in *To War With Whitaker: The Wartime Diaries of the Countess of Ranfurly 1939–45* (London: Mandarin, 1997), p. 123

14. Sir Philip Neame, *Playing With Strife: The Autobiography of a Soldier* (London: George G. Harrap & Sons Ltd, 1947), p. 289

15. Brigadier E.J. Todhunter to Mr B.E. Todhunter, 30 September 1941

16. Brigadier E.J. Todhunter to Mr B.E. Todhunter, 7 November 1941

17. Sir Adrian Carton de Wiart, *Happy Odyssey* (London: Jonathan Cape Ltd, 1950), p. 192

18. 'Camp for British Generals at Vincigliata', Red Cross Report, 29 November 1941, WO 32/10706 (The National Archives [Public Record Office], Kew)

19. 'Brief Narrative of Events at the British Generals' Prisoner of War Camps in Italy, Apl. 1941 to Sept. 1943' (unpublished), private papers of Lieutenant-General Sir Philip Neame

20. Sir Adrian Carton de Wiart, *Happy Odyssey* (London: Jonathan Cape Ltd, 1950), p. 192

21. The Earl of Ranfurly to The Countess of Ranfurly, 3 October 1941, in *To War With Whitaker: The Wartime Diaries of the Countess of Ranfurly 1939–45* (London: Mandarin, 1997), p. 123

22. Sir Adrian Carton de Wiart, *Happy Odyssey* (London: Jonathan Cape Ltd, 1950), p. 196

23. Brigadier E.J. Todhunter to Mr B.E. Todhunter, 30 September 1941

24. 'Escape Narrative' by General Sir Richard O'Connor (OCONNOR 4/5/1 1941 Apr–1943 Apr), Liddell Hart Centre for Military History, King's College London

25. Ibid.

26. Ibid.

27. Ibid.

28. John Leeming, *Always To-Morrow* (London: George G. Harrap & Co. Ltd, 1951), p. 114

29. The Earl of Ranfurly to The Countess of Ranfurly, 3 October 1941, in *To War With Whitaker: The Wartime Diaries of the Countess of Ranfurly 1939–45* (London: Mandarin, 1997), p. 123

30. 'Escape Narrative' by General Sir Richard O'Connor (OCONNOR 4/5/1 1941 Apr–1943 Apr), Liddell Hart Centre for Military History, King's College London

31. John Leeming, *Always To-Morrow* (London: George G. Harrap & Co. Ltd, 1951), p. 113

32. 'Escape Narrative' by General Sir Richard O'Connor (OCONNOR 4/5/1 1941 Apr–1943 Apr), Liddell Hart Centre for Military History, King's College London

33. Ibid.
34. 'Brief Narrative of Events at the British Generals' Prisoner of War Camps in Italy, Apl. 1941 to Sept. 1943' (unpublished), private papers of Lieutenant-General Sir Philip Neame
35. Sir Adrian Carton de Wiart, *Happy Odyssey* (London: Jonathan Cape Ltd, 1950), p. 194
36. John Leeming, *Always To-Morrow* (London: George G. Harrap & Co. Ltd, 1951), p. 116
37. 'Camp for British Generals at Vincigliata', Red Cross Report, 30 May 1942, WO 32/10706 (The National Archives [Public Record Office], Kew)
38. 'Escape Narrative' by General Sir Richard O'Connor (OCONNOR 4/5/1 1941 Apr–1943 Apr), Liddell Hart Centre for Military History, King's College London
39. 'De Wiart tells how they dug a tunnel for seven months' by Stuart Gelder, *News Chronicle*, 27 January 1944, front page
40. 'Escape Narrative' by General Sir Richard O'Connor (OCONNOR 4/5/1 1941 Apr–1943 Apr), Liddell Hart Centre for Military History, King's College London
41. Sir Adrian Carton de Wiart, *Happy Odyssey* (London: Jonathan Cape Ltd, 1950), p. 197
42. John Leeming, *Always To-Morrow* (London: George G. Harrap & Co. Ltd, 1951), p. 116
43. Ibid: p. 116
44. Brigadier E.J. Todhunter to Mr B.E. Todhunter, 7 November 1941
45. Brigadier E.J. Todhunter to Mr B.E. Todhunter, 30 September 1941
46. Brigadier E.J. Todhunter to Mr B.E. Todhunter, 7 November 1941
47. The Earl of Ranfurly to The Countess of Ranfurly, 26 December 1941, in *To War With Whitaker: The Wartime Diaries of the Countess of Ranfurly 1939–45* (London: Mandarin, 1997), pp. 124–5
48. Ibid: p. 125
49. Brigadier E.J. Todhunter to Mr B.E. Todhunter, undated [late 1941]
50. Ibid.
51. 'Brief Narrative of Events at the British Generals' Prisoner of War Camps in Italy, Apl. 1941 to Sept. 1943' (unpublished), private papers of Lieutenant-General Sir Philip Neame
52. Ibid.
53. Ibid.
54. Ibid.

Chapter 8

1. 'Brief Narrative of Events at the British Generals' Prisoner of War Camps in Italy, Apl. 1941 to Sept. 1943' (unpublished), private papers of Lieutenant-General Sir Philip Neame
2. Brigadier E.J. Todhunter to Mr B.E. Todhunter, 17 March 1942
3. James Hargest, *Farewell Campo 12* (London: Michael Joseph, 1954), p. 72

4. 'Report No. 2 On Inspection of Prisoner of War Camp No. 12', 1 July 1942, WO 32/10706 (The National Archives [Public Record Office], Kew)

5. James Hargest, *Farewell Campo 12* (London: Michael Joseph, 1954), p. 72

6. The Earl of Ranfurly to The Countess of Ranfurly, 13 March 1942, in *To War With Whitaker: The Wartime Diaries of the Countess of Ranfurly 1939–45* (London: Mandarin, 1997), p. 130

7. James Hargest, *Farewell Campo 12* (London: Michael Joseph, 1954), pp. 72–3

8. Ibid: p. 73

9. 'Camp for British Generals at Vincigliata', Red Cross Report, 30 May 1942, WO 32/10706 (The National Archives [Public Record Office], Kew)

10. John Leeming, *Always To-Morrow* (London: George G. Harrap & Co. Ltd, 1951), p. 117

11. 'Brief Narrative of Events at the British Generals' Prisoner of War Camps in Italy, Apl. 1941 to Sept. 1943' (unpublished), private papers of Lieutenant-General Sir Philip Neame

12. Sir Philip Neame, *Playing With Strife: The Autobiography of a Soldier* (London: George G. Harrap & Sons Ltd, 1947), p. 290

13. John Leeming, *Always To-Morrow* (London: George G. Harrap & Co. Ltd, 1951), p. 118

14. Ibid: p. 290

15. Ibid: p. 119

16. 'Report No. 2 On Inspection of Prisoner of War Camp No. 12', 1 July 1942, WO 32/10706 (The National Archives [Public Record Office], Kew)

17. James Hargest, *Farewell Campo 12* (London: Michael Joseph, 1954), p. 74

18. Ibid.

19. Sir Philip Neame, *Playing With Strife: The Autobiography of a Soldier* (London: George G. Harrap & Sons Ltd, 1947), p. 290

20. John Leeming, *Always To-Morrow* (London: George G. Harrap & Co. Ltd, 1951), p. 119

21. Ibid: p. 120

22. James Hargest, *Farewell Campo 12* (London: Michael Joseph, 1954), p. 75

23. Sir Philip Neame, *Playing With Strife: The Autobiography of a Soldier* (London: George G. Harrap & Sons Ltd, 1947), p. 291

24. Sir Adrian Carton de Wiart, *Happy Odyssey* (London: Jonathan Cape Ltd, 1950), p. 199

25. James Hargest, *Farewell Campo 12* (London: Michael Joseph, 1954), p. 76

26. 'Brief Narrative of Events at the British Generals' Prisoner of War Camps in Italy, Apl. 1941 to Sept. 1943' (unpublished), private papers of Lieutenant-General Sir Philip Neame

27. Ibid.

28. Sir Philip Neame, *Playing With Strife: The Autobiography of a Soldier* (London: George G. Harrap & Sons Ltd, 1947), p. 291

29. Sir Adrian Carton de Wiart, *Happy Odyssey* (London: Jonathan Cape Ltd, 1950), p. 198

30. John Leeming, *Always To-Morrow* (London: George G. Harrap & Co. Ltd, 1951), p. 124
31. Ibid.
32. Sir Philip Neame, *Playing With Strife: The Autobiography of a Soldier* (London: George G. Harrap & Sons Ltd, 1947), p. 292
33. Ibid.
34. Sir Adrian Carton de Wiart, *Happy Odyssey* (London: Jonathan Cape Ltd, 1950), pp. 199–200
35. James Hargest, *Farewell Campo 12* (London: Michael Joseph, 1954), p. 76
36. 'Camp for British Generals at Vincigliata', Red Cross Report, 29 November 1941', WO 32/10706 (The National Archives [Public Record Office], Kew)

Chapter 9

1. John Leeming, *Always To-Morrow* (London: George G. Harrap & Co. Ltd, 1951), p. 129
2. Ibid: p. 130
3. James Hargest, *Farewell Campo 12* (London: Michael Joseph, 1954), p. 79
4. John Leeming, *Always To-Morrow* (London: George G. Harrap & Co. Ltd, 1951), p. 133
5. Ibid.
6. 'Escape Narrative' by General Sir Richard O'Connor (OCONNOR 4/5/1 1941 Apr–1943 Apr), Liddell Hart Centre for Military History, King's College London
7. John Leeming, *Always To-Morrow* (London: George G. Harrap & Co. Ltd, 1951), p. 134
8. Ibid: p. 135
9. Ibid: p. 135
10. 'Report of Captain Leonardo Trippi', Assistant Military Attaché, Swiss Legation, Rome, 3 June 1942, WO 32/10706 (The National Archives [Public Record Office], Kew)
11. John Leeming, *Always To-Morrow* (London: George G. Harrap & Co. Ltd, 1951), p. 136
12. James Hargest, *Farewell Campo 12* (London: Michael Joseph, 1954), p. 86
13. Ibid: p. 87
14. Ibid: p. 88
15. Ibid: p. 88
16. Ibid: p. 90
17. Sir Philip Neame, *Playing With Strife: The Autobiography of a Soldier* (London: George G. Harrap & Sons Ltd, 1947), p. 294
18. James Hargest, *Farewell Campo 12* (London: Michael Joseph, 1954), p. 90
19. Ibid: p. 91
20. Ibid: p. 92
21. Sir Philip Neame, *Playing With Strife: The Autobiography of a Soldier* (London: George G. Harrap & Sons Ltd, 1947), p. 294

22. John Leeming, *Always To-Morrow* (London: George G. Harrap & Co. Ltd, 1951), p. 150
23. Sir Philip Neame, *Playing With Strife: The Autobiography of a Soldier* (London: George G. Harrap & Sons Ltd, 1947), p. 294
24. John Leeming, *Always To-Morrow* (London: George G. Harrap & Co. Ltd, 1951), p. 150

Chapter 10

1. 'Escape Narrative' by General Sir Richard O'Connor (OCONNOR 4/5/1 1941 Apr–1943 Apr), Liddell Hart Centre for Military History, King's College London
2. Ibid.
3. Ibid.
4. Ibid.
5. Ibid.
6. Ibid.
7. Ibid.
8. John Leeming, *Always To-Morrow* (London: George G. Harrap & Co. Ltd, 1951), p. 152
9. 'Escape Narrative' by General Sir Richard O'Connor (OCONNOR 4/5/1 1941 Apr–1943 Apr), Liddell Hart Centre for Military History, King's College London
10. Ibid.
11. Ibid.
12. Ibid.
13. Ibid.
14. Ibid.
15. Ibid.
16. Ibid.
17. Ibid.
18. John Leeming, *Always To-Morrow* (London: George G. Harrap & Co. Ltd, 1951), p. 154
19. 'Escape Narrative' by General Sir Richard O'Connor (OCONNOR 4/5/1 1941 Apr–1943 Apr), Liddell Hart Centre for Military History, King's College London
20. 'De Wiart tells how they dug a tunnel for seven months' by Stuart Gelder, *News Chronicle*, 27 January 1944, front page
21. John Leeming, *Always To-Morrow* (London: George G. Harrap & Co. Ltd, 1951), p. 157
22. Lieutenant-General P. Neame to the Protecting Power, 14 May 1942, WO 32/10706 (The National Archives [Public Record Office], Kew)
23. Ibid.
24. Ibid.
25. Ibid.

26. Sir Philip Neame, *Playing With Strife: The Autobiography of a Soldier* (London: George G. Harrap & Sons Ltd, 1947), p. 292

27. 'Memorandum from the Italian Ministry of Foreign Affairs to the Swiss Legation Rome, 25 July 1942', WO 32/10706 (The National Archives [Public Record Office], Kew)

28. Ibid.

29. 'War Office (Directorate of Prisoners of War) to the Foreign Office (Prisoners of War Department): Treatment of British Generals in Italian Hands', November 1942, WO 32/10706 (The National Archives [Public Record Office], Kew)

30. John Baynes, *The Forgotten Victor: General Sir Richard O'Connor* (London: Brassey's, 1989), p. 147

31. Ibid.

32. Ibid.

33. Sir Philip Neame, *Playing With Strife: The Autobiography of a Soldier* (London: George G. Harrap & Sons Ltd, 1947), p. 293

34. 'Escape Narrative' by General Sir Richard O'Connor (OCONNOR 4/5/1 1941 Apr–1943 Apr), Liddell Hart Centre for Military History, King's College London

Chapter 11

1. John Baynes, *The Forgotten Victor: General Sir Richard O'Connor* (London: Brassey's, 1989), p. 147

2. 'Escape Narrative' by General Sir Richard O'Connor (OCONNOR 4/5/1 1941 Apr–1943 Apr), Liddell Hart Centre for Military History, King's College London

3. John Baynes, *The Forgotten Victor: General Sir Richard O'Connor* (London: Brassey's, 1989), p. 147

4. Sir Philip Neame, *Playing With Strife: The Autobiography of a Soldier* (London: George G. Harrap & Sons Ltd, 1947), p. 293

5. Sir Adrian Carton de Wiart, *Happy Odyssey* (London: Jonathan Cape Ltd, 1950), p. 205

6. John Baynes, *The Forgotten Victor: General Sir Richard O'Connor* (London: Brassey's, 1989), p. 147

7. 'Escape Narrative' by General Sir Richard O'Connor (OCONNOR 4/5/1 1941 Apr–1943 Apr), Liddell Hart Centre for Military History, King's College London

8. 'Brief Narrative of Events at the British Generals' Prisoner of War Camps in Italy, Apl. 1941 to Sept. 1943' (unpublished), private papers of Lieutenant-General Sir Philip Neame

9. 'Escape Narrative' by General Sir Richard O'Connor (OCONNOR 4/5/1 1941 Apr–1943 Apr), Liddell Hart Centre for Military History, King's College London

10. John Baynes, *The Forgotten Victor: General Sir Richard O'Connor* (London: Brassey's, 1989), p. 148

11. 'Escape Narrative' by General Sir Richard O'Connor (OCONNOR 4/5/1 1941 Apr–1943 Apr), Liddell Hart Centre for Military History, King's College London

12. Sir Philip Neame, *Playing With Strife: The Autobiography of a Soldier* (London: George G. Harrap & Sons Ltd, 1947), p. 293

13. John Baynes, *The Forgotten Victor: General Sir Richard O'Connor* (London: Brassey's, 1989), p. 148

14. 'Escape Narrative' by General Sir Richard O'Connor (OCONNOR 4/5/1 1941 Apr–1943 Apr), Liddell Hart Centre for Military History, King's College London

15. John Baynes, *The Forgotten Victor: General Sir Richard O'Connor* (London: Brassey's, 1989), p. 148

16. 'Escape Narrative' by General Sir Richard O'Connor (OCONNOR 4/5/1 1941 Apr–1943 Apr), Liddell Hart Centre for Military History, King's College London

17. Ibid.

18. John Baynes, *The Forgotten Victor: General Sir Richard O'Connor* (London: Brassey's, 1989), p. 148

19. 'Escape Narrative' by General Sir Richard O'Connor (OCONNOR 4/5/1 1941 Apr–1943 Apr), Liddell Hart Centre for Military History, King's College London

20. 'Brief Narrative of Events at the British Generals' Prisoner of War Camps in Italy, Apl. 1941 to Sept. 1943' (unpublished), private papers of Lieutenant-General Sir Philip Neame

21. 'Report No. 4 on Inspection of Prisoners of War Camp No. 12', 15 October 1942, WO 32/10706 (The National Archives [Public Record Office], Kew)

22. Sir Philip Neame, *Playing With Strife: The Autobiography of a Soldier* (London: George G. Harrap & Sons Ltd, 1947), p. 295

23. Sir Adrian Carton de Wiart, *Happy Odyssey* (London: Jonathan Cape Ltd, 1950), p. 207

24. Ibid: p. 207

25. 'Escape Narrative' by General Sir Richard O'Connor (OCONNOR 4/5/1 1941 Apr–1943 Apr), Liddell Hart Centre for Military History, King's College London

26. Sir Philip Neame, *Playing With Strife: The Autobiography of a Soldier* (London: George G. Harrap & Sons Ltd, 1947), p. 295

27. Ibid: p. 295

28. James Hargest, *Farewell Campo 12* (London: Michael Joseph, 1954), p. 104

29. Sir Philip Neame, *Playing With Strife: The Autobiography of a Soldier* (London: George G. Harrap & Sons Ltd, 1947), p. 296

30. Ibid: p. 296

31. Ibid: p. 296

32. John Baynes, *The Forgotten Victor: General Sir Richard O'Connor* (London: Brassey's, 1989), p. 151

33. Sir Philip Neame, *Playing With Strife: The Autobiography of a Soldier* (London: George G. Harrap & Sons Ltd, 1947), p. 296

34. Ibid: p. 297

35. James Hargest, *Farewell Campo 12* (London: Michael Joseph, 1954), p. 104

36. Sir Philip Neame, *Playing With Strife: The Autobiography of a Soldier* (London: George G. Harrap & Sons Ltd, 1947), p. 297

37. James Hargest, *Farewell Campo 12* (London: Michael Joseph, 1954), p. 105

38. Sir Adrian Carton de Wiart, *Happy Odyssey* (London: Jonathan Cape Ltd, 1950), p. 207

39. James Hargest, *Farewell Campo 12* (London: Michael Joseph, 1954), pp. 104–5

40. 'Escape Narrative' by General Sir Richard O'Connor (OCONNOR 4/5/1 1941 Apr–1943 Apr), Liddell Hart Centre for Military History, King's College London

41. James Hargest, *Farewell Campo 12* (London: Michael Joseph, 1954), p. 106

42. 'Escape Narrative' by General Sir Richard O'Connor (OCONNOR 4/5/1 1941 Apr–1943 Apr), Liddell Hart Centre for Military History, King's College London

43. Ibid.

44. Sir Philip Neame, *Playing With Strife: The Autobiography of a Soldier* (London: George G. Harrap & Sons Ltd, 1947), p. 298

45. Ibid: 299

46. 'Escape Narrative' by General Sir Richard O'Connor (OCONNOR 4/5/1 1941 Apr–1943 Apr), Liddell Hart Centre for Military History, King's College London

47. Sir Philip Neame, *Playing With Strife: The Autobiography of a Soldier* (London: George G. Harrap & Sons Ltd, 1947), p. 298

48. 'Escape Narrative' by General Sir Richard O'Connor (OCONNOR 4/5/1 1941 Apr–1943 Apr), Liddell Hart Centre for Military History, King's College London

49. Ibid.

50. James Hargest, *Farewell Campo 12* (London: Michael Joseph, 1954), p. 108

51. 'Escape Narrative' by General Sir Richard O'Connor (OCONNOR 4/5/1 1941 Apr–1943 Apr), Liddell Hart Centre for Military History, King's College London

52. Brigadier E.J. Todhunter to Mr B.E. Todhunter, 7 October 1942

53. Ibid.

54. 'Escape Narrative' by General Sir Richard O'Connor (OCONNOR 4/5/1 1941 Apr–1943 Apr), Liddell Hart Centre for Military History, King's College London

55. Sir Philip Neame, *Playing With Strife: The Autobiography of a Soldier* (London: George G. Harrap & Sons Ltd, 1947), p. 299

56. Ibid: p. 300

57. Ibid: p. 299

Chapter 12

1. Sir Philip Neame, *Playing With Strife: The Autobiography of a Soldier* (London: George G. Harrap & Sons Ltd, 1947), p. 301

2. 'Escape Narrative' by General Sir Richard O'Connor (OCONNOR 4/5/1 1941 Apr–1943 Apr), Liddell Hart Centre for Military History, King's College London

3. James Hargest, *Farewell Campo 12* (London: Michael Joseph, 1954), pp. 114–15

4. Ibid: p. 115

5. Sir Philip Neame, *Playing With Strife: The Autobiography of a Soldier* (London: George G. Harrap & Sons Ltd, 1947), p. 300

6. Ibid.

7. 'Escape Narrative' by General Sir Richard O'Connor (OCONNOR 4/5/1 1941 Apr–1943 Apr), Liddell Hart Centre for Military History, King's College London

8. Sir Philip Neame, *Playing With Strife: The Autobiography of a Soldier* (London: George G. Harrap & Sons Ltd, 1947), p. 301

9. Sir Adrian Carton de Wiart, *Happy Odyssey* (London: Jonathan Cape Ltd, 1950), p. 209

10. Sir Philip Neame, *Playing With Strife: The Autobiography of a Soldier* (London: George G. Harrap & Sons Ltd, 1947), p. 301

11. Sir Adrian Carton de Wiart, *Happy Odyssey* (London: Jonathan Cape Ltd, 1950), p. 209

12. 'Escape Narrative' by General Sir Richard O'Connor (OCONNOR 4/5/1 1941 Apr–1943 Apr), Liddell Hart Centre for Military History, King's College London

13. Brigadier E.J. Todhunter to Mr B.E. Todhunter, 7 November 1942

14. Brigadier E.J. Todhunter to Mrs Todhunter, 19 December 1942

15. Sir Philip Neame, *Playing With Strife: The Autobiography of a Soldier* (London: George G. Harrap & Sons Ltd, 1947), p. 300

16. 'Escape Narrative' by General Sir Richard O'Connor (OCONNOR 4/5/1 1941 Apr–1943 Apr), Liddell Hart Centre for Military History, King's College London

17. Brigadier E.J. Todhunter to Mr B.E. Todhunter, 2 January 1943

18. James Hargest, *Farewell Campo 12* (London: Michael Joseph, 1954), p. 114

19. Brigadier E.J. Todhunter to Mr B.E. Todhunter, 2 January 1943

20. James Hargest, *Farewell Campo 12* (London: Michael Joseph, 1954), p. 120

21. Sir Adrian Carton de Wiart, *Happy Odyssey* (London: Jonathan Cape Ltd, 1950), p. 210

22. War Office (Directorate of Prisoners of War) to the Foreign Office (Prisoners of War Department), 'Treatment of British Generals in Italian Hands', November 1942, WO 32/10706, (The National Archives [Public Record Office], Kew)

23. 'Escape Narrative' by General Sir Richard O'Connor (OCONNOR 4/5/1 1941 Apr–1943 Apr), Liddell Hart Centre for Military History, King's College London

24. James Hargest, *Farewell Campo 12* (London: Michael Joseph, 1954), p. 120

25. 'Escape Narrative' by General Sir Richard O'Connor (OCONNOR 4/5/1 1941 Apr–1943 Apr), Liddell Hart Centre for Military History, King's College London

26. Sir Adrian Carton de Wiart, *Happy Odyssey* (London: Jonathan Cape Ltd, 1950), p. 212

27. Ibid.

28. 'Escape Narrative' by General Sir Richard O'Connor (OCONNOR 4/5/1 1941 Apr–1943 Apr), Liddell Hart Centre for Military History, King's College London

29. Ibid.

30. James Hargest, *Farewell Campo 12* (London: Michael Joseph, 1954), p. 116

31. Ibid.

32. Ibid.

33. 'Escape Narrative' by General Sir Richard O'Connor (OCONNOR 4/5/1 1941 Apr–1943 Apr), Liddell Hart Centre for Military History, King's College London

34. Ibid.

35. Ibid.

36. Sir Philip Neame, *Playing With Strife: The Autobiography of a Soldier* (London: George G. Harrap & Sons Ltd, 1947), p. 301

37. 'Escape Narrative' by General Sir Richard O'Connor (OCONNOR 4/5/1 1941 Apr–1943 Apr), Liddell Hart Centre for Military History, King's College London

Chapter 13

1. James Hargest, *Farewell Campo 12* (London: Michael Joseph, 1954), p. 119

2. Sir Philip Neame, *Playing With Strife: The Autobiography of a Soldier* (London: George G. Harrap & Sons Ltd, 1947), p. 302

3. Ibid.

4. Ibid.

5. James Hargest, *Farewell Campo 12* (London: Michael Joseph, 1954), p. 121

6. Sir Philip Neame, *Playing With Strife: The Autobiography of a Soldier* (London: George G. Harrap & Sons Ltd, 1947), p. 304

7. War Office (Directorate of Prisoners of War) to the Foreign Office (Prisoners of War Department): 'Treatment of British Generals in Italian Hands', November 1942, WO 32/10706 (The National Archives [Public Record Office], Kew)

8. 'Escape Narrative' by General Sir Richard O'Connor (OCONNOR 4/5/1 1941 Apr–1943 Apr), Liddell Hart Centre for Military History, King's College London

9. 'De Wiart tells how they dug a tunnel for seven months' by Stuart Gelder, *News Chronicle*, 27 January 1944, front page

10. 'Escape Narrative' by General Sir Richard O'Connor (OCONNOR 4/5/1 1941 Apr–1943 Apr), Liddell Hart Centre for Military History, King's College London

11. Ibid.
12. James Hargest, *Farewell Campo 12* (London: Michael Joseph, 1954), p. 122
13. Sir Philip Neame, *Playing With Strife: The Autobiography of a Soldier* (London: George G. Harrap & Sons Ltd, 1947), p. 304
14. 'Escape Narrative' by General Sir Richard O'Connor (OCONNOR 4/5/1 1941 Apr–1943 Apr), Liddell Hart Centre for Military History, King's College London
15. James Hargest, *Farewell Campo 12* (London: Michael Joseph, 1954), p. 122
16. 'Escape Narrative' by General Sir Richard O'Connor (OCONNOR 4/5/1 1941 Apr–1943 Apr), Liddell Hart Centre for Military History, King's College London
17. James Hargest, *Farewell Campo 12* (London: Michael Joseph, 1954), p. 122
18. Sir Philip Neame, *Playing With Strife: The Autobiography of a Soldier* (London: George G. Harrap & Sons Ltd, 1947), p. 305
19. Ibid.
20. Sir Adrian Carton de Wiart, *Happy Odyssey* (London: Jonathan Cape Ltd, 1950), pp. 213–14
21. Sir Philip Neame, *Playing With Strife: The Autobiography of a Soldier* (London: George G. Harrap & Sons Ltd, 1947), p. 305
22. James Hargest, *Farewell Campo 12* (London: Michael Joseph, 1954), p. 119
23. Ibid: p. 124

Chapter 14

1. James Hargest, *Farewell Campo 12* (London: Michael Joseph, 1954), p. 124
2. Ibid.
3. Sir Philip Neame, *Playing With Strife: The Autobiography of a Soldier* (London: George G. Harrap & Sons Ltd, 1947), p. 305
4. John Leeming, *Always To-Morrow* (London: George G. Harrap & Co. Ltd, 1951), p. 164
5. 'Escape Narrative' by General Sir Richard O'Connor (OCONNOR 4/5/1 1941 Apr–1943 Apr), Liddell Hart Centre for Military History, King's College London
6. James Hargest, *Farewell Campo 12* (London: Michael Joseph, 1954), p. 125
7. Sir Philip Neame, *Playing With Strife: The Autobiography of a Soldier* (London: George G. Harrap & Sons Ltd, 1947), p. 306
8. James Hargest, *Farewell Campo 12* (London: Michael Joseph, 1954), p. 125
9. Ibid.
10. Sir Adrian Carton de Wiart, *Happy Odyssey* (London: Jonathan Cape Ltd, 1950), p. 213
11. Ibid.
12. 'Escape Narrative' by General Sir Richard O'Connor (OCONNOR 4/5/1 1941 Apr–1943 Apr), Liddell Hart Centre for Military History, King's College London
13. James Hargest, *Farewell Campo 12* (London: Michael Joseph, 1954), p. 126

NOTES

14. Sir Philip Neame, *Playing With Strife: The Autobiography of a Soldier* (London: George G. Harrap & Sons Ltd, 1947), p. 306
15. James Hargest, *Farewell Campo 12* (London: Michael Joseph, 1954), p. 126
16. Ibid: p. 126
17. Ibid: p. 127
18. 'Escape Narrative' by General Sir Richard O'Connor (OCONNOR 4/5/1 1941 Apr–1943 Apr), Liddell Hart Centre for Military History, King's College London
19. Sir Adrian Carton de Wiart, *Happy Odyssey* (London: Jonathan Cape Ltd, 1950), p. 215
20. Ibid.
21. 'Escape Narrative' by General Sir Richard O'Connor (OCONNOR 4/5/1 1941 Apr–1943 Apr), Liddell Hart Centre for Military History, King's College London
22. James Hargest, *Farewell Campo 12* (London: Michael Joseph, 1954), p. 127
23. Ibid: p. 128
24. Ibid: pp. 128–9
25. Sir Adrian Carton de Wiart, *Happy Odyssey* (London: Jonathan Cape Ltd, 1950), p. 215
26. James Hargest, *Farewell Campo 12* (London: Michael Joseph, 1954), p. 129
27. Ibid: p. 129
28. Ibid: p. 130
29. Sir Adrian Carton de Wiart, *Happy Odyssey* (London: Jonathan Cape Ltd, 1950), p. 215
30. 'Escape Narrative' by General Sir Richard O'Connor (OCONNOR 4/5/1 1941 Apr–1943 Apr), Liddell Hart Centre for Military History, King's College London
31. 'De Wiart tells how they dug a tunnel for seven months' by Stuart Gelder, *News Chronicle*, 27 January 1944, front page
32. 'Escape Narrative' by General Sir Richard O'Connor (OCONNOR 4/5/1 1941 Apr–1943 Apr), Liddell Hart Centre for Military History, King's College London

Chapter 15

1. James Hargest, *Farewell Campo 12* (London: Michael Joseph, 1954), p. 131
2. Ibid.
3. Statement by Lt.-Col. (Acting Brigadier) John Frederick Boyce Combe, DSO (and bar), 11th Hussars, WO 208/3319/1921, (The National Archives [Public Record Office], Kew)
4. James Hargest, *Farewell Campo 12* (London: Michael Joseph, 1954), p. 131
5. Statement by Lt.-Col. (Acting Brigadier) John Frederick Boyce Combe, DSO (and bar), 11th Hussars, WO 208/3319/1921, (The National Archives [Public Record Office], Kew)
6. Ibid.
7. Ibid.

8. James Hargest, *Farewell Campo 12* (London: Michael Joseph, 1954), p. 131
9. Statement by Lt.-Col. (Acting Brigadier) John Frederick Boyce Combe, DSO (and bar), 11th Hussars, WO 208/3319/1921, (The National Archives [Public Record Office], Kew)
10. Ibid.
11. Ibid.
12. Ibid.
13. Sir Philip Neame, *Playing With Strife: The Autobiography of a Soldier* (London: George G. Harrap & Sons Ltd, 1947), p. 306
14. Ibid.
15. James Hargest, *Farewell Campo 12* (London: Michael Joseph, 1954), p. 132

Chapter 16
1. Statement by Lt.-Col. (Acting Brigadier) John Frederick Boyce Combe, DSO (and bar), 11th Hussars, WO 208/3319/1921, (The National Archives [Public Record Office], Kew)
2. Ibid.
3. James Hargest, *Farewell Campo 12* (London: Michael Joseph, 1954), p. 132
4. 'Escape Narrative' by General Sir Richard O'Connor (OCONNOR 4/5/1 1941 Apr–1943 Apr), Liddell Hart Centre for Military History, King's College London
5. James Hargest, *Farewell Campo 12* (London: Michael Joseph, 1954), p. 133
6. 'Escape Narrative' by General Sir Richard O'Connor (OCONNOR 4/5/1 1941 Apr–1943 Apr), Liddell Hart Centre for Military History, King's College London
7. Ibid.
8. Statement by Lt.-Col. (Acting Brigadier) John Frederick Boyce Combe, DSO (and bar), 11th Hussars, WO 208/3319/1921, (The National Archives [Public Record Office], Kew)
9. Sir Adrian Carton de Wiart, *Happy Odyssey* (Barnsley: Pen & Sword Books, 2013), p. 222
10. Statement by Lt.-Col. (Acting Brigadier) John Frederick Boyce Combe, DSO (and bar), 11th Hussars, WO 208/3319/1921, (The National Archives [Public Record Office], Kew)
11. James Hargest, *Farewell Campo 12* (London: Michael Joseph, 1954), p. 133
12. Ibid: p. 133
13. Ibid: p. 134
14. John Leeming, *Always To-Morrow* (London: George G. Harrap & Co. Ltd, 1951), p. 163
15. James Hargest, *Farewell Campo 12* (London: Michael Joseph, 1954), p. 134
16. Ibid.
17. Sir Philip Neame, *Playing With Strife: The Autobiography of a Soldier* (London: George G. Harrap & Sons Ltd, 1947), pp. 306–7
18. John Leeming, *Always To-Morrow* (London: George G. Harrap & Co. Ltd, 1951), p. 163

19. 'Escape Narrative' by General Sir Richard O'Connor (OCONNOR 4/5/1 1941 Apr–1943 Apr), Liddell Hart Centre for Military History, King's College London

20. James Hargest, *Farewell Campo 12* (London: Michael Joseph, 1954), p. 135

21. Ibid.

22. Ibid.

23. Sir Philip Neame, *Playing With Strife: The Autobiography of a Soldier* (London: George G. Harrap & Sons Ltd, 1947), p. 307

Chapter 17

1. Sir Adrian Carton de Wiart, *Happy Odyssey* (London: Jonathan Cape Ltd, 1950), p. 222

2. Sir Philip Neame, *Playing With Strife: The Autobiography of a Soldier* (London: George G. Harrap & Sons Ltd, 1947), p. 307

3. Ibid.

4. 'Escape Narrative' by General Sir Richard O'Connor (OCONNOR 4/5/1 1941 Apr–1943 Apr), Liddell Hart Centre for Military History, King's College London

5. Sir Philip Neame, *Playing With Strife: The Autobiography of a Soldier* (London: George G. Harrap & Sons Ltd, 1947), p. 307

6. John Baynes, *The Forgotten Victor: General Sir Richard O'Connor* (London: Brassey's, 1989), p. 160

7. Sir Adrian Carton de Wiart, *Happy Odyssey* (London: Jonathan Cape Ltd, 1950), p. 216

8. James Hargest, *Farewell Campo 12* (London: Michael Joseph, 1954), p. 135

9. Ibid.

10. Ibid.

11. Ibid.

12. Ibid: pp. 135–6

13. Ibid: p. 136

14. John Leeming, *Always To-Morrow* (London: George G. Harrap & Co. Ltd, 1951), p. 163

15. James Hargest, *Farewell Campo 12* (London: Michael Joseph, 1954), p. 147

16. Ibid: p. 136

17. Ibid: p. 136

18. 'Escape Narrative' by General Sir Richard O'Connor (OCONNOR 4/5/1 1941 Apr–1943 Apr), Liddell Hart Centre for Military History, King's College London

19. Sir Adrian Carton de Wiart, *Happy Odyssey* (London: Jonathan Cape Ltd, 1950), p. 222

20. 'Escape Narrative' by General Sir Richard O'Connor (OCONNOR 4/5/1 1941 Apr–1943 Apr), Liddell Hart Centre for Military History, King's College London

21. James Hargest, *Farewell Campo 12* (London: Michael Joseph, 1954), pp. 136–7

22. Ibid: p. 137

23. 'Escape Narrative' by General Sir Richard O'Connor (OCONNOR 4/5/1 1941 Apr–1943 Apr), Liddell Hart Centre for Military History, King's College London

24. James Hargest, *Farewell Campo 12* (London: Michael Joseph, 1954), p. 137

25. 'Escape Narrative' by General Sir Richard O'Connor (OCONNOR 4/5/1 1941 Apr–1943 Apr), Liddell Hart Centre for Military History, King's College London

26. James Hargest, *Farewell Campo 12* (London: Michael Joseph, 1954), p. 145

27. Ibid: p. 137

Chapter 18

1. James Hargest, *Farewell Campo 12* (London: Michael Joseph, 1954), p. 137

2. Ibid.

3. Ibid.

4. Statement by Lt.-Col. (Acting Brigadier) John Frederick Boyce Combe, DSO (and bar), 11th Hussars, WO 208/3319/1921 (The National Archives [Public Record Office], Kew)

5. James Hargest, *Farewell Campo 12* (London: Michael Joseph, 1954), p. 145

6. 'Escape Narrative' by General Sir Richard O'Connor (OCONNOR 4/5/1 1941 Apr–1943 Apr), Liddell Hart Centre for Military History, King's College London

7. Ibid.

8. James Hargest, *Farewell Campo 12* (London: Michael Joseph, 1954), p. 138

9. Ibid: p. 138

10. Ibid: p. 139

11. Ibid: p. 139

12. Ibid: p. 139

13. Ibid: pp. 139–40

14. 'Escape Narrative' by General Sir Richard O'Connor (OCONNOR 4/5/1 1941 Apr–1943 Apr), Liddell Hart Centre for Military History, King's College London

15. Sir Adrian Carton de Wiart, *Happy Odyssey* (Barnsley: Pen & Sword Books, 2013), p. 216

16. 'Escape Narrative' by General Sir Richard O'Connor (OCONNOR 4/5/1 1941 Apr–1943 Apr), Liddell Hart Centre for Military History, King's College London

17. James Hargest, *Farewell Campo 12* (London: Michael Joseph, 1954), p. 140

18. Ibid: p. 140

19. Ibid: p. 140

20. Ibid: p. 141

21. Sir Adrian Carton de Wiart, *Happy Odyssey* (London: Jonathan Cape Ltd, 1950), p. 216

22. 'Escape Narrative' by General Sir Richard O'Connor (OCONNOR 4/5/1 1941 Apr–1943 Apr), Liddell Hart Centre for Military History, King's College London

23. Sir Adrian Carton de Wiart, *Happy Odyssey* (London: Jonathan Cape Ltd, 1950), p. 216

24. Ibid: p. 217

25. James Hargest, *Farewell Campo 12* (London: Michael Joseph, 1954), p. 142

26. Sir Adrian Carton de Wiart, *Happy Odyssey* (London: Jonathan Cape Ltd, 1950), p. 217

27. Statement by Lt.-Col. (Acting Brigadier) John Frederick Boyce Combe, DSO (and bar), 11th Hussars, WO 208/3319/1921 (The National Archives [Public Record Office], Kew)

28. 'De Wiart tells how they dug a tunnel for seven months' by Stuart Gelder, *News Chronicle*, 27 January 1944, front page

29. 'Brief Narrative of Events at the British Generals' Prisoner of War Camps in Italy, Apl. 1941 to Sept. 1943' (unpublished), private papers of Lieutenant-General Sir Philip Neame

30. Ibid.

31. Lieutenant-General Sir Philip Neame to The Italian War Ministry, Rome, 13 April 1943, WO 32/10706 (The National Archives [Public Record Office], Kew)

32. Sir Philip Neame, *Playing With Strife: The Autobiography of a Soldier* (London: George G. Harrap & Sons Ltd, 1947), p. 310

33. 'Brief Narrative of Events at the British Generals' Prisoner of War Camps in Italy, Apl. 1941 to Sept. 1943' (unpublished), private papers of Lieutenant-General Sir Philip Neame

34. Lieutenant-General Sir Philip Neame to The Italian War Ministry, Rome, 13 April 1943, WO 32/10706, (The National Archives (Public Record Office), Kew)

35. Statement by Lt.-Col. (Acting Brigadier) John Frederick Boyce Combe, DSO (and bar), 11th Hussars, WO 208/3319/1921 (The National Archives [Public Record Office], Kew)

36. James Hargest, *Farewell Campo 12* (London: Michael Joseph, 1954), p. 146

37. Sir Adrian Carton de Wiart, *Happy Odyssey* (Barnsley: Pen & Sword Books, 2013), p. 217

38. Ibid.

39. James Hargest, *Farewell Campo 12* (London: Michael Joseph, 1954), p. 143

40. Ibid.

41. Ibid.

Epilogue

1. Sir Adrian Carton de Wiart, *Happy Odyssey* (London: Jonathan Cape Ltd, 1950), p. 218

2. Ibid: p. 218

3. Ibid: p. 219

4. Ibid: p. 219

5. 'Escape Narrative' by General Sir Richard O'Connor (OCONNOR 4/5/1 1941 Apr–1943 Apr), Liddell Hart Centre for Military History, King's College London

6. Sir Adrian Carton de Wiart, *Happy Odyssey* (London: Jonathan Cape Ltd, 1950), p. 220

7. Ibid: p. 221

8. 'Escape Narrative' by General Sir Richard O'Connor (OCONNOR 4/5/1 1941 Apr–1943 Apr), Liddell Hart Centre for Military History, King's College London